hawkeye

HAWKEYES

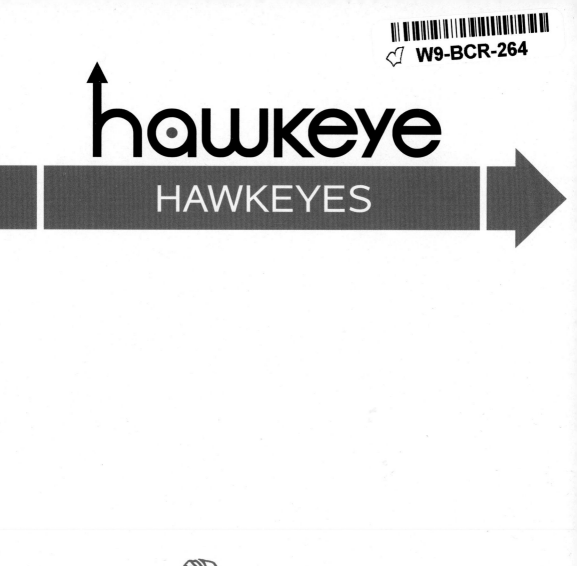

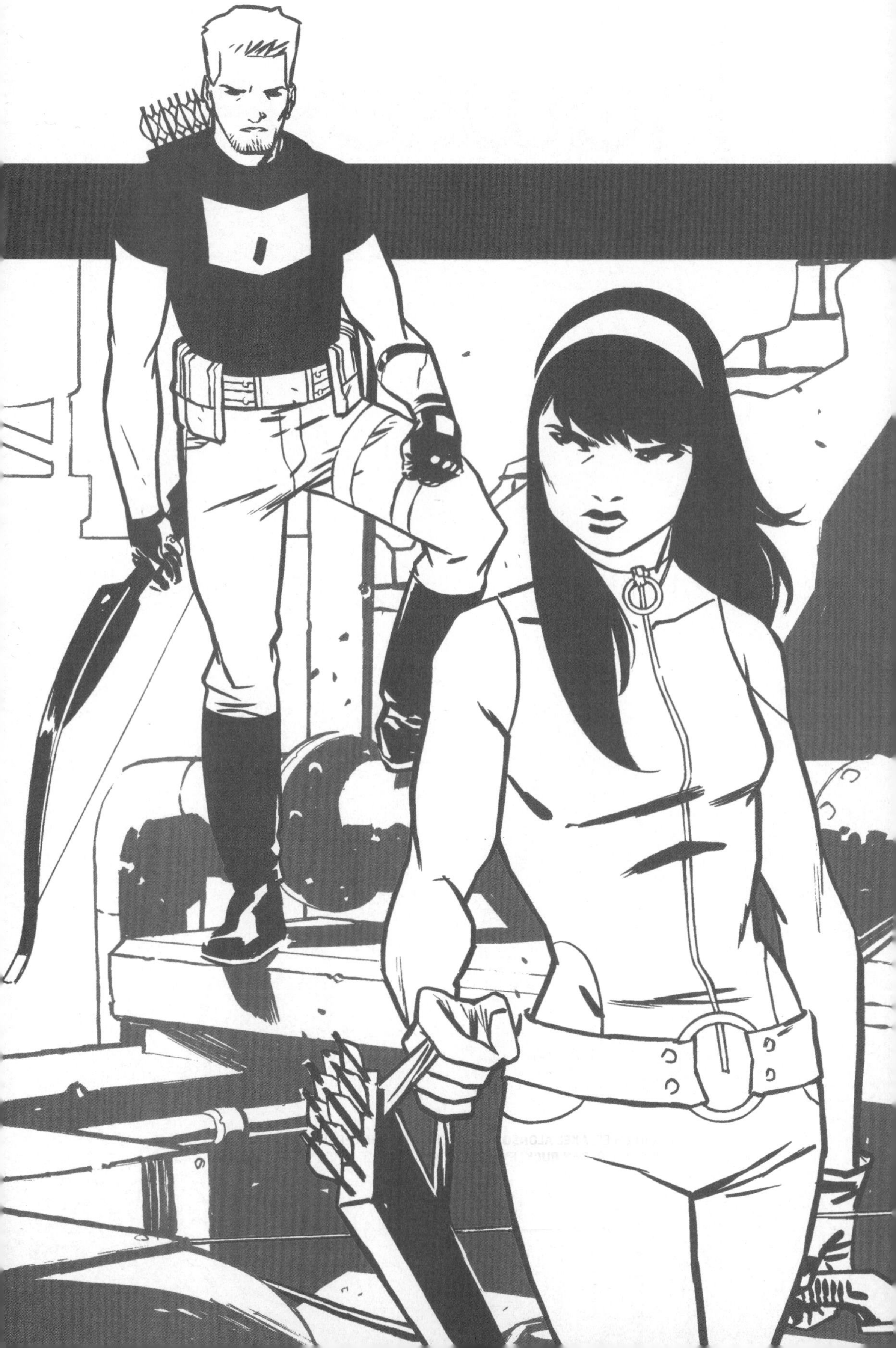

hawkeye

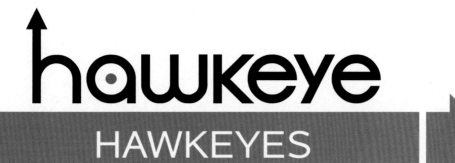

HAWKEYES

JEFF LEMIRE
WRITER

RAMÓN PÉREZ
ARTIST

IAN HERRING WITH **RAMÓN PÉREZ** (#4-6)
COLOR ARTISTS

VC's JOE SABINO
LETTERER

RAMÓN PÉREZ
COVER ART

CHARLES BEACHAM
ASSISTANT EDITOR

SANA AMANAT & DARREN SHAN
EDITORS

COLLECTION EDITOR: **JENNIFER GRÜNWALD** • ASSOCIATE EDITOR: **SARAH BRUNSTAD**
ASSOCIATE MANAGING EDITOR: **ALEX STARBUCK** • EDITOR, SPECIAL PROJECTS: **MARK D. BEAZLEY**
VP, PRODUCTION & SPECIAL PROJECTS: **JEFF YOUNGQUIST** • SVP PRINT, SALES & MARKETING: **DAVID GABRIEL**
BOOK DESIGNER: **JAY BOWEN**

EDITOR IN CHIEF: **AXEL ALONSO** • CHIEF CREATIVE OFFICER: **JOE QUESADA**
PUBLISHER: **DAN BUCKLEY** • EXECUTIVE PRODUCER: **ALAN FINE**

KEYE VOL. 6: HAWKEYES. Contains material originally published in magazine form as ALL-NEW HAWKEYE #1-6. First printing 2016. ISBN# 978-0-7851-9946-5. Published by MARVEL WORLDWIDE, INC., a subsidiary RVEL ENTERTAINMENT, LLC. OFFICE OF PUBLICATION: 135 West 50th Street, New York, NY 10020. Copyright © 2016 MARVEL No similarity between any of the names, characters, persons, and/or institutions in this zine with those of any living or dead person or institution is intended, and any such similarity which may exist is purely coincidental. **Printed in Canada**. ALAN FINE, President, Marvel Entertainment; DAN BUCKLEY, ent, TV, Publishing & Brand Management; JOE QUESADA, Chief Creative Officer; TOM BREVOORT, SVP of Publishing; DAVID BOGART, SVP of Business Affairs & Operations, Publishing & Partnership; C.B. CEBULSKI, Brand Management & Development, Asia; DAVID GABRIEL, SVP of Sales & Marketing, Publishing; JEFF YOUNGQUIST, VP of Production & Special Projects; DAN CARR, Executive Director of Publishing Technology; ALEX LES, Director of Publishing Operations; SUSAN CRESPI, Production Manager; STAN LEE, Chairman Emeritus. For information regarding advertising in Marvel Comics or on Marvel.com, please contact Vit DeBellis, ated Sales Manager, at vdebellis@marvel.com. For Marvel subscription inquiries, please call 888-511-5480. **Manufactured between 4/22/2016 and 5/30/2016 by SOLISCO PRINTERS, SCOTT, QC, CANADA.**

7654321

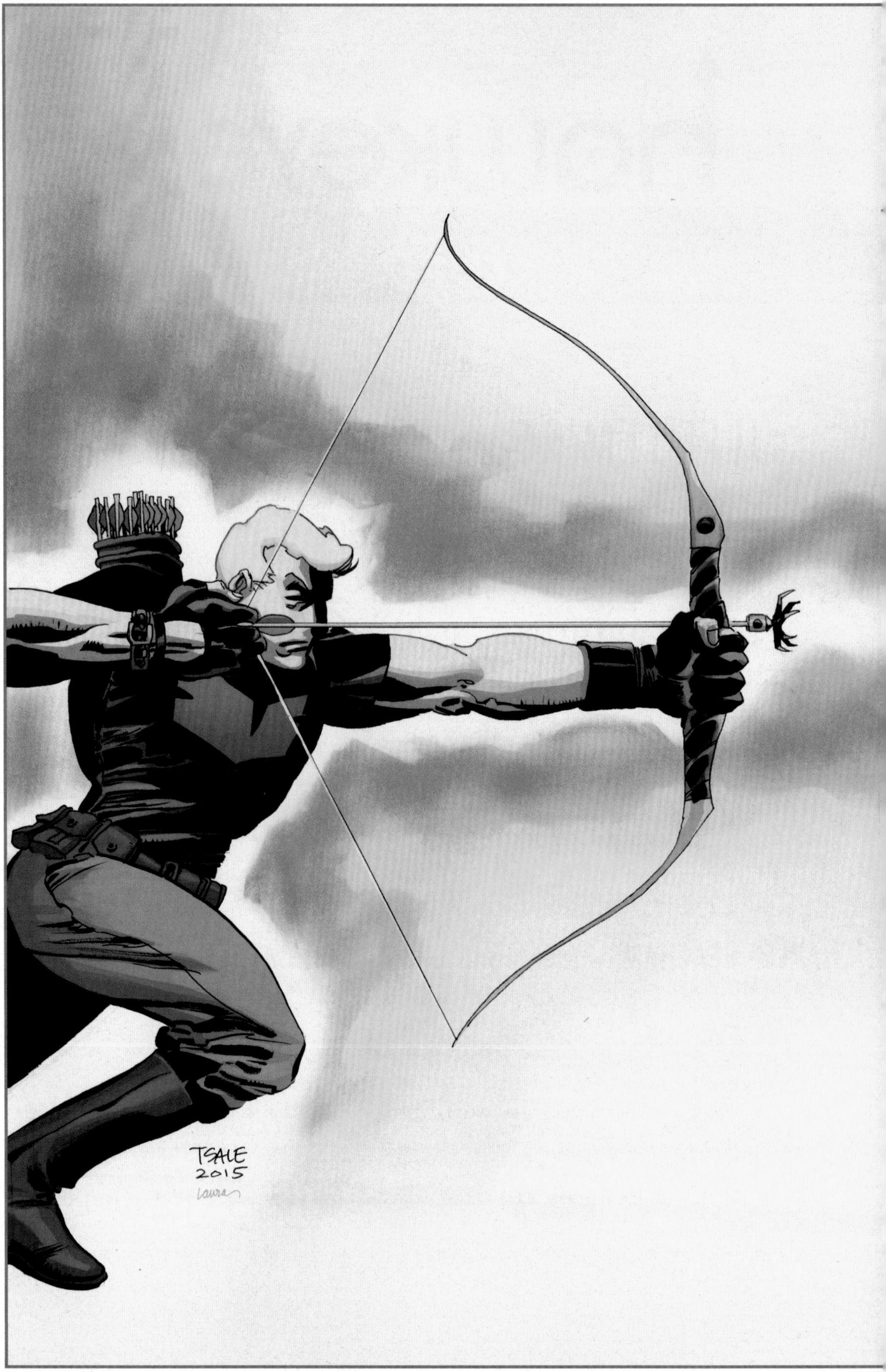
TSALE
2015

ALL-NEW HAWKEYE #1 VARIANT BY **TIM SALE** & **LAURA MARTIN**

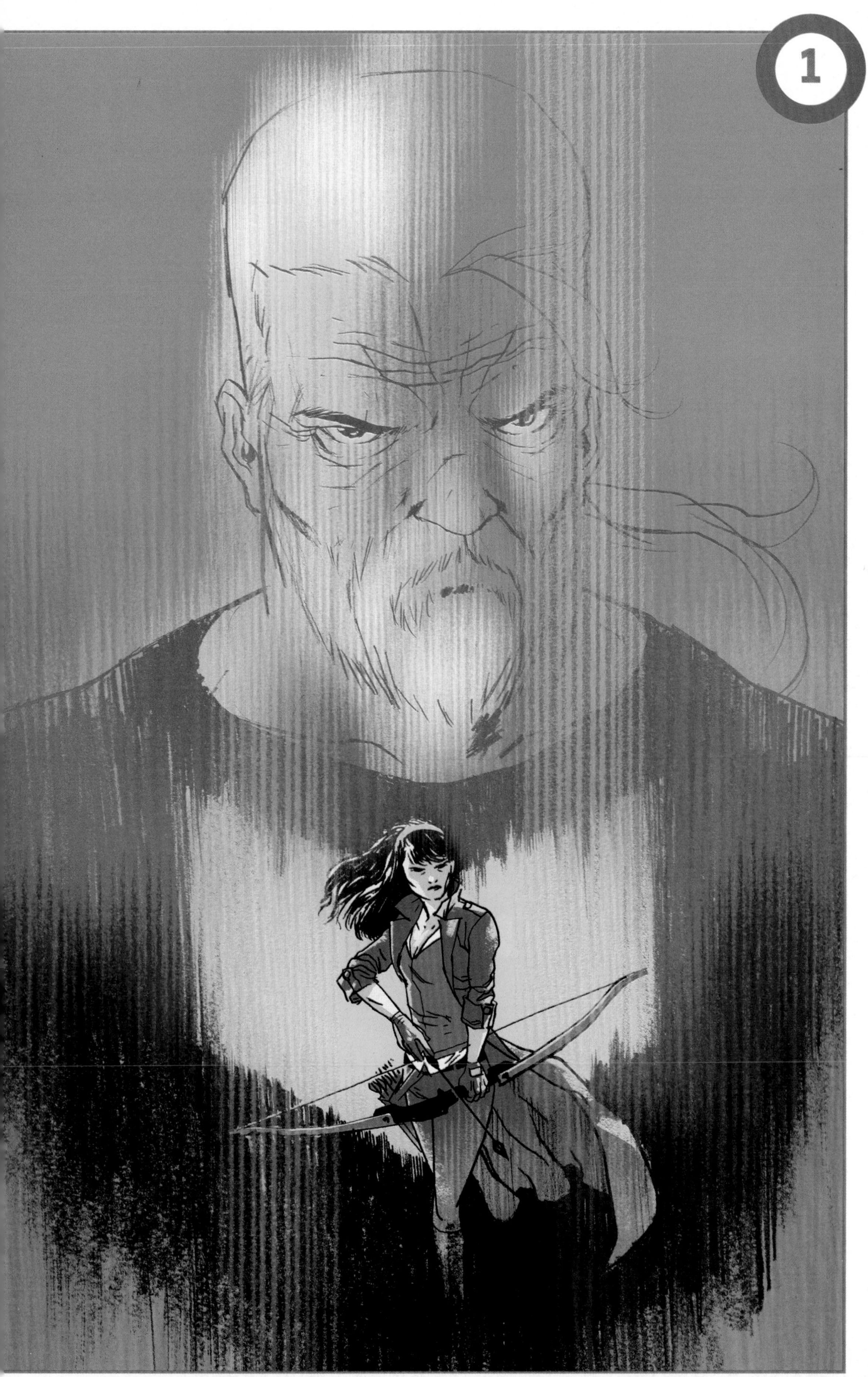
1

Clint Barton, a.k.a.

hawkeye

is one of the two greatest sharpshooters known to man.
He's also an Avenger.

Kate Bishop, a.k.a.

hawkeye

is the other one. (Some might say the better one.)

This is what they do when they do what they do best.

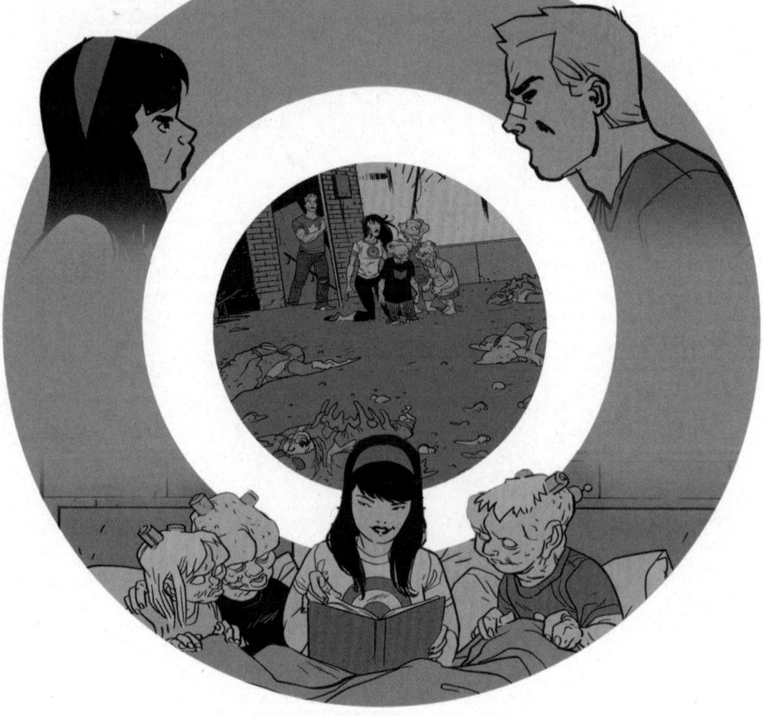

Following a disagreement during a secret mission for S.H.I.E.L.D., Kate and Clint have found it hard to nock arrows for even the most routine of missions.

With a rift growing between them, the future looks bleak for Team Hawkeye.

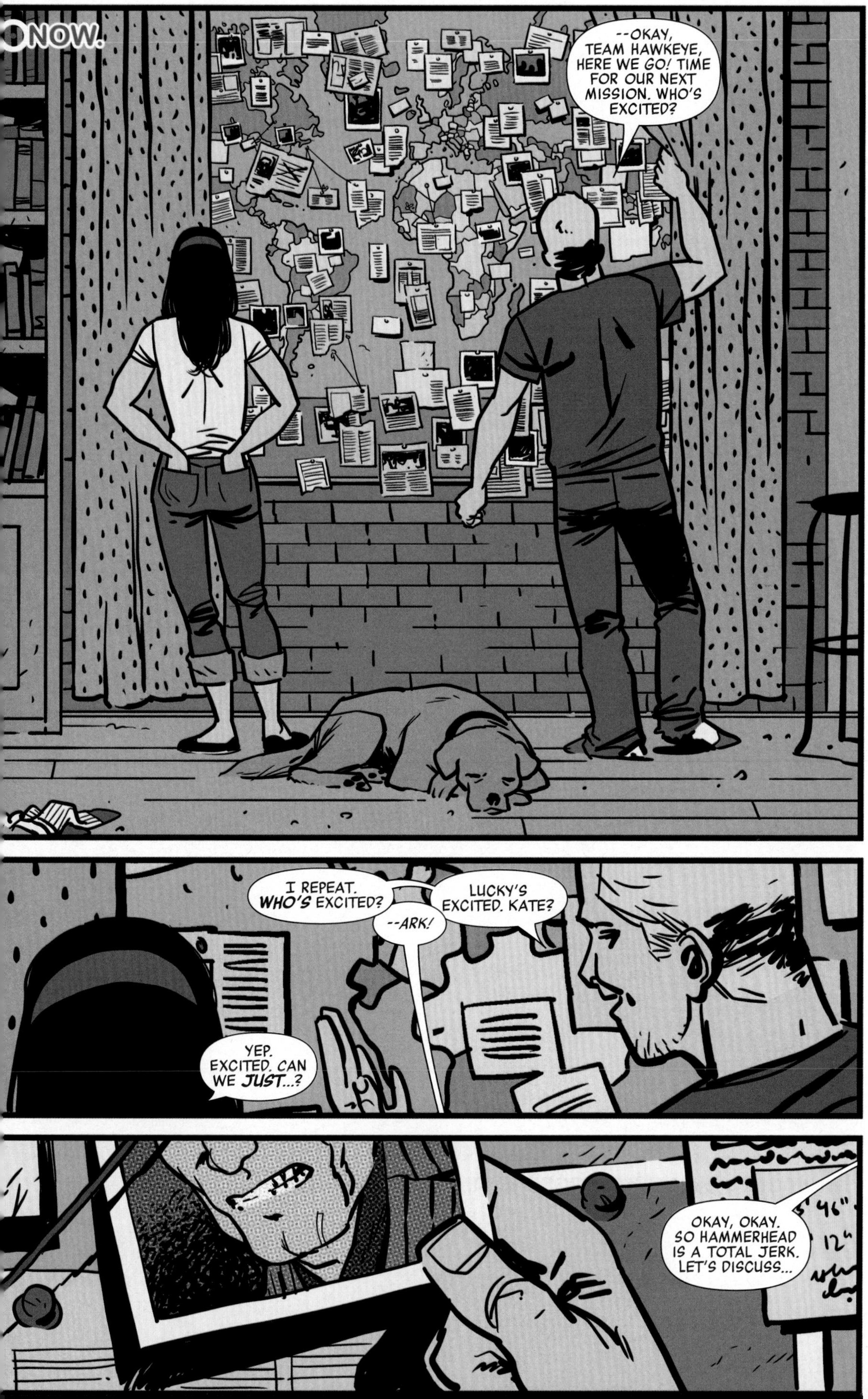
NOW.
--OKAY, TEAM HAWKEYE, HERE WE GO! TIME FOR OUR NEXT MISSION. WHO'S EXCITED?
I REPEAT. WHO'S EXCITED?
--ARK!
LUCKY'S EXCITED. KATE?
YEP. EXCITED. CAN WE JUST...?
OKAY, OKAY. SO HAMMERHEAD IS A TOTAL JERK. LET'S DISCUSS...

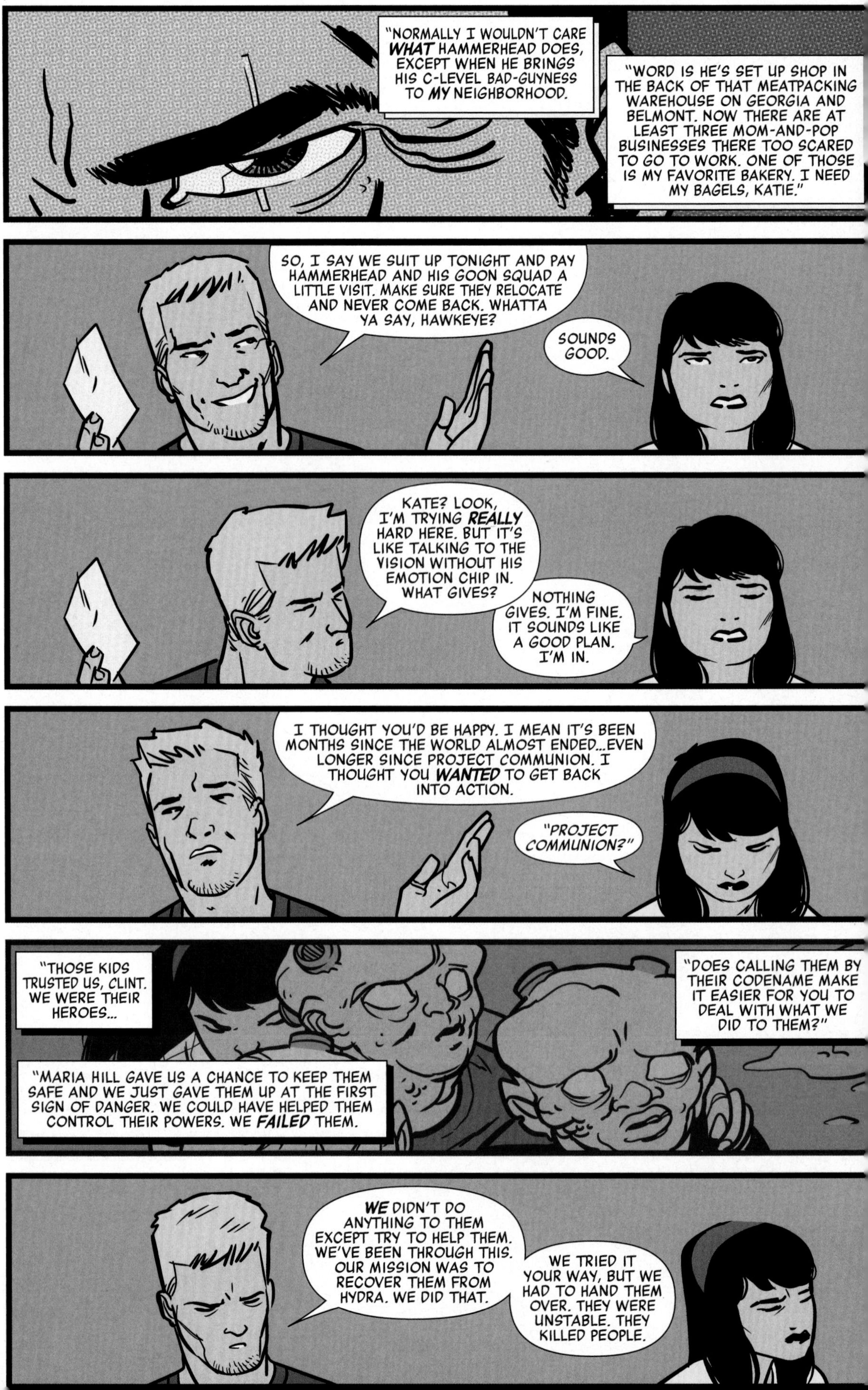
"NORMALLY I WOULDN'T CARE WHAT HAMMERHEAD DOES, EXCEPT WHEN HE BRINGS HIS C-LEVEL BAD-GUYNESS TO MY NEIGHBORHOOD.
"WORD IS HE'S SET UP SHOP IN THE BACK OF THAT MEATPACKING WAREHOUSE ON GEORGIA AND BELMONT. NOW THERE ARE AT LEAST THREE MOM-AND-POP BUSINESSES THERE TOO SCARED TO GO TO WORK. ONE OF THOSE IS MY FAVORITE BAKERY. I NEED MY BAGELS, KATIE."
SO, I SAY WE SUIT UP TONIGHT AND PAY HAMMERHEAD AND HIS GOON SQUAD A LITTLE VISIT. MAKE SURE THEY RELOCATE AND NEVER COME BACK. WHATTA YA SAY, HAWKEYE?
SOUNDS GOOD.
KATE? LOOK, I'M TRYING REALLY HARD HERE. BUT IT'S LIKE TALKING TO THE VISION WITHOUT HIS EMOTION CHIP IN. WHAT GIVES?
NOTHING GIVES. I'M FINE. IT SOUNDS LIKE A GOOD PLAN. I'M IN.
I THOUGHT YOU'D BE HAPPY. I MEAN IT'S BEEN MONTHS SINCE THE WORLD ALMOST ENDED...EVEN LONGER SINCE PROJECT COMMUNION. I THOUGHT YOU WANTED TO GET BACK INTO ACTION.
"PROJECT COMMUNION?"
"THOSE KIDS TRUSTED US, CLINT. WE WERE THEIR HEROES...
"MARIA HILL GAVE US A CHANCE TO KEEP THEM SAFE AND WE JUST GAVE THEM UP AT THE FIRST SIGN OF DANGER. WE COULD HAVE HELPED THEM CONTROL THEIR POWERS. WE FAILED THEM.
"DOES CALLING THEM BY THEIR CODENAME MAKE IT EASIER FOR YOU TO DEAL WITH WHAT WE DID TO THEM?"
WE DIDN'T DO ANYTHING TO THEM EXCEPT TRY TO HELP THEM. WE'VE BEEN THROUGH THIS. OUR MISSION WAS TO RECOVER THEM FROM HYDRA. WE DID THAT.
WE TRIED IT YOUR WAY, BUT WE HAD TO HAND THEM OVER. THEY WERE UNSTABLE. THEY KILLED PEOPLE.

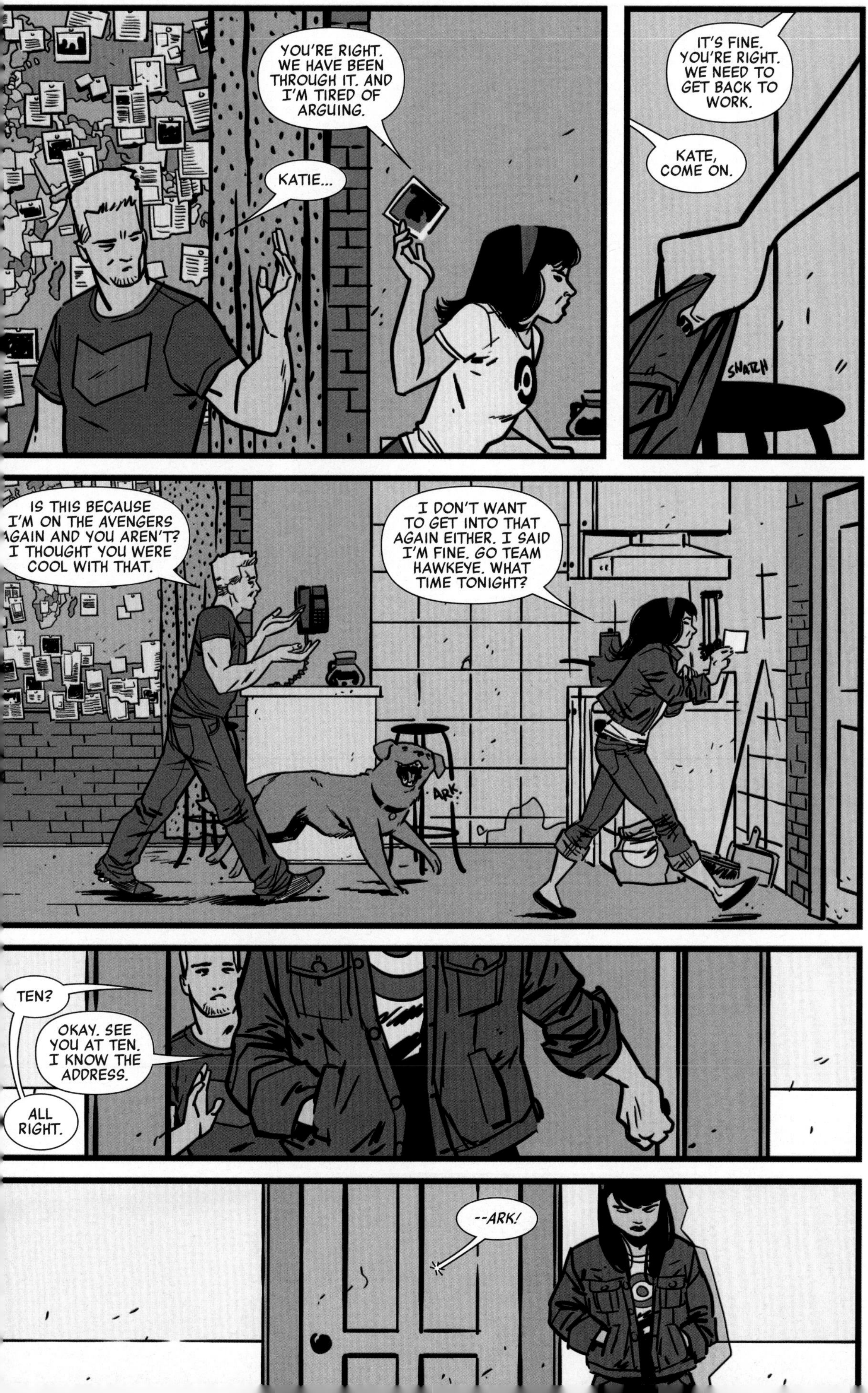
YOU'RE RIGHT. WE HAVE BEEN THROUGH IT. AND I'M TIRED OF ARGUING.
KATIE...
IT'S FINE. YOU'RE RIGHT. WE NEED TO GET BACK TO WORK.
KATE, COME ON.
SNATCH
IS THIS BECAUSE I'M ON THE AVENGERS AGAIN AND YOU AREN'T? I THOUGHT YOU WERE COOL WITH THAT.
I DON'T WANT TO GET INTO THAT AGAIN EITHER. I SAID I'M FINE. GO TEAM HAWKEYE. WHAT TIME TONIGHT?
ARK.
TEN?
OKAY. SEE YOU AT TEN. I KNOW THE ADDRESS.
ALL RIGHT.
--ARK!

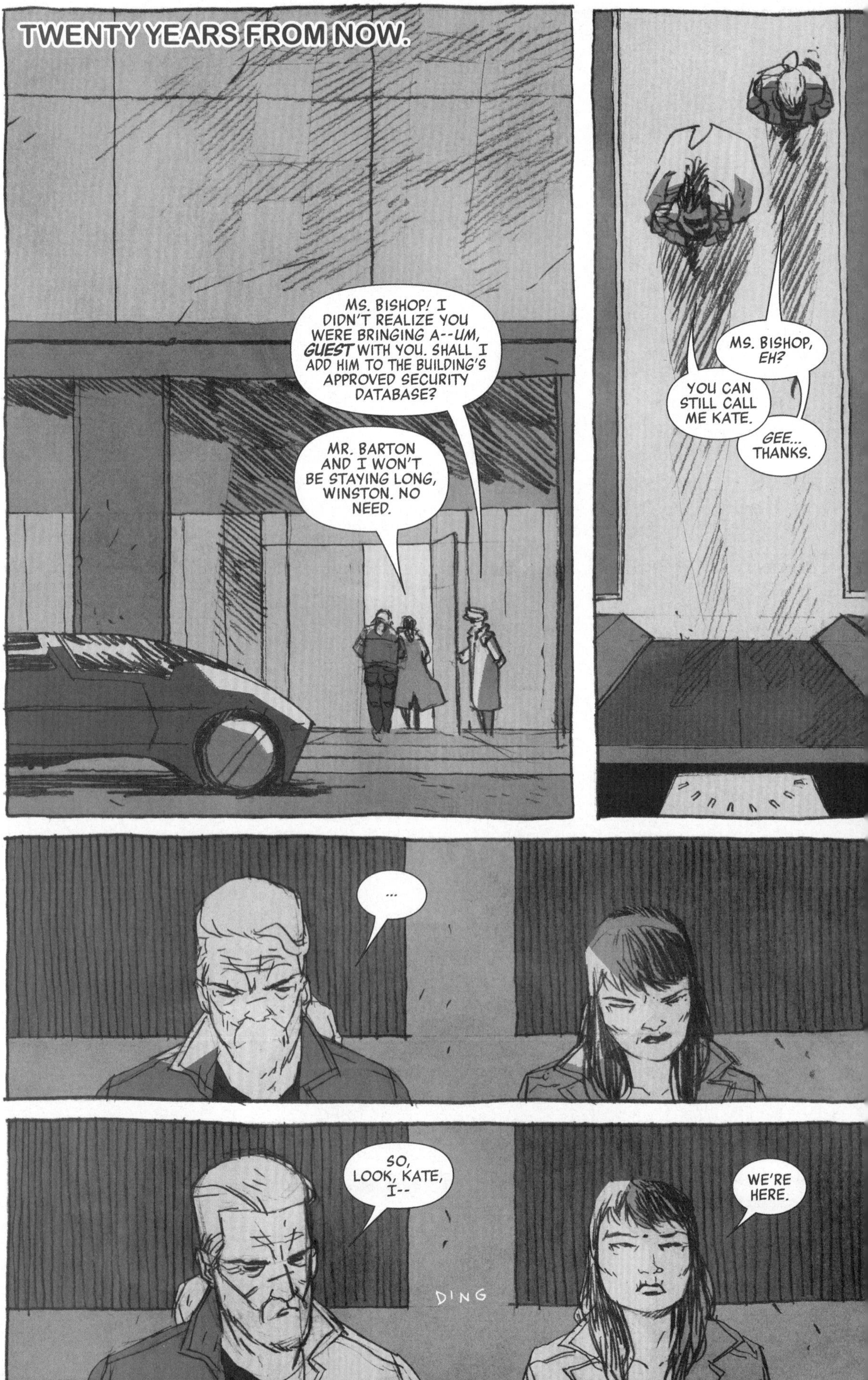
TWENTY YEARS FROM NOW.
MS. BISHOP! I DIDN'T REALIZE YOU WERE BRINGING A--UM, GUEST WITH YOU. SHALL I ADD HIM TO THE BUILDING'S APPROVED SECURITY DATABASE?
MR. BARTON AND I WON'T BE STAYING LONG, WINSTON. NO NEED.
MS. BISHOP, EH?
YOU CAN STILL CALL ME KATE.
GEE... THANKS.
...
SO, LOOK, KATE, I--
DING
WE'RE HERE.

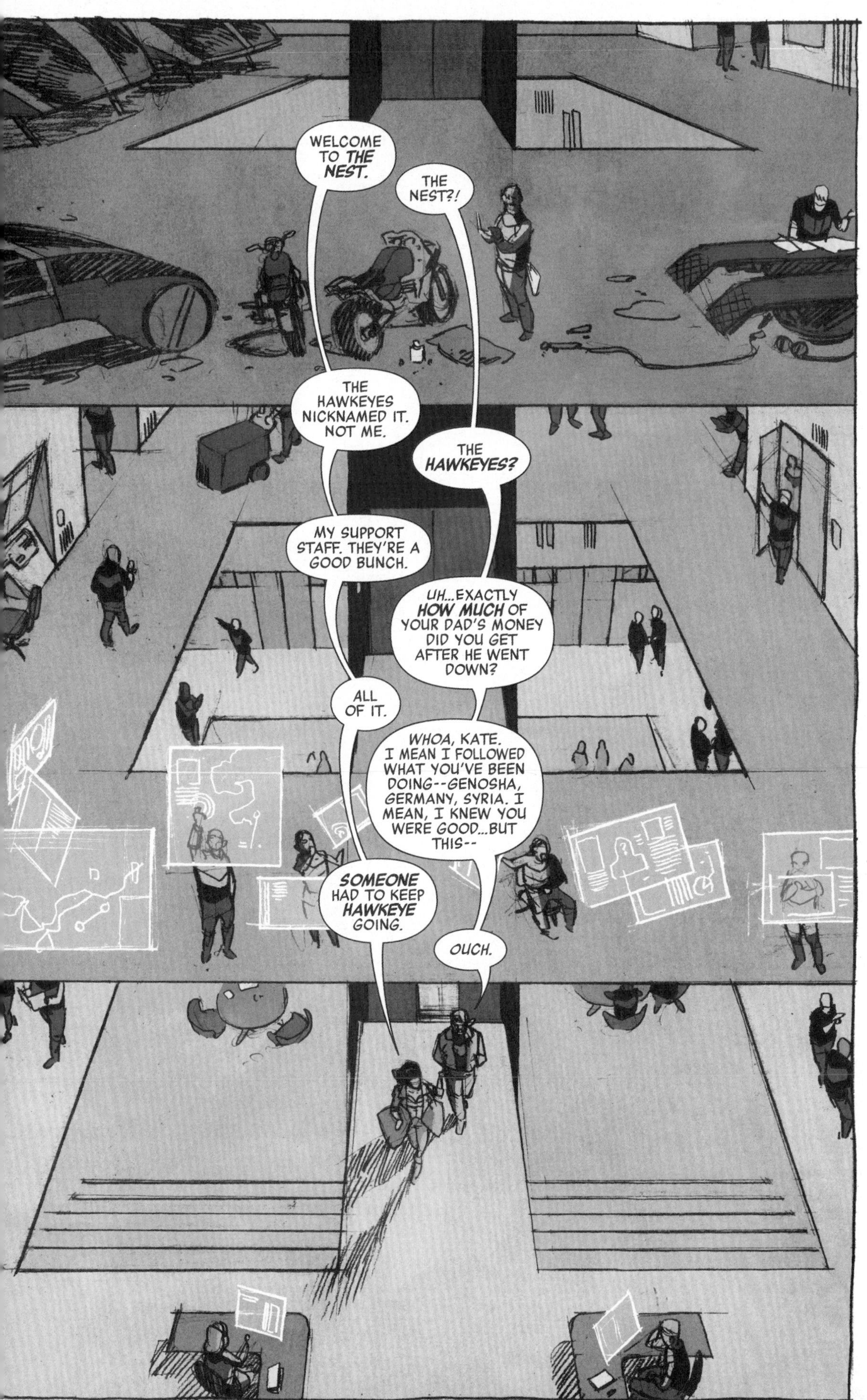

WELCOME TO THE NEST.
THE NEST?!
THE HAWKEYES NICKNAMED IT. NOT ME.
THE HAWKEYES?
MY SUPPORT STAFF. THEY'RE A GOOD BUNCH.
UH...EXACTLY HOW MUCH OF YOUR DAD'S MONEY DID YOU GET AFTER HE WENT DOWN?
ALL OF IT.
WHOA, KATE. I MEAN I FOLLOWED WHAT YOU'VE BEEN DOING--GENOSHA, GERMANY, SYRIA. I MEAN, I KNEW YOU WERE GOOD...BUT THIS--
SOMEONE HAD TO KEEP HAWKEYE GOING.
OUCH.

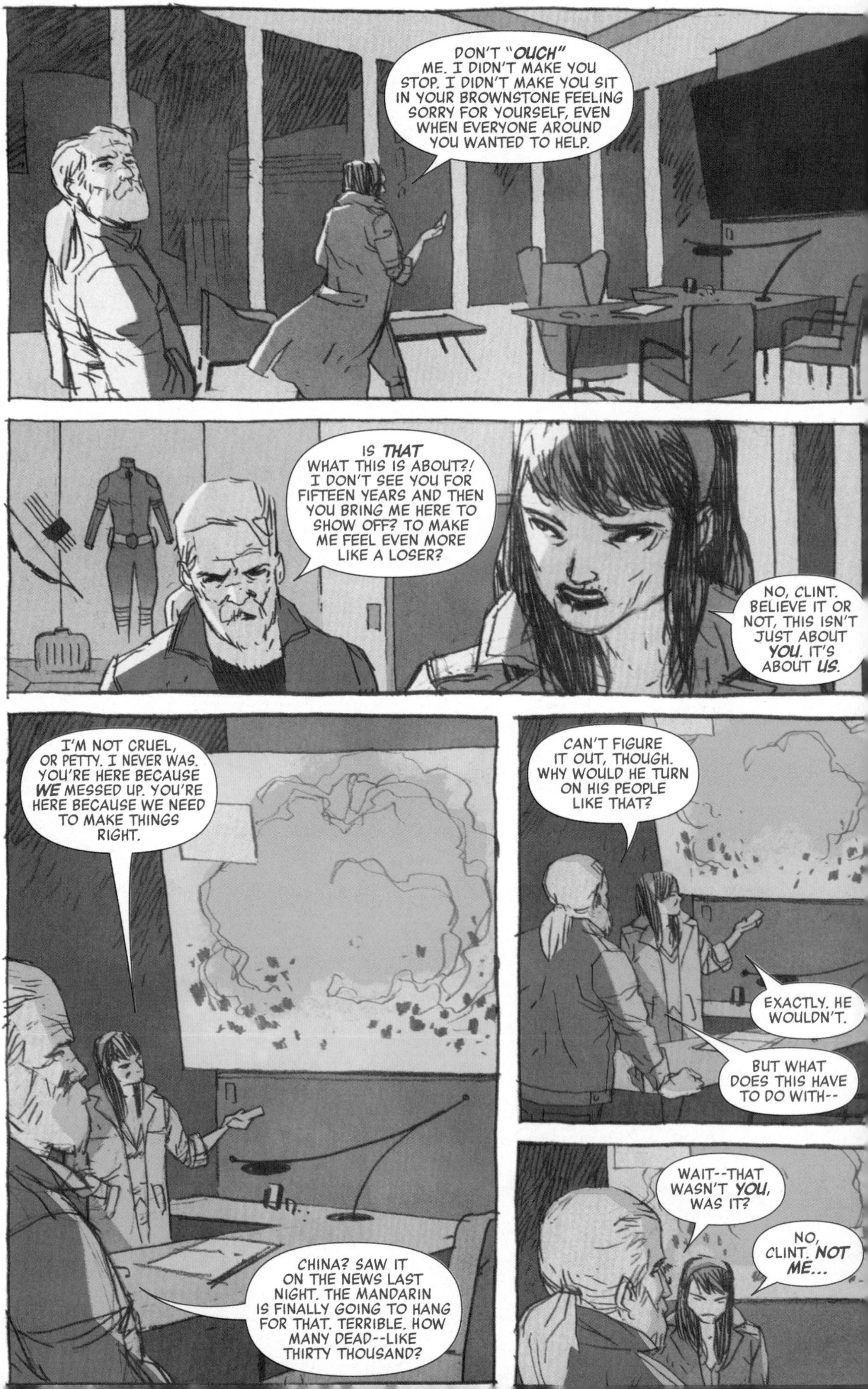

DON'T "OUCH" ME. I DIDN'T MAKE YOU STOP. I DIDN'T MAKE YOU SIT IN YOUR BROWNSTONE FEELING SORRY FOR YOURSELF, EVEN WHEN EVERYONE AROUND YOU WANTED TO HELP.
IS THAT WHAT THIS IS ABOUT?! I DON'T SEE YOU FOR FIFTEEN YEARS AND THEN YOU BRING ME HERE TO SHOW OFF? TO MAKE ME FEEL EVEN MORE LIKE A LOSER?
NO, CLINT. BELIEVE IT OR NOT, THIS ISN'T JUST ABOUT YOU. IT'S ABOUT US.
I'M NOT CRUEL, OR PETTY. I NEVER WAS. YOU'RE HERE BECAUSE WE MESSED UP. YOU'RE HERE BECAUSE WE NEED TO MAKE THINGS RIGHT.
CHINA? SAW IT ON THE NEWS LAST NIGHT. THE MANDARIN IS FINALLY GOING TO HANG FOR THAT. TERRIBLE. HOW MANY DEAD--LIKE THIRTY THOUSAND?
CAN'T FIGURE IT OUT, THOUGH. WHY WOULD HE TURN ON HIS PEOPLE LIKE THAT?
EXACTLY. HE WOULDN'T.
BUT WHAT DOES THIS HAVE TO DO WITH--
WAIT--THAT WASN'T YOU, WAS IT?
NO, CLINT. NOT ME...

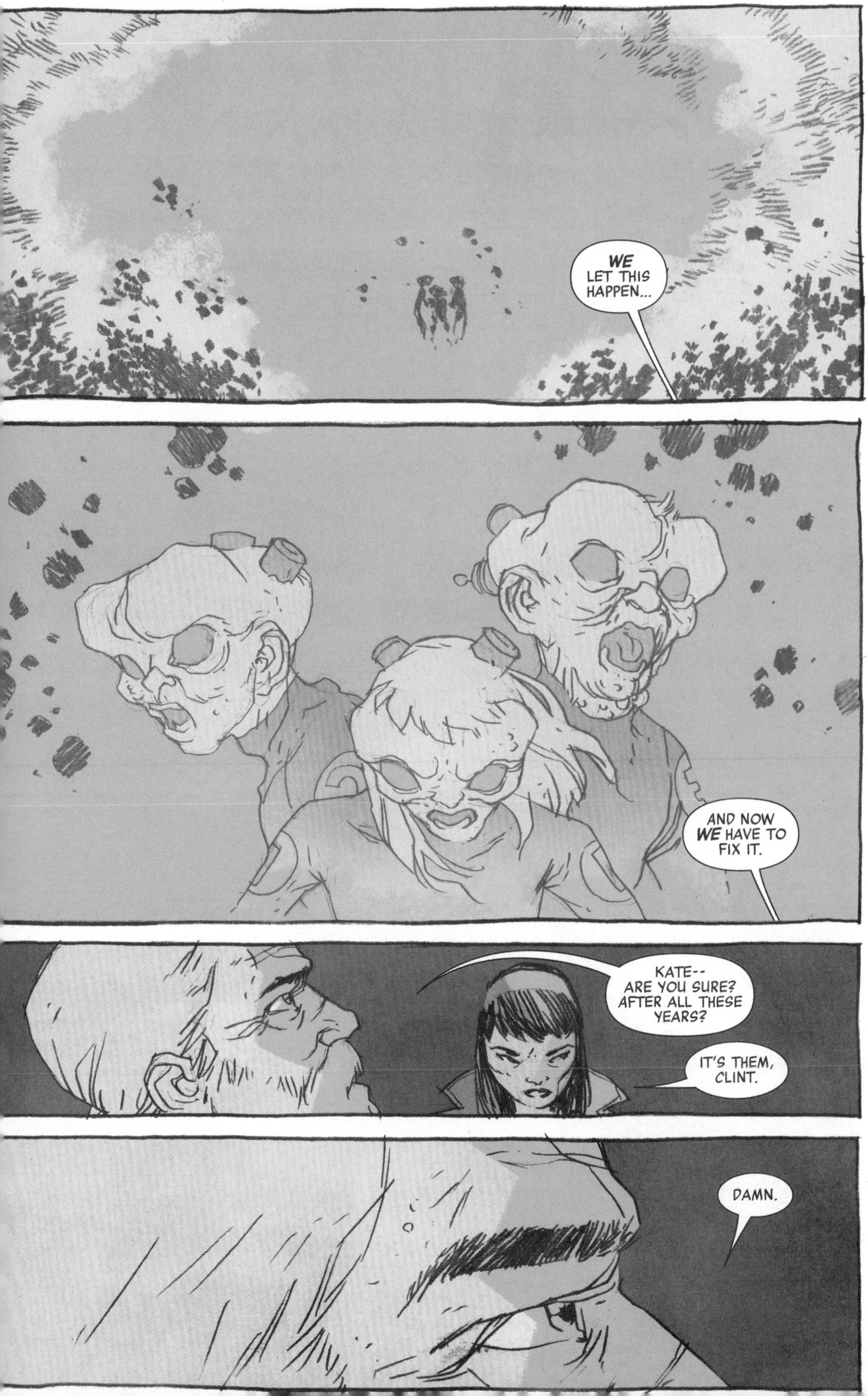
WE LET THIS HAPPEN...
AND NOW WE HAVE TO FIX IT.
KATE-- ARE YOU SURE? AFTER ALL THESE YEARS?
IT'S THEM, CLINT.
DAMN.

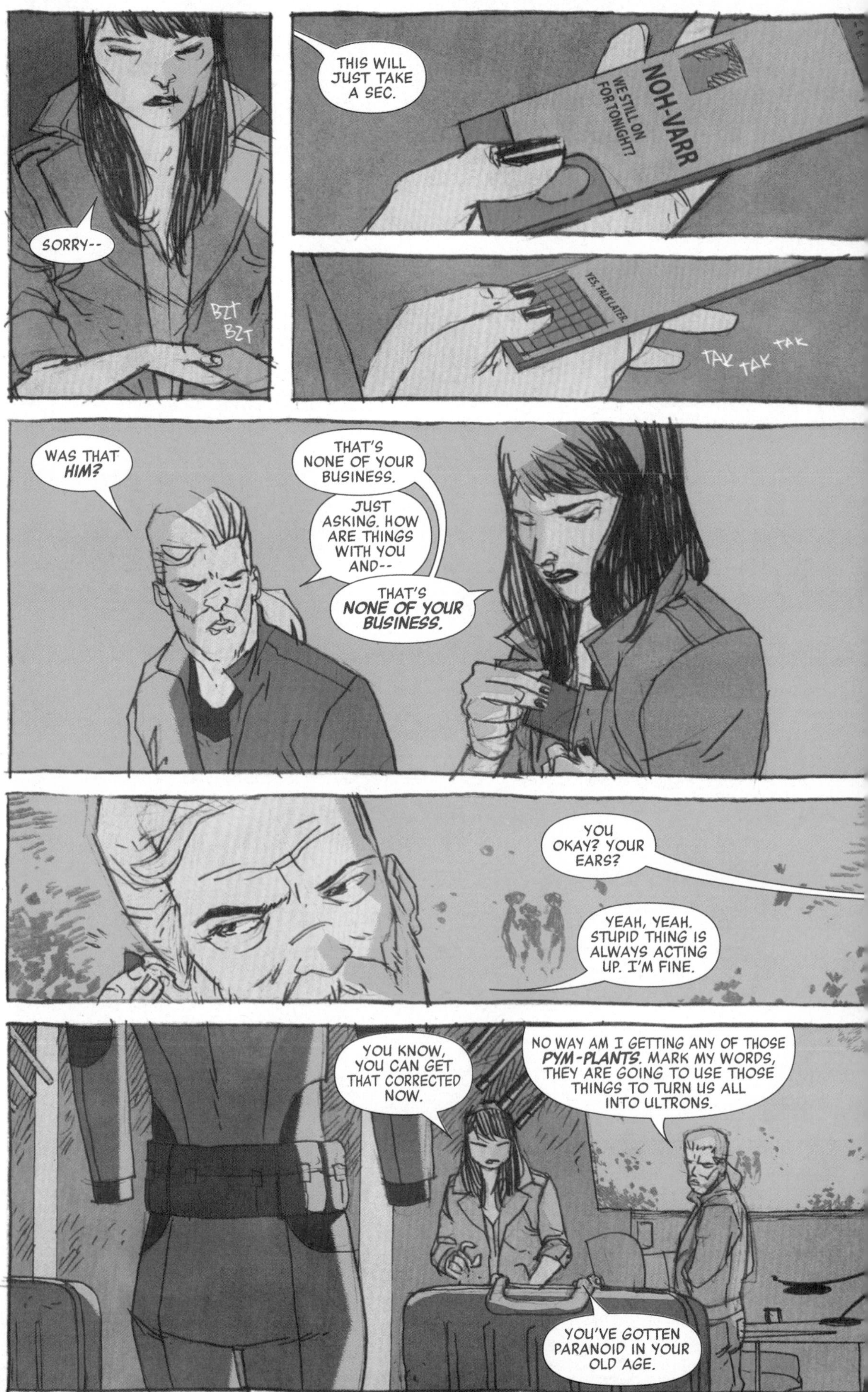
SORRY--
BZT BZT
THIS WILL JUST TAKE A SEC.
NOH-VARR
WE STILL ON FOR TONIGHT?
YES. TALK LATER.
TAK TAK TAK
WAS THAT HIM?
THAT'S NONE OF YOUR BUSINESS.
JUST ASKING. HOW ARE THINGS WITH YOU AND--
THAT'S NONE OF YOUR BUSINESS.
YOU OKAY? YOUR EARS?
YEAH, YEAH. STUPID THING IS ALWAYS ACTING UP. I'M FINE.
YOU KNOW, YOU CAN GET THAT CORRECTED NOW.
NO WAY AM I GETTING ANY OF THOSE PYM-PLANTS. MARK MY WORDS, THEY ARE GOING TO USE THOSE THINGS TO TURN US ALL INTO ULTRONS.
YOU'VE GOTTEN PARANOID IN YOUR OLD AGE.

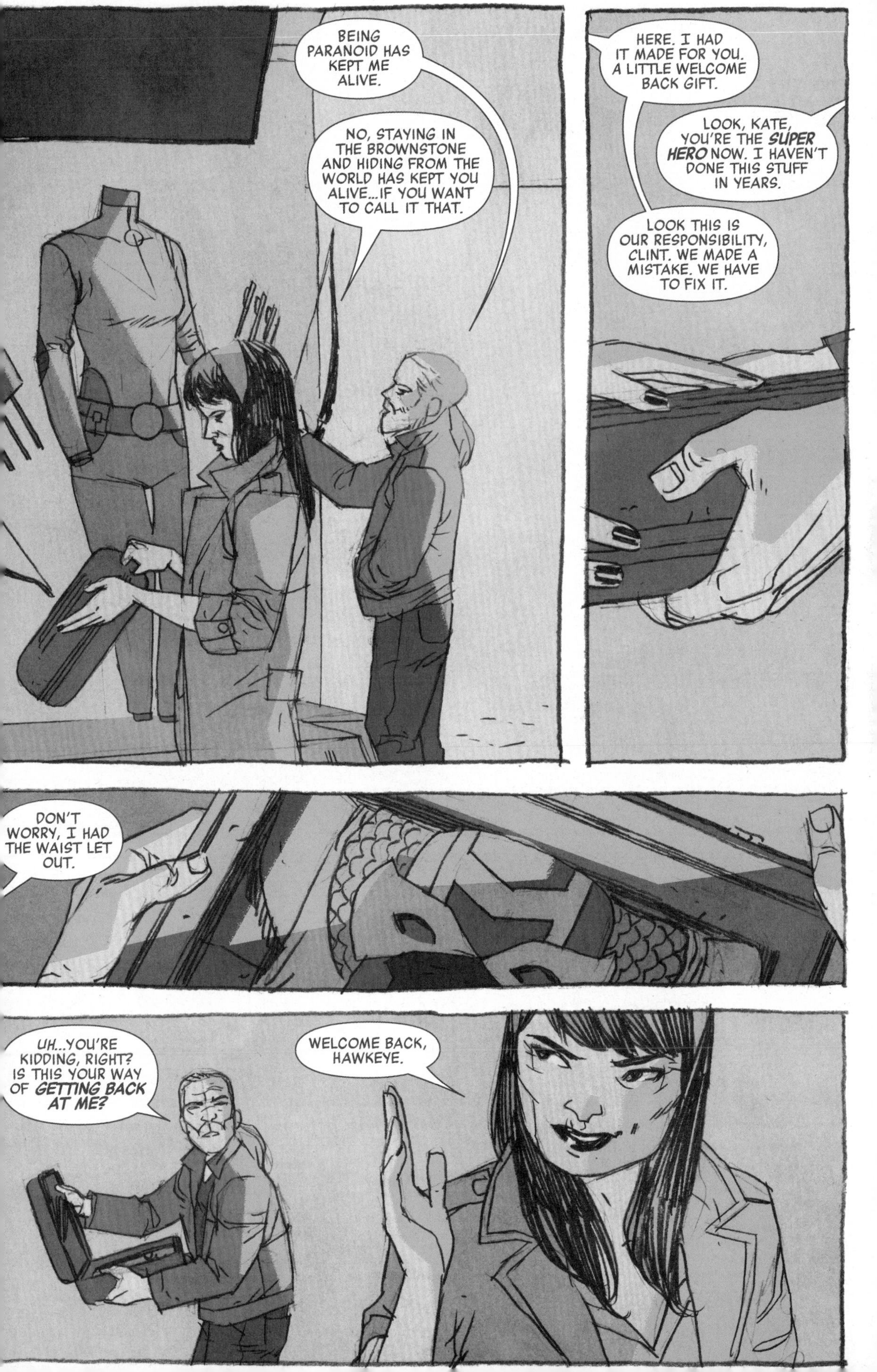
BEING PARANOID HAS KEPT ME ALIVE.
NO, STAYING IN THE BROWNSTONE AND HIDING FROM THE WORLD HAS KEPT YOU ALIVE...IF YOU WANT TO CALL IT THAT.
HERE. I HAD IT MADE FOR YOU. A LITTLE WELCOME BACK GIFT.
LOOK, KATE, YOU'RE THE SUPER HERO NOW. I HAVEN'T DONE THIS STUFF IN YEARS.
LOOK THIS IS OUR RESPONSIBILITY, CLINT. WE MADE A MISTAKE. WE HAVE TO FIX IT.
DON'T WORRY, I HAD THE WAIST LET OUT.
UH...YOU'RE KIDDING, RIGHT? IS THIS YOUR WAY OF GETTING BACK AT ME?
WELCOME BACK, HAWKEYE.

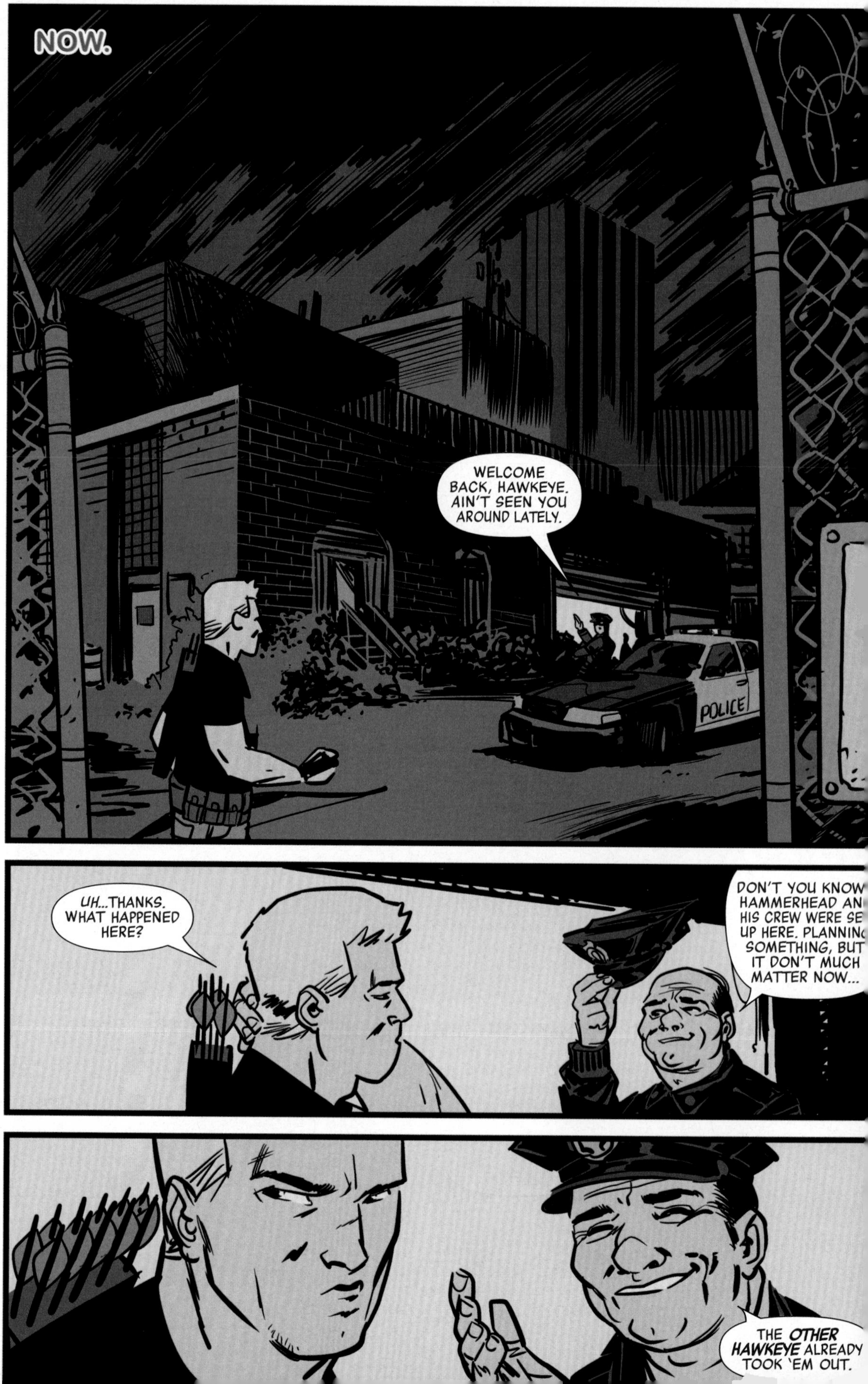
NOW.
WELCOME BACK, HAWKEYE. AIN'T SEEN YOU AROUND LATELY.
POLICE
UH...THANKS. WHAT HAPPENED HERE?
DON'T YOU KNOW HAMMERHEAD AN HIS CREW WERE SE UP HERE. PLANNIN SOMETHING, BUT IT DON'T MUCH MATTER NOW...
THE OTHER HAWKEYE ALREADY TOOK 'EM OUT.

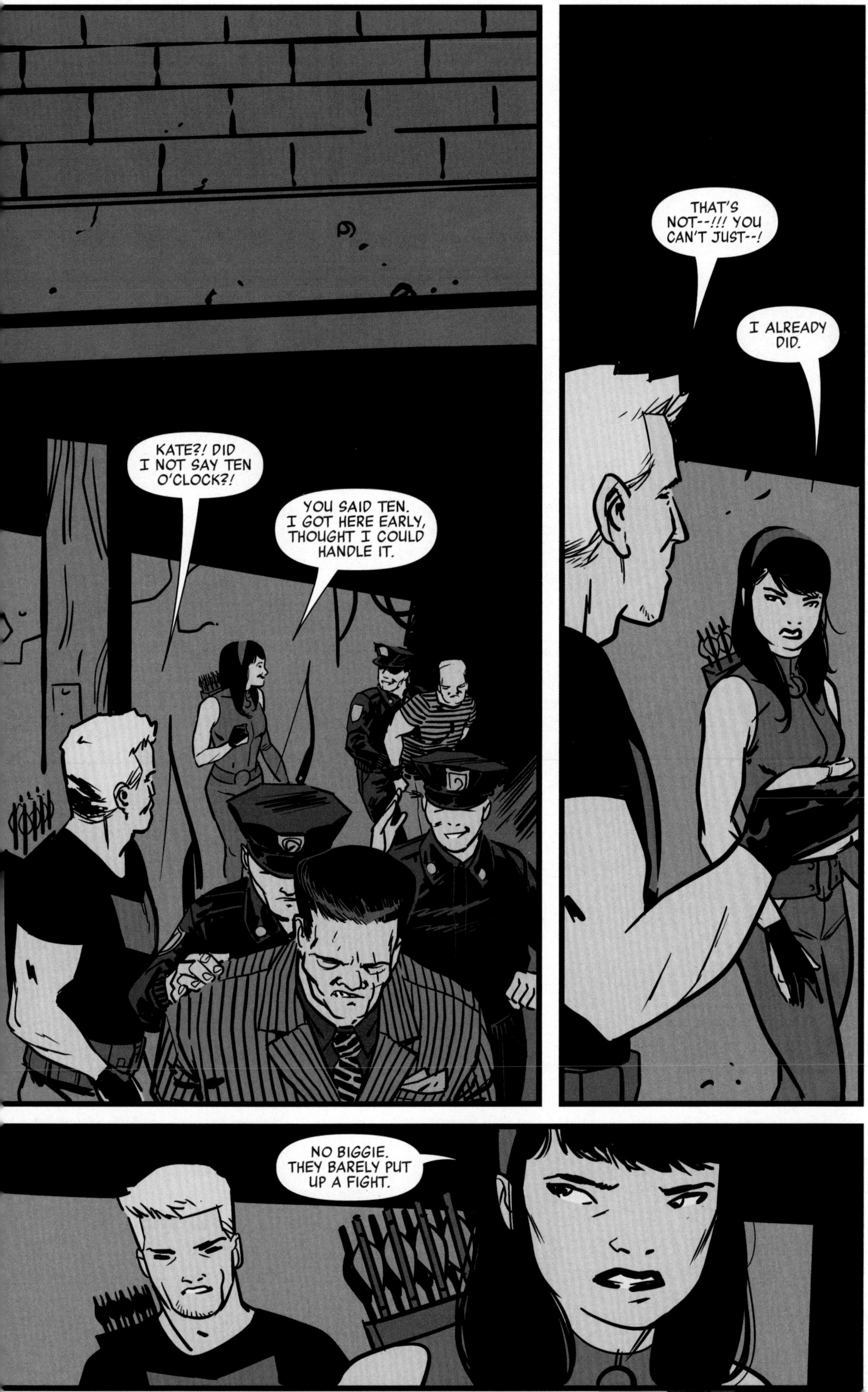
KATE?! DID I NOT SAY TEN O'CLOCK?!
YOU SAID TEN. I GOT HERE EARLY, THOUGHT I COULD HANDLE IT.
THAT'S NOT--!!! YOU CAN'T JUST--!
I ALREADY DID.
NO BIGGIE. THEY BARELY PUT UP A FIGHT.

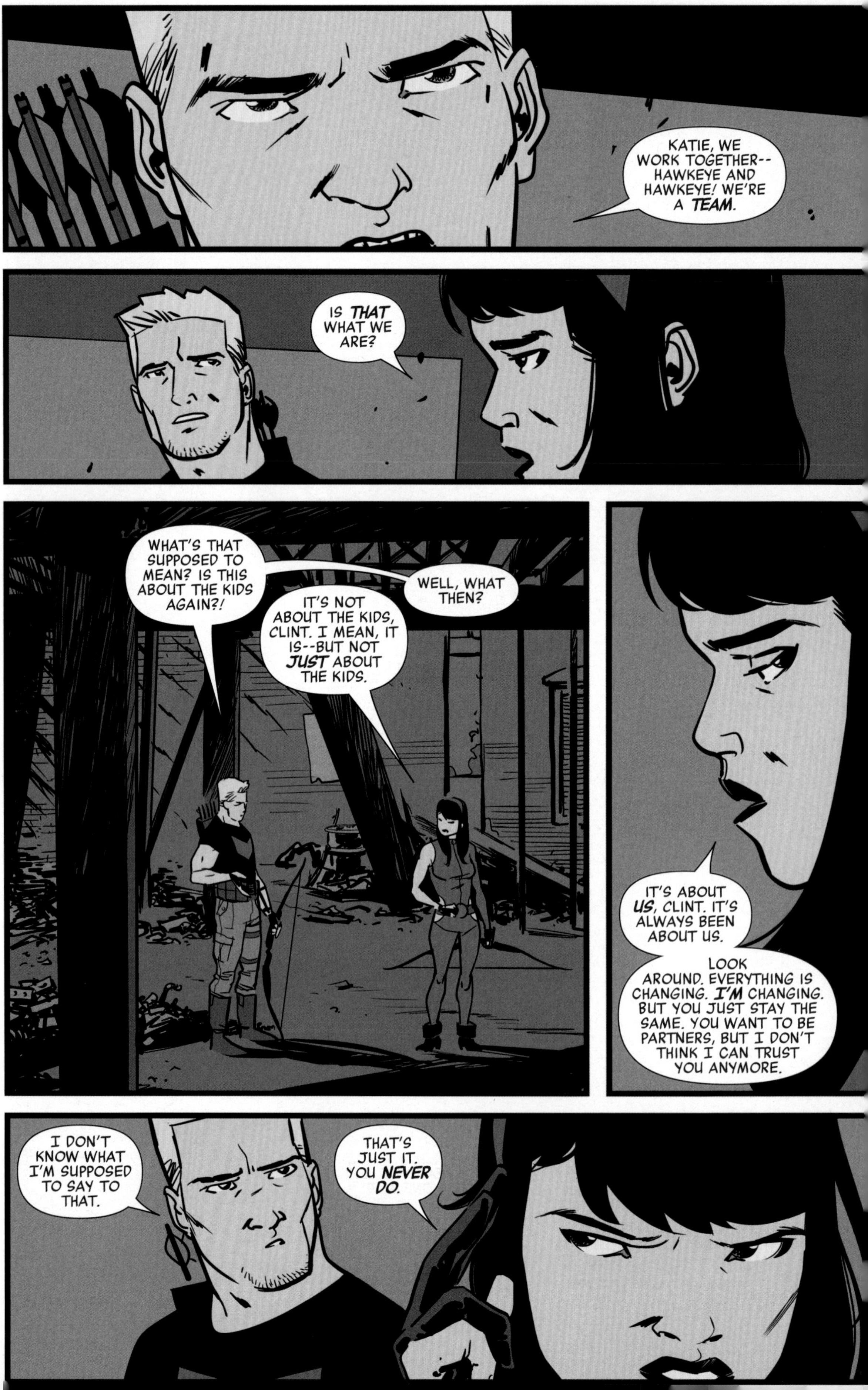
KATIE, WE WORK TOGETHER-- HAWKEYE AND HAWKEYE! WE'RE A TEAM.
IS THAT WHAT WE ARE?
WHAT'S THAT SUPPOSED TO MEAN? IS THIS ABOUT THE KIDS AGAIN?!
IT'S NOT ABOUT THE KIDS, CLINT. I MEAN, IT IS--BUT NOT JUST ABOUT THE KIDS.
WELL, WHAT THEN?
IT'S ABOUT US, CLINT. IT'S ALWAYS BEEN ABOUT US.
LOOK AROUND. EVERYTHING IS CHANGING. I'M CHANGING. BUT YOU JUST STAY THE SAME. YOU WANT TO BE PARTNERS, BUT I DON'T THINK I CAN TRUST YOU ANYMORE.
I DON'T KNOW WHAT I'M SUPPOSED TO SAY TO THAT.
THAT'S JUST IT. YOU NEVER DO.

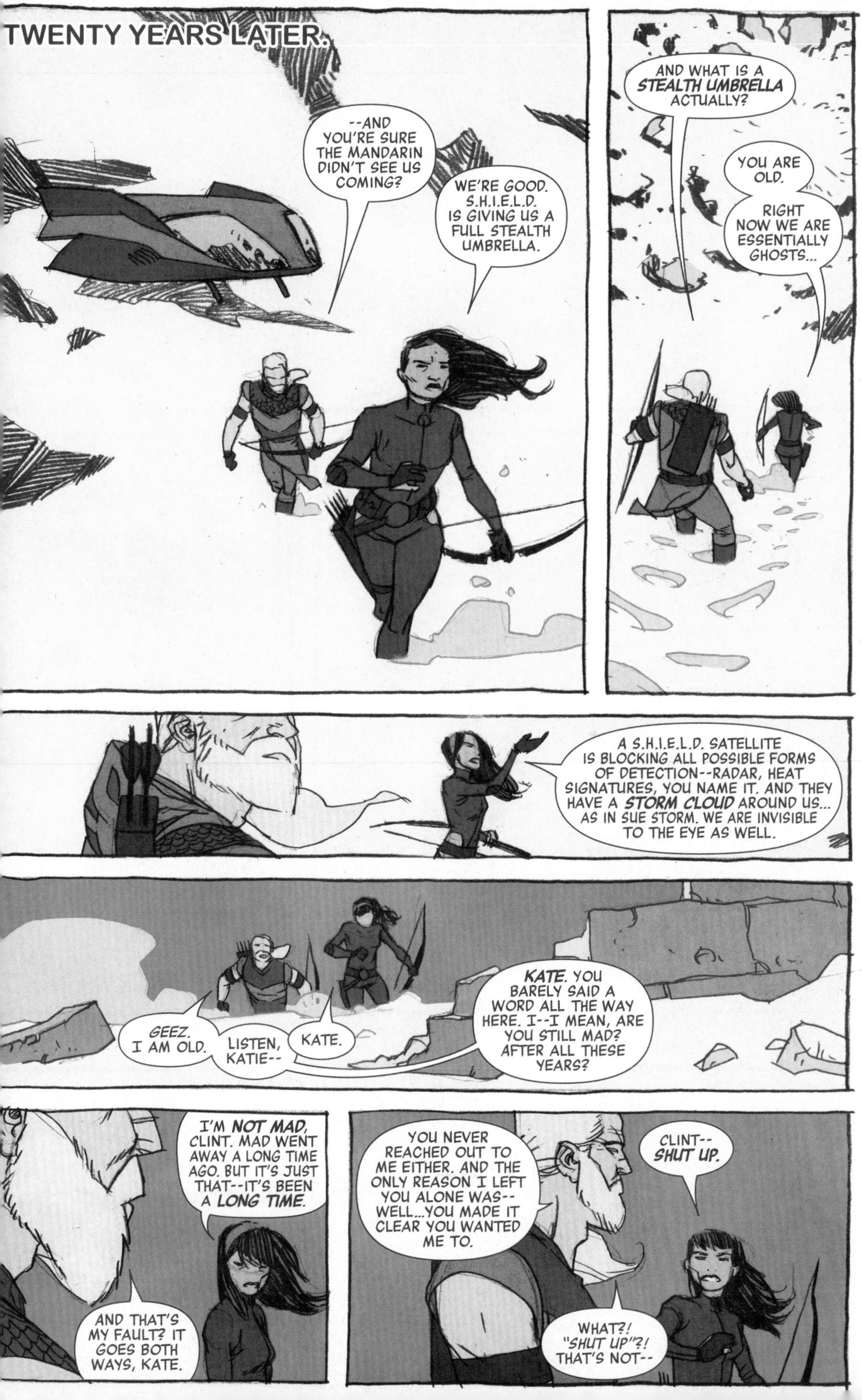
TWENTY YEARS LATER.
--AND YOU'RE SURE THE MANDARIN DIDN'T SEE US COMING?
WE'RE GOOD. S.H.I.E.L.D. IS GIVING US A FULL STEALTH UMBRELLA.
AND WHAT IS A STEALTH UMBRELLA ACTUALLY?
YOU ARE OLD.
RIGHT NOW WE ARE ESSENTIALLY GHOSTS...
A S.H.I.E.L.D. SATELLITE IS BLOCKING ALL POSSIBLE FORMS OF DETECTION--RADAR, HEAT SIGNATURES, YOU NAME IT. AND THEY HAVE A STORM CLOUD AROUND US... AS IN SUE STORM. WE ARE INVISIBLE TO THE EYE AS WELL.
GEEZ. I AM OLD.
LISTEN, KATIE--
KATE.
KATE. YOU BARELY SAID A WORD ALL THE WAY HERE. I--I MEAN, ARE YOU STILL MAD? AFTER ALL THESE YEARS?
I'M NOT MAD, CLINT. MAD WENT AWAY A LONG TIME AGO. BUT IT'S JUST THAT--IT'S BEEN A LONG TIME.
AND THAT'S MY FAULT? IT GOES BOTH WAYS, KATE.
YOU NEVER REACHED OUT TO ME EITHER. AND THE ONLY REASON I LEFT YOU ALONE WAS--WELL...YOU MADE IT CLEAR YOU WANTED ME TO.
CLINT--SHUT UP.
WHAT?! "SHUT UP"?! THAT'S NOT--

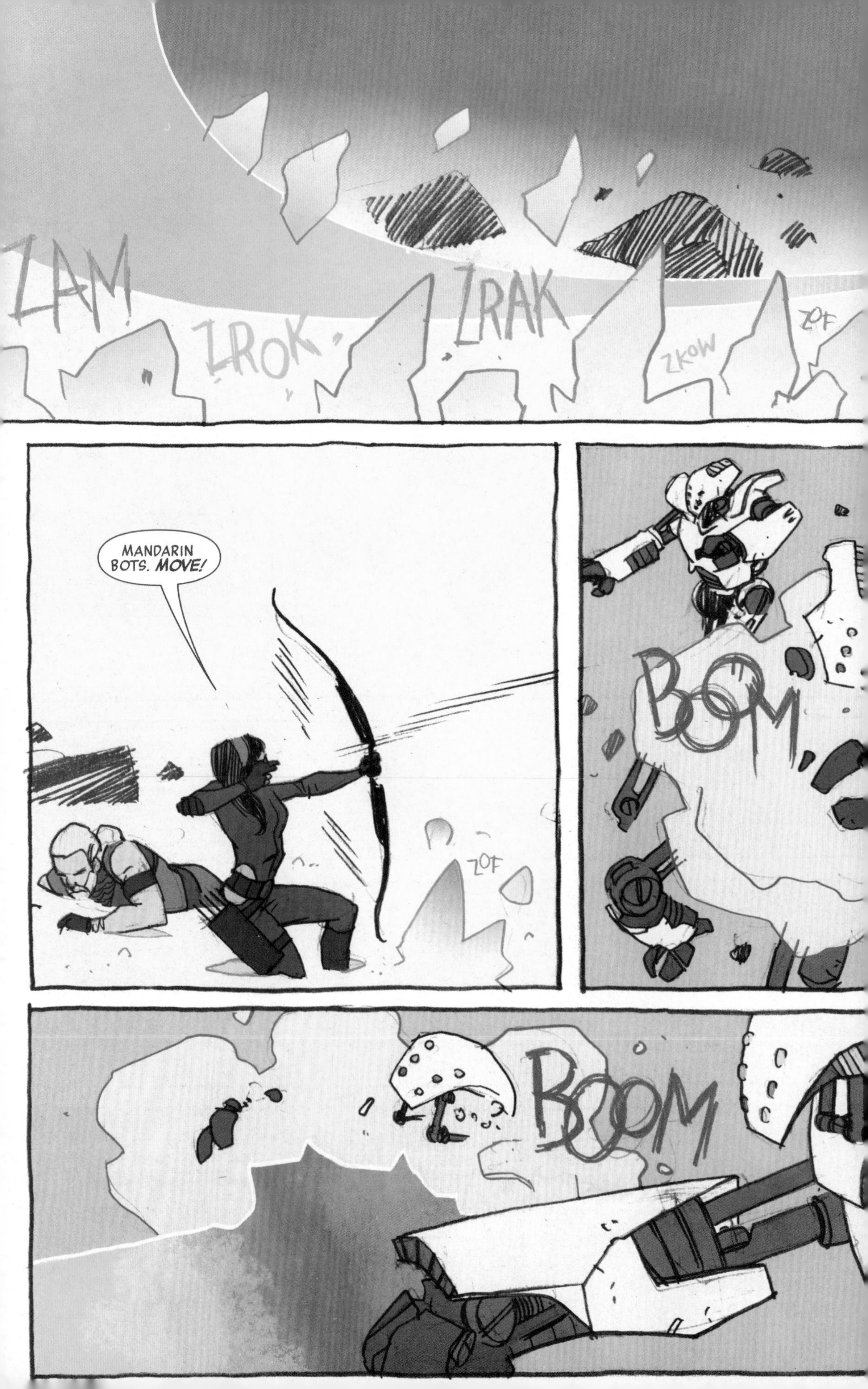
ZAM
ZROK
ZRAK
ZKOW
ZOF
MANDARIN BOTS. MOVE!
ZOF
BOOM
BOOM

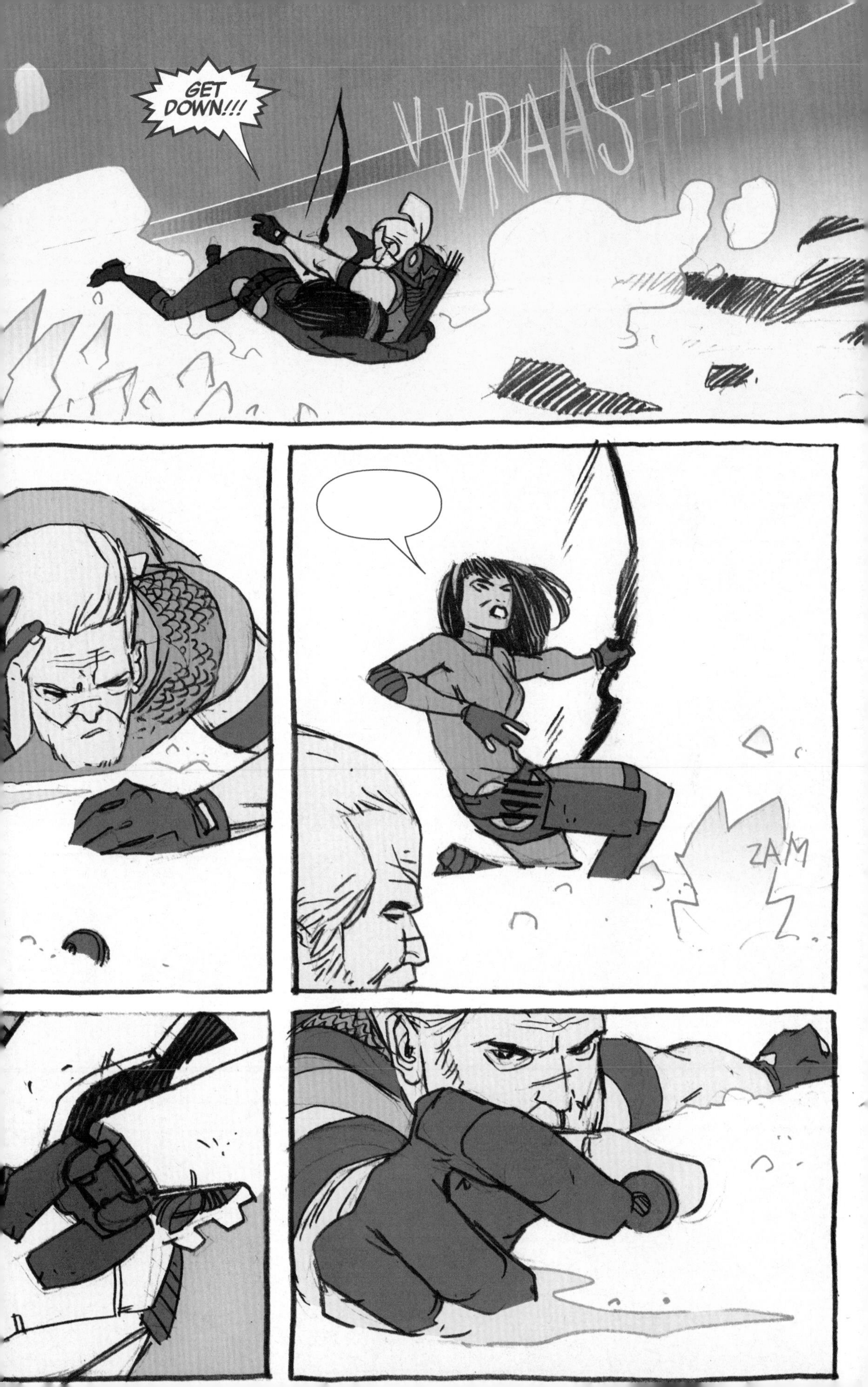
GET DOWN!!!
VVRAASHHHHH
ZAM

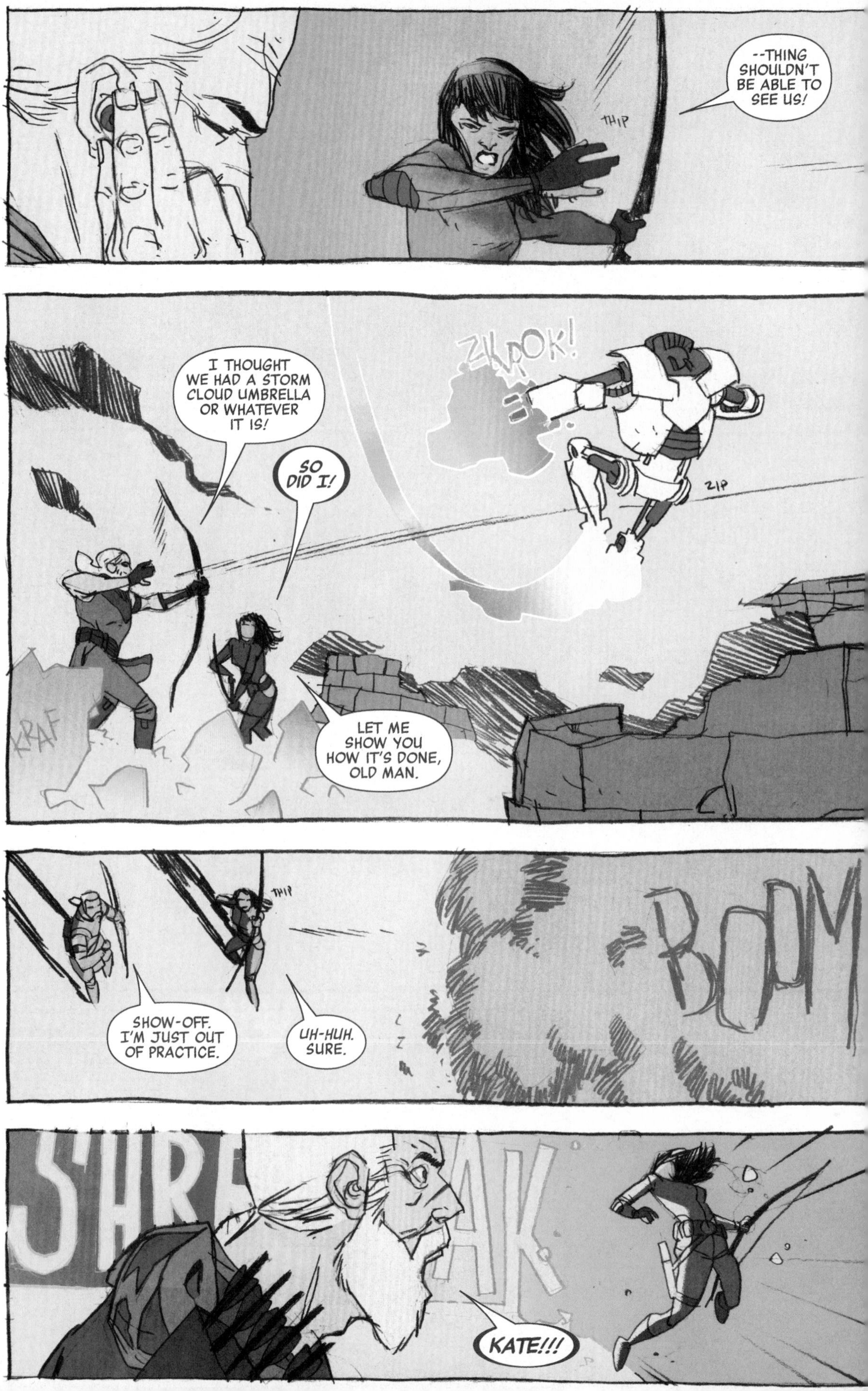
--THING SHOULDN'T BE ABLE TO SEE US!
THIP
I THOUGHT WE HAD A STORM CLOUD UMBRELLA OR WHATEVER IT IS!
SO DID I!
ZIP
KRAF
LET ME SHOW YOU HOW IT'S DONE, OLD MAN.
THIP
SHOW-OFF. I'M JUST OUT OF PRACTICE.
UH-HUH. SURE.
BOOM
KATE!!!

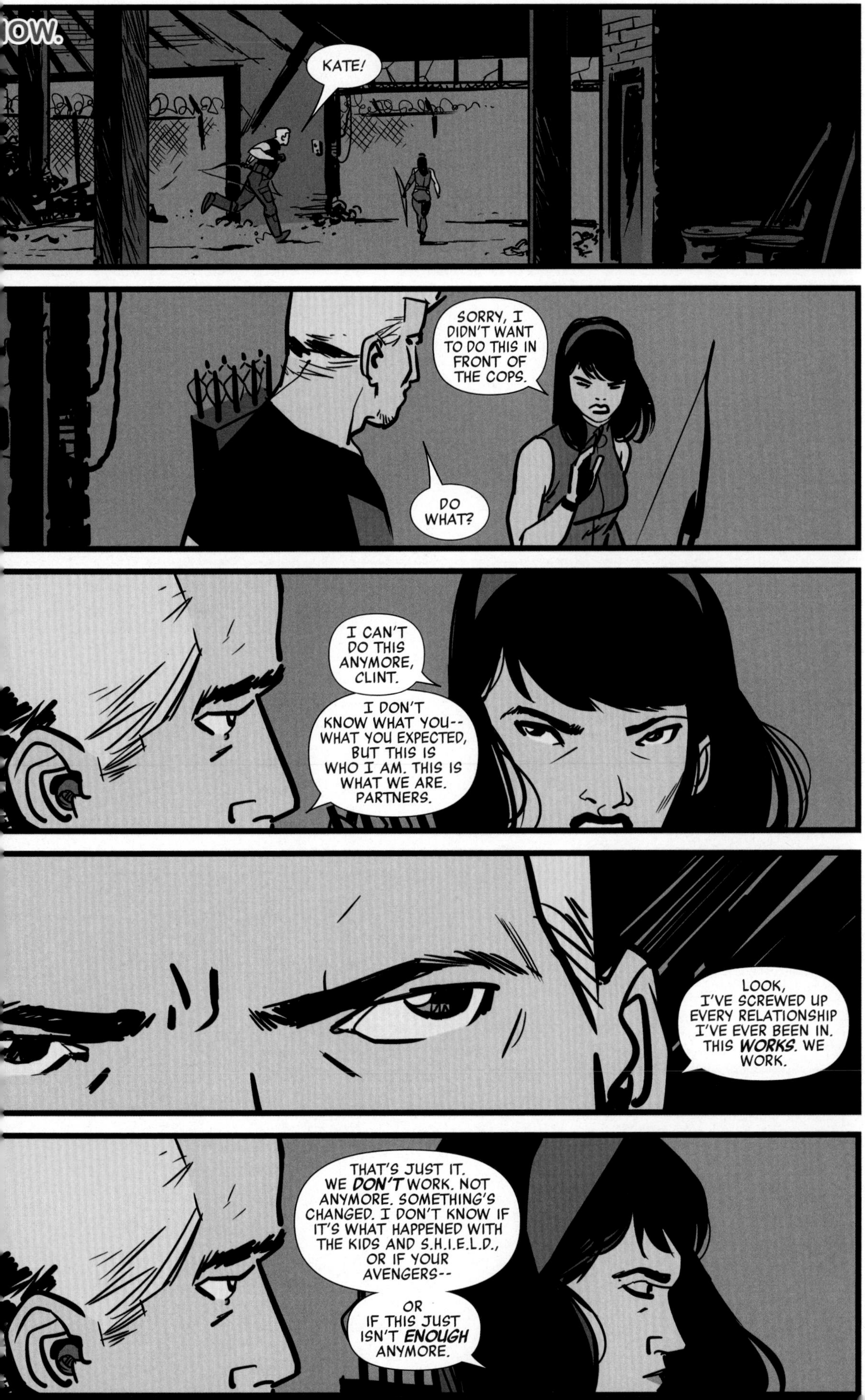
OW.
KATE!
SORRY, I DIDN'T WANT TO DO THIS IN FRONT OF THE COPS.
DO WHAT?
I CAN'T DO THIS ANYMORE, CLINT.
I DON'T KNOW WHAT YOU-- WHAT YOU EXPECTED, BUT THIS IS WHO I AM. THIS IS WHAT WE ARE. PARTNERS.
LOOK, I'VE SCREWED UP EVERY RELATIONSHIP I'VE EVER BEEN IN. THIS WORKS. WE WORK.
THAT'S JUST IT. WE DON'T WORK. NOT ANYMORE. SOMETHING'S CHANGED. I DON'T KNOW IF IT'S WHAT HAPPENED WITH THE KIDS AND S.H.I.E.L.D., OR IF YOUR AVENGERS--
OR IF THIS JUST ISN'T ENOUGH ANYMORE.

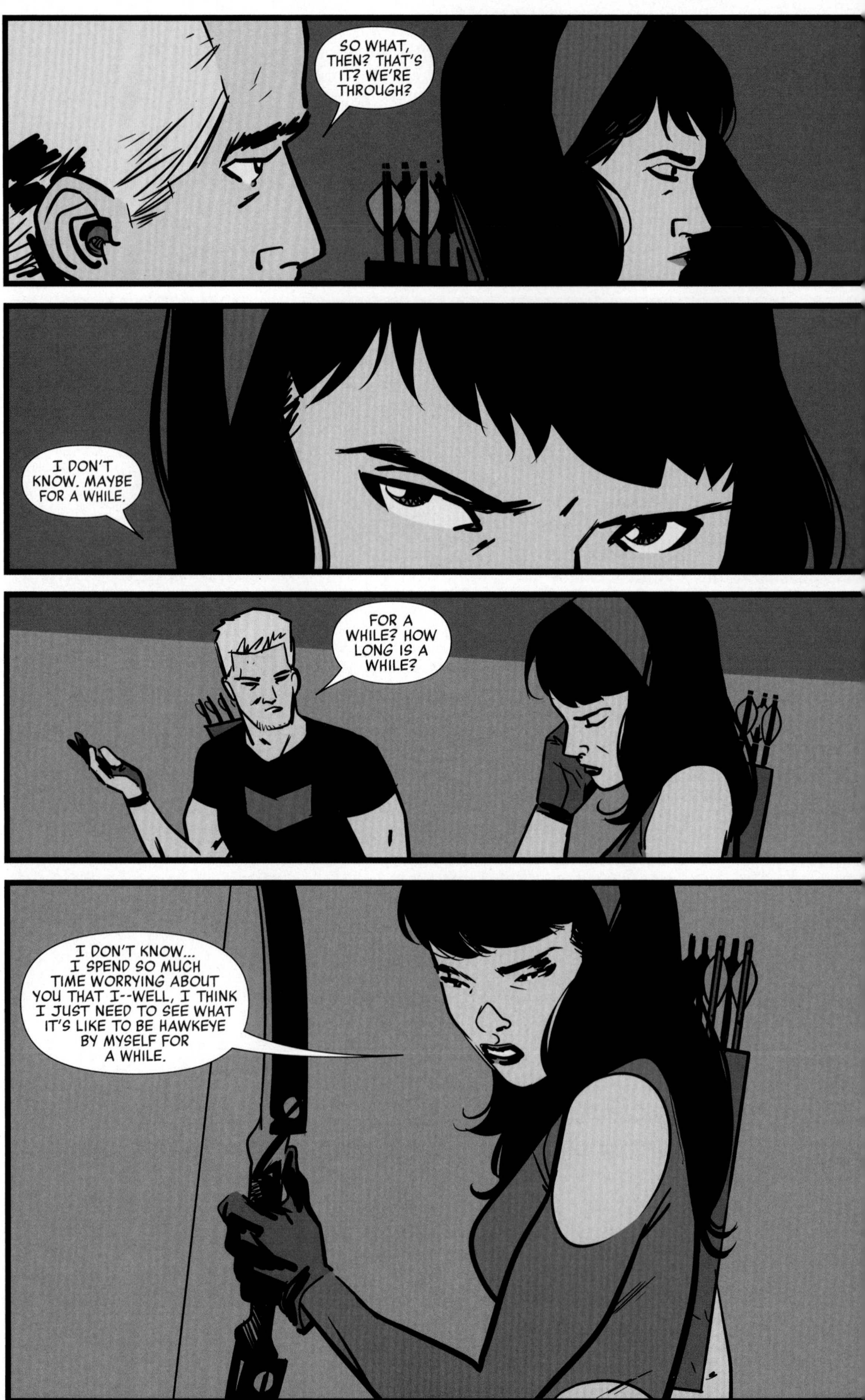
SO WHAT, THEN? THAT'S IT? WE'RE THROUGH?
I DON'T KNOW. MAYBE FOR A WHILE.
FOR A WHILE? HOW LONG IS A WHILE?
I DON'T KNOW... I SPEND SO MUCH TIME WORRYING ABOUT YOU THAT I--WELL, I THINK I JUST NEED TO SEE WHAT IT'S LIKE TO BE HAWKEYE BY MYSELF FOR A WHILE.

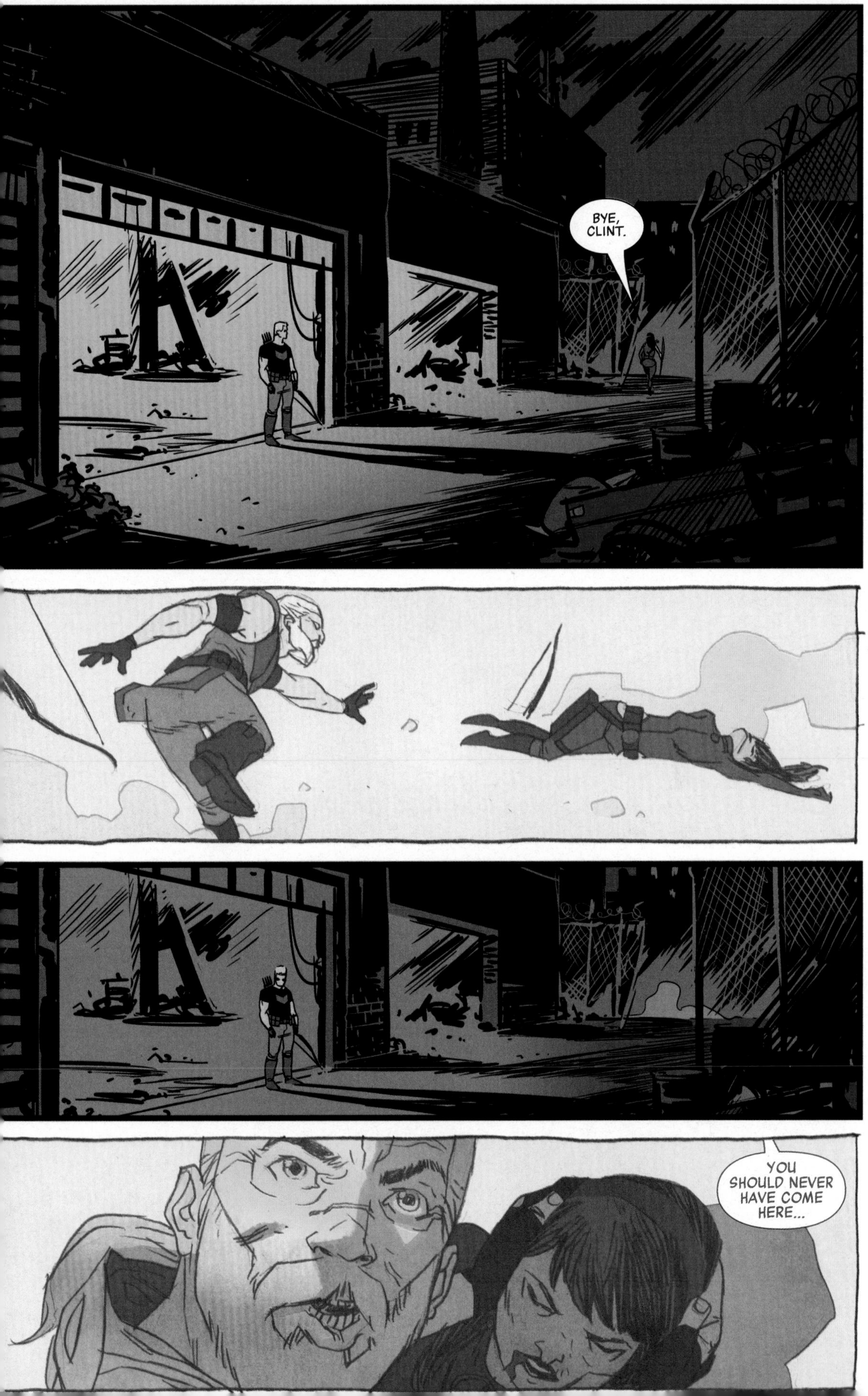
BYE, CLINT.
YOU SHOULD NEVER HAVE COME HERE...

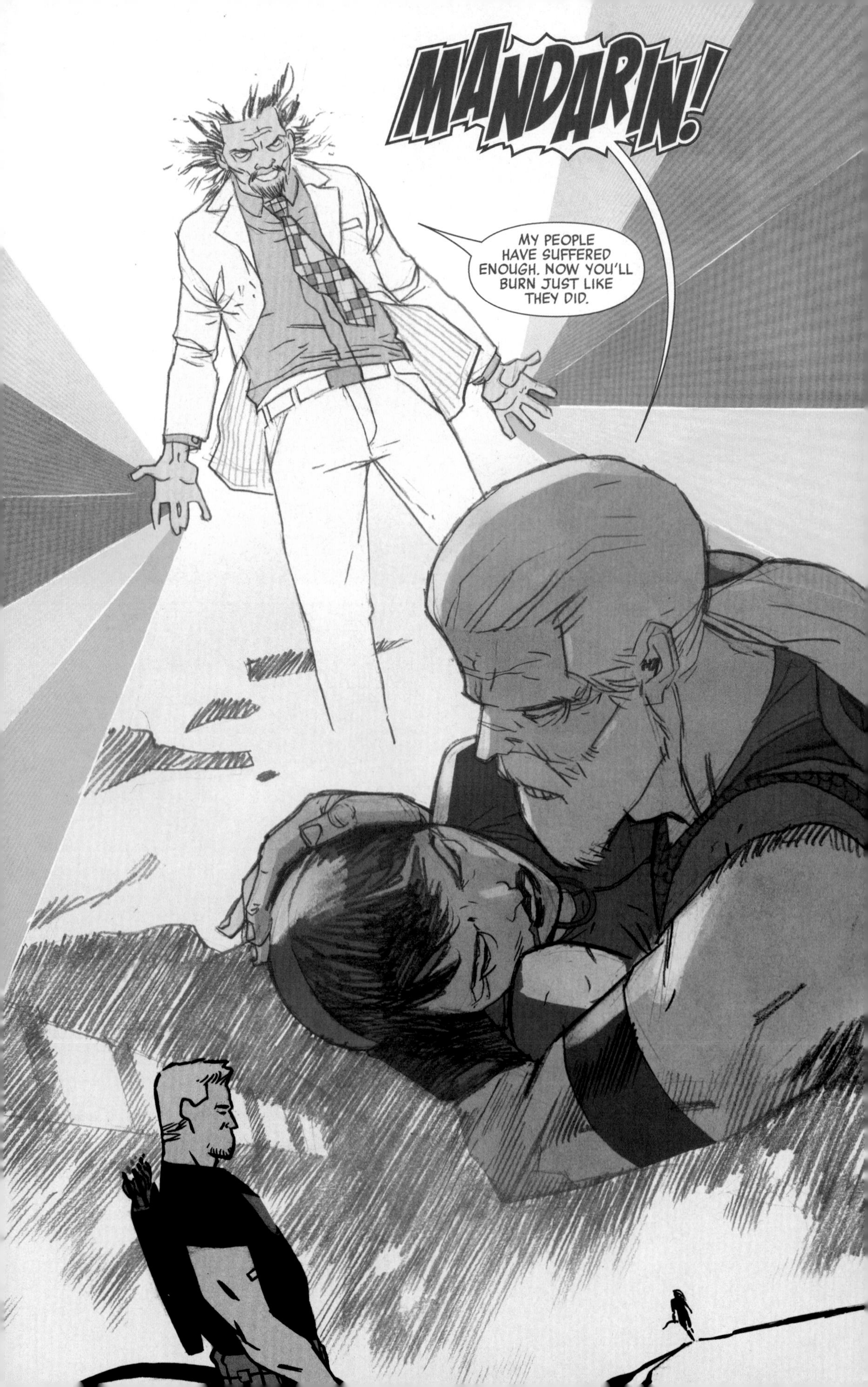
MANDARIN!
MY PEOPLE HAVE SUFFERED ENOUGH. NOW YOU'LL BURN JUST LIKE THEY DID.

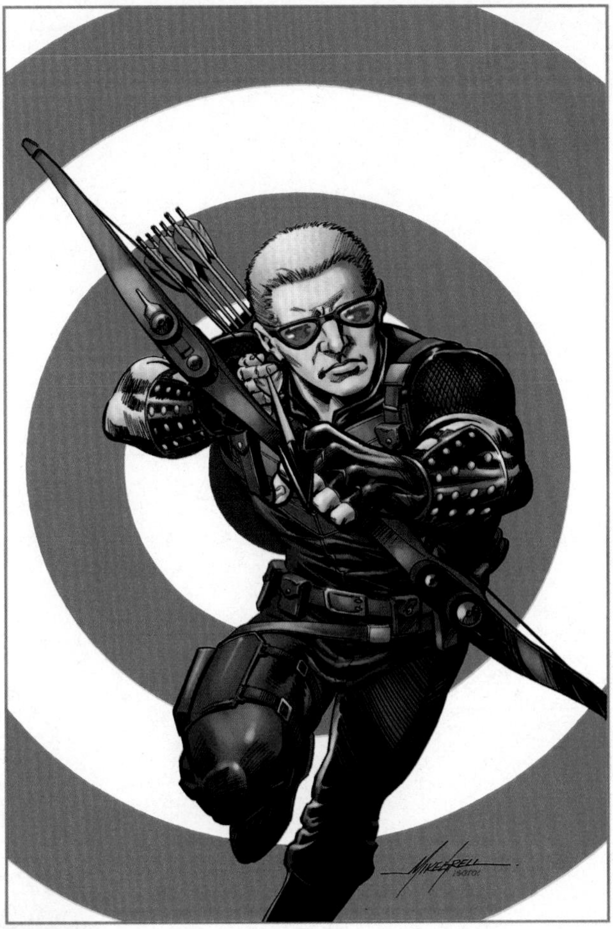

ALL-NEW HAWKEYE #1
VARIANT BY **MIKE GRELL**
& **CHRIS SOTOMAYOR**

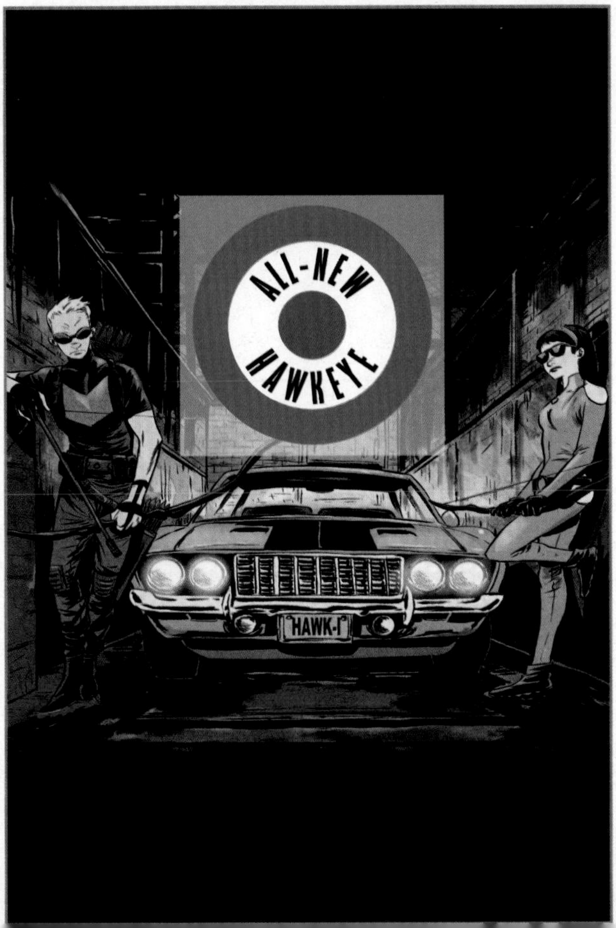
ALL-NEW
HAWKEYE
HAWK-I

ALL-NEW HAWKEYE #1
HIP-HOP VARIANT
BY **SANFORD GREENE**

2

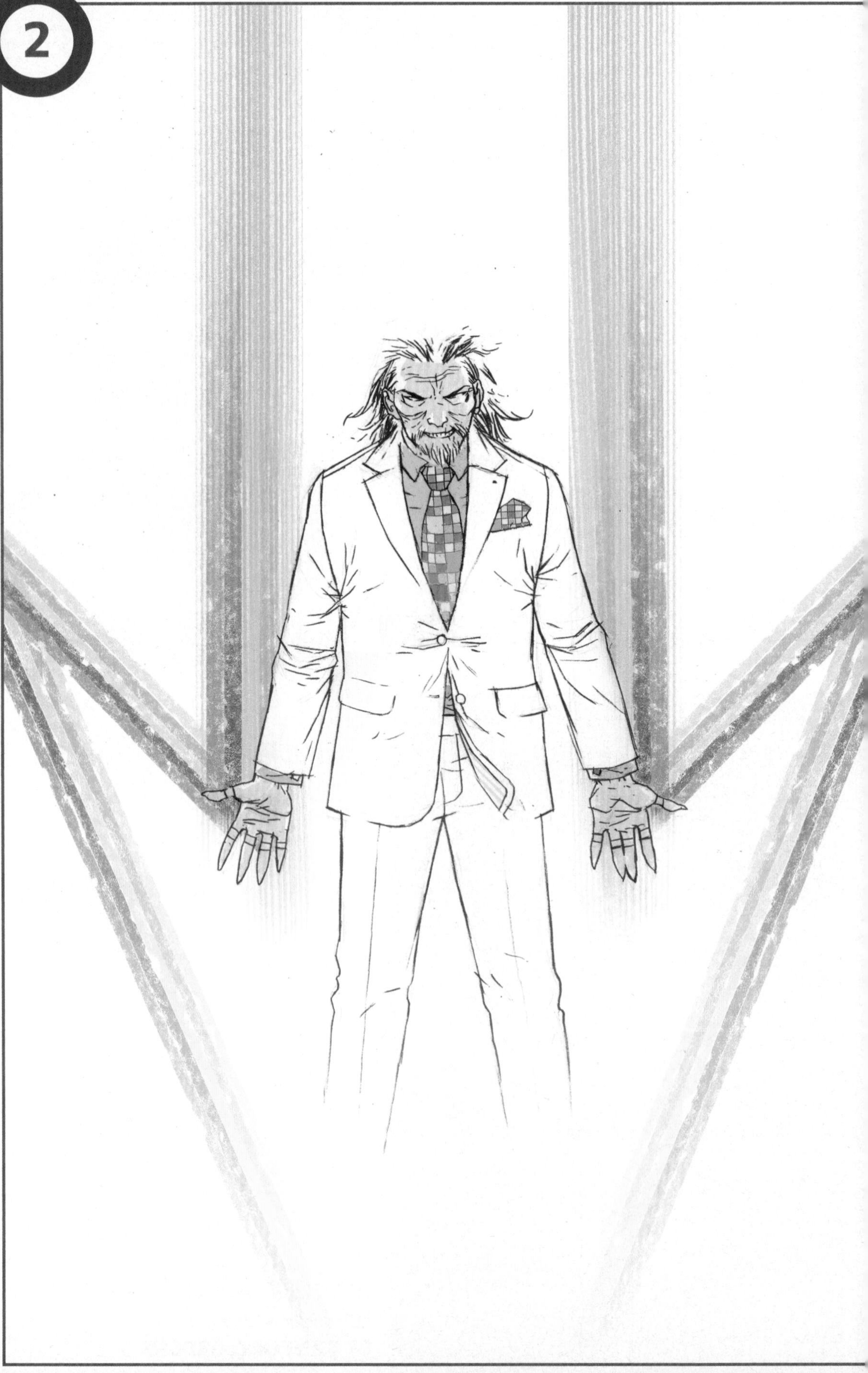

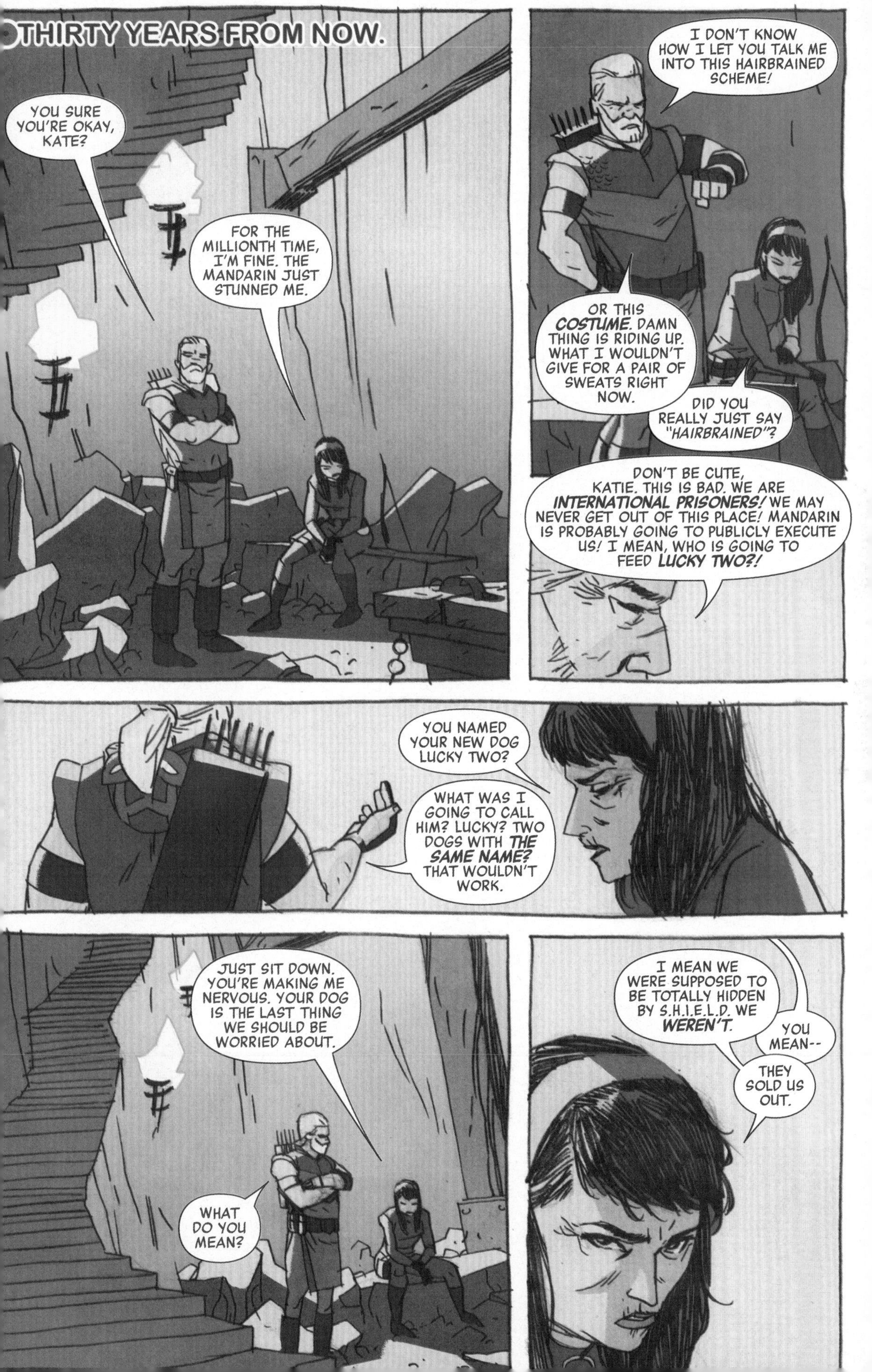
THIRTY YEARS FROM NOW.
YOU SURE YOU'RE OKAY, KATE?
FOR THE MILLIONTH TIME, I'M FINE. THE MANDARIN JUST STUNNED ME.
I DON'T KNOW HOW I LET YOU TALK ME INTO THIS HAIRBRAINED SCHEME!
OR THIS COSTUME. DAMN THING IS RIDING UP. WHAT I WOULDN'T GIVE FOR A PAIR OF SWEATS RIGHT NOW.
DID YOU REALLY JUST SAY "HAIRBRAINED"?
DON'T BE CUTE, KATIE. THIS IS BAD. WE ARE INTERNATIONAL PRISONERS! WE MAY NEVER GET OUT OF THIS PLACE! MANDARIN IS PROBABLY GOING TO PUBLICLY EXECUTE US! I MEAN, WHO IS GOING TO FEED LUCKY TWO?!
YOU NAMED YOUR NEW DOG LUCKY TWO?
WHAT WAS I GOING TO CALL HIM? LUCKY? TWO DOGS WITH THE SAME NAME? THAT WOULDN'T WORK.
JUST SIT DOWN. YOU'RE MAKING ME NERVOUS. YOUR DOG IS THE LAST THING WE SHOULD BE WORRIED ABOUT.
WHAT DO YOU MEAN?
I MEAN WE WERE SUPPOSED TO BE TOTALLY HIDDEN BY S.H.I.E.L.D. WE WEREN'T.
YOU MEAN--
THEY SOLD US OUT.

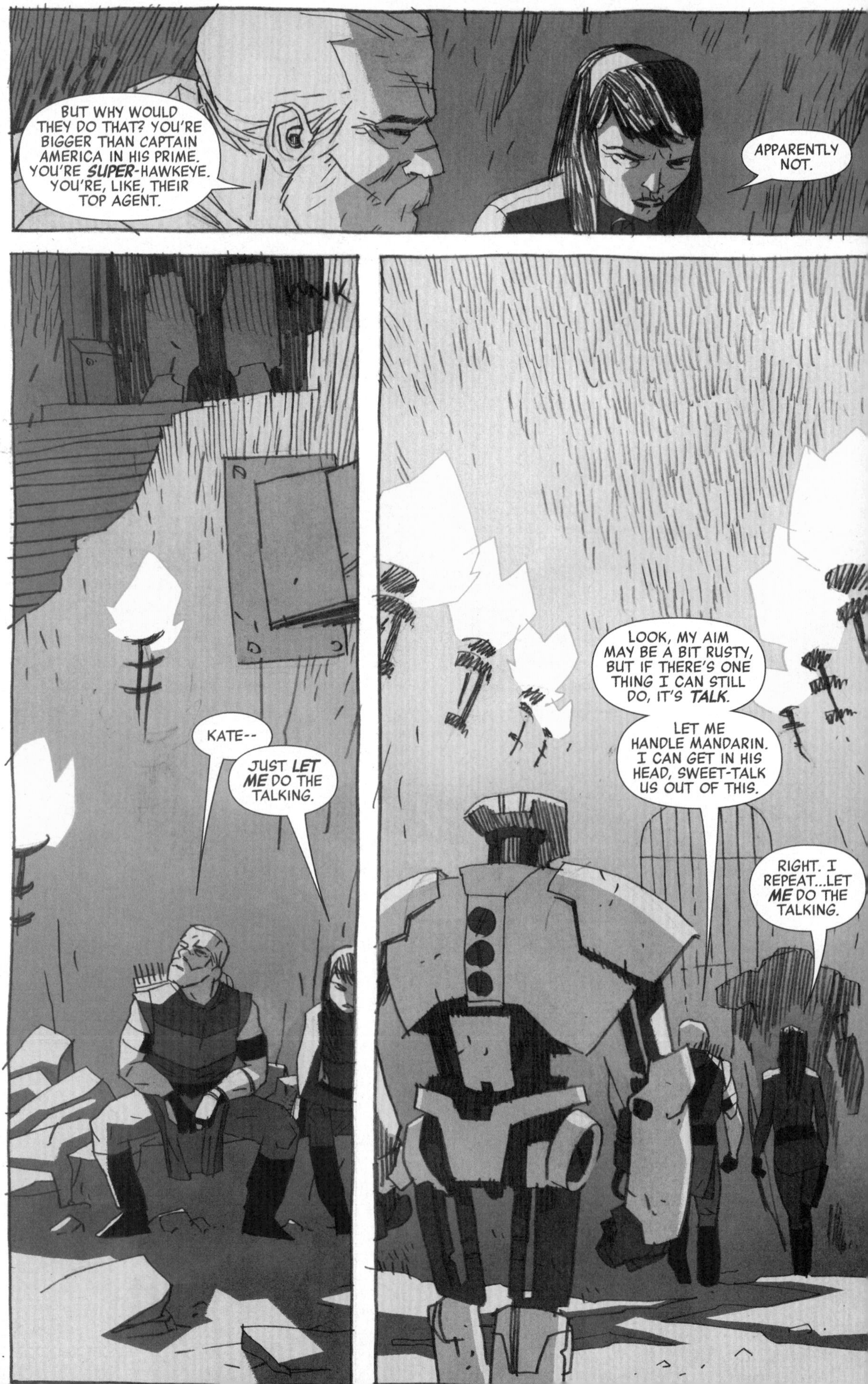
BUT WHY WOULD THEY DO THAT? YOU'RE BIGGER THAN CAPTAIN AMERICA IN HIS PRIME. YOU'RE SUPER-HAWKEYE. YOU'RE, LIKE, THEIR TOP AGENT.
APPARENTLY NOT.
KATE--
JUST LET ME DO THE TALKING.
LOOK, MY AIM MAY BE A BIT RUSTY, BUT IF THERE'S ONE THING I CAN STILL DO, IT'S TALK.
LET ME HANDLE MANDARIN. I CAN GET IN HIS HEAD, SWEET-TALK US OUT OF THIS.
RIGHT. I REPEAT...LET ME DO THE TALKING.

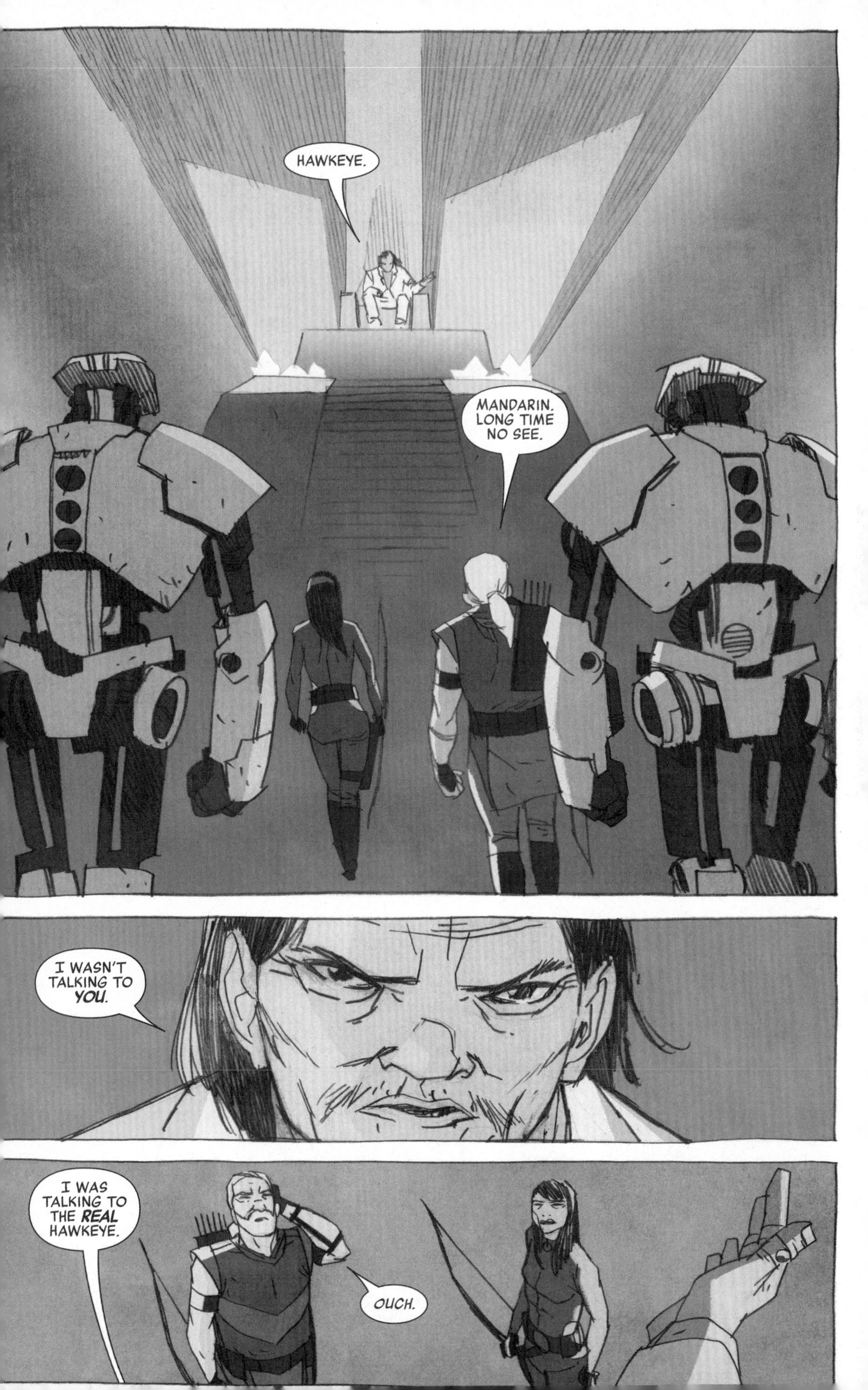
HAWKEYE.
MANDARIN. LONG TIME NO SEE.
I WASN'T TALKING TO *YOU*.
I WAS TALKING TO THE *REAL* HAWKEYE.
OUCH.

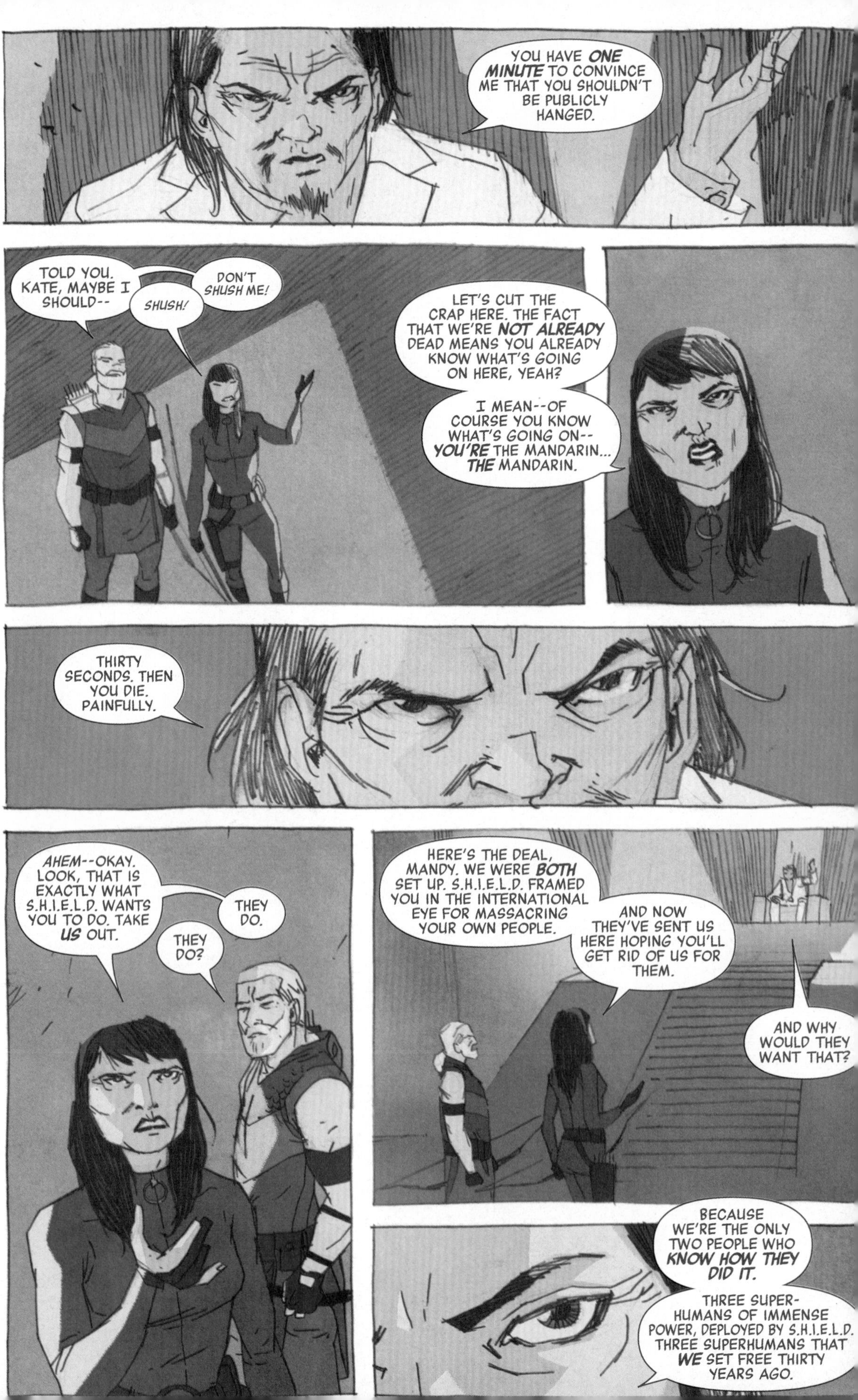
YOU HAVE ONE MINUTE TO CONVINCE ME THAT YOU SHOULDN'T BE PUBLICLY HANGED.
TOLD YOU. KATE, MAYBE I SHOULD--
SHUSH!
DON'T SHUSH ME!
LET'S CUT THE CRAP HERE. THE FACT THAT WE'RE NOT ALREADY DEAD MEANS YOU ALREADY KNOW WHAT'S GOING ON HERE, YEAH?
I MEAN--OF COURSE YOU KNOW WHAT'S GOING ON-- YOU'RE THE MANDARIN... THE MANDARIN.
THIRTY SECONDS. THEN YOU DIE. PAINFULLY.
AHEM--OKAY. LOOK, THAT IS EXACTLY WHAT S.H.I.E.L.D. WANTS YOU TO DO. TAKE US OUT.
THEY DO?
THEY DO.
HERE'S THE DEAL, MANDY. WE WERE BOTH SET UP. S.H.I.E.L.D. FRAMED YOU IN THE INTERNATIONAL EYE FOR MASSACRING YOUR OWN PEOPLE.
AND NOW THEY'VE SENT US HERE HOPING YOU'LL GET RID OF US FOR THEM.
AND WHY WOULD THEY WANT THAT?
BECAUSE WE'RE THE ONLY TWO PEOPLE WHO KNOW HOW THEY DID IT.
THREE SUPER-HUMANS OF IMMENSE POWER, DEPLOYED BY S.H.I.E.L.D. THREE SUPERHUMANS THAT WE SET FREE THIRTY YEARS AGO.

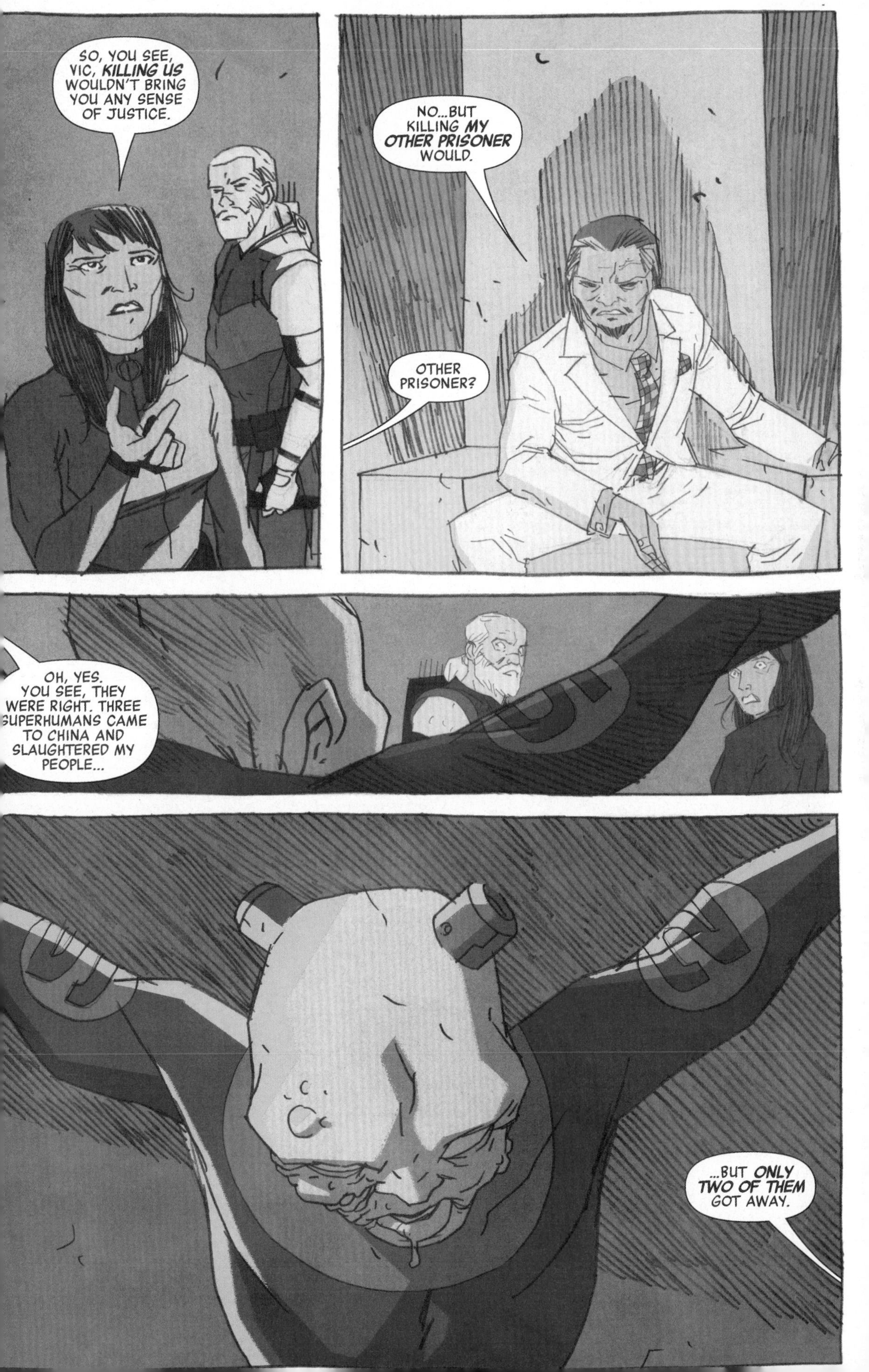
SO, YOU SEE, VIC, KILLING US WOULDN'T BRING YOU ANY SENSE OF JUSTICE.
NO...BUT KILLING MY OTHER PRISONER WOULD.
OTHER PRISONER?
OH, YES. YOU SEE, THEY WERE RIGHT. THREE SUPERHUMANS CAME TO CHINA AND SLAUGHTERED MY PEOPLE...
...BUT ONLY TWO OF THEM GOT AWAY.

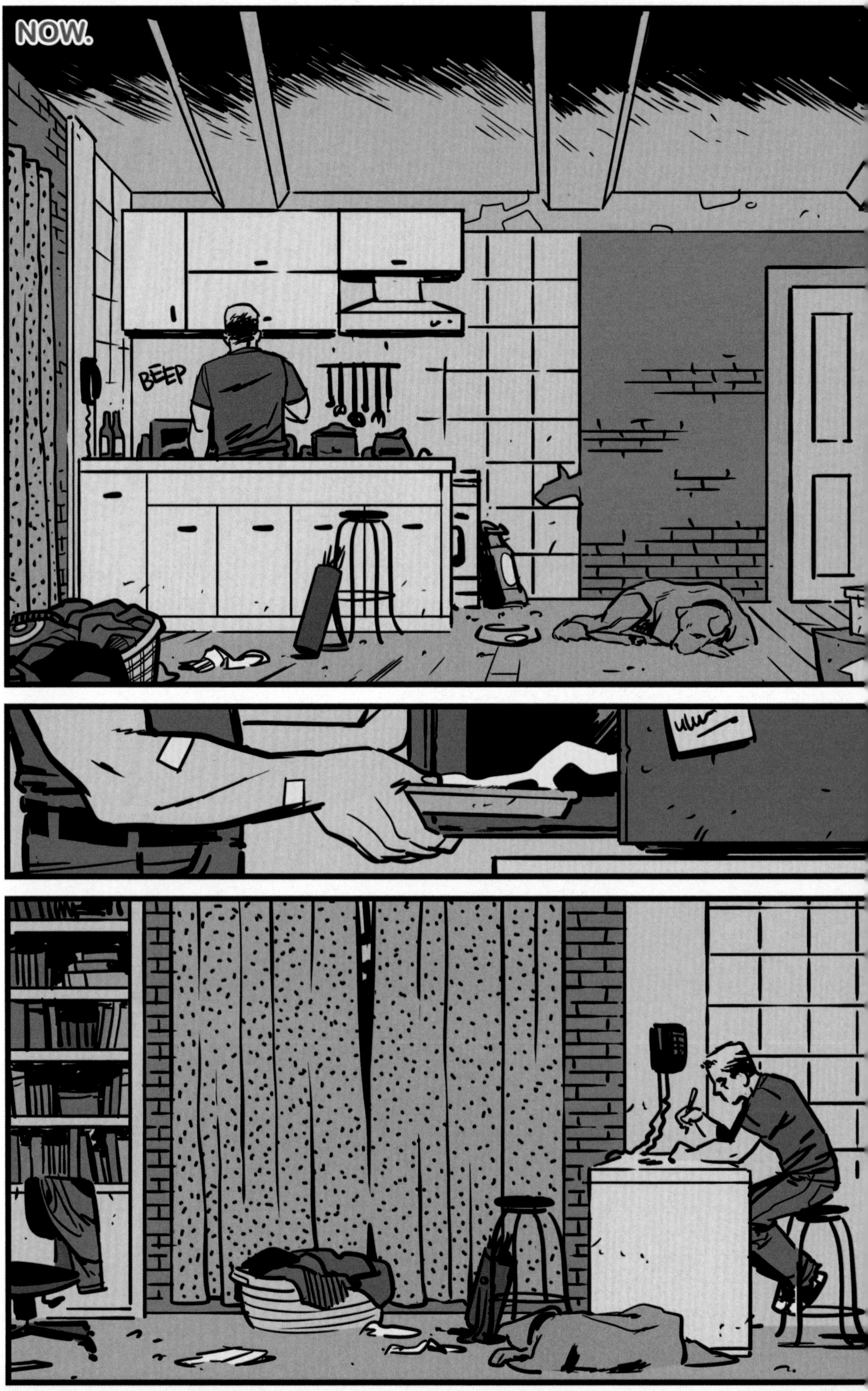
NOW.
BEEP

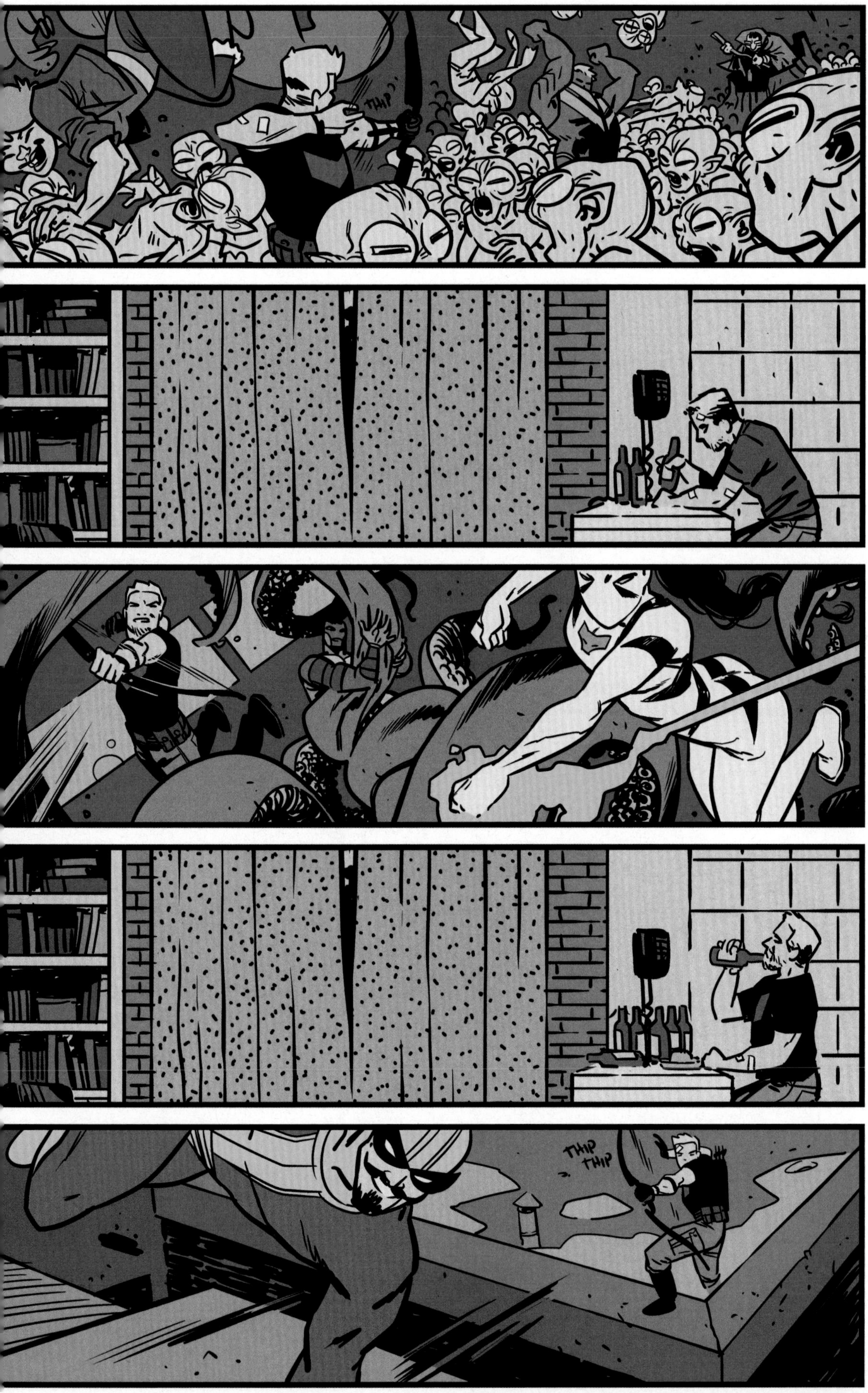
THIP
THIP THIP

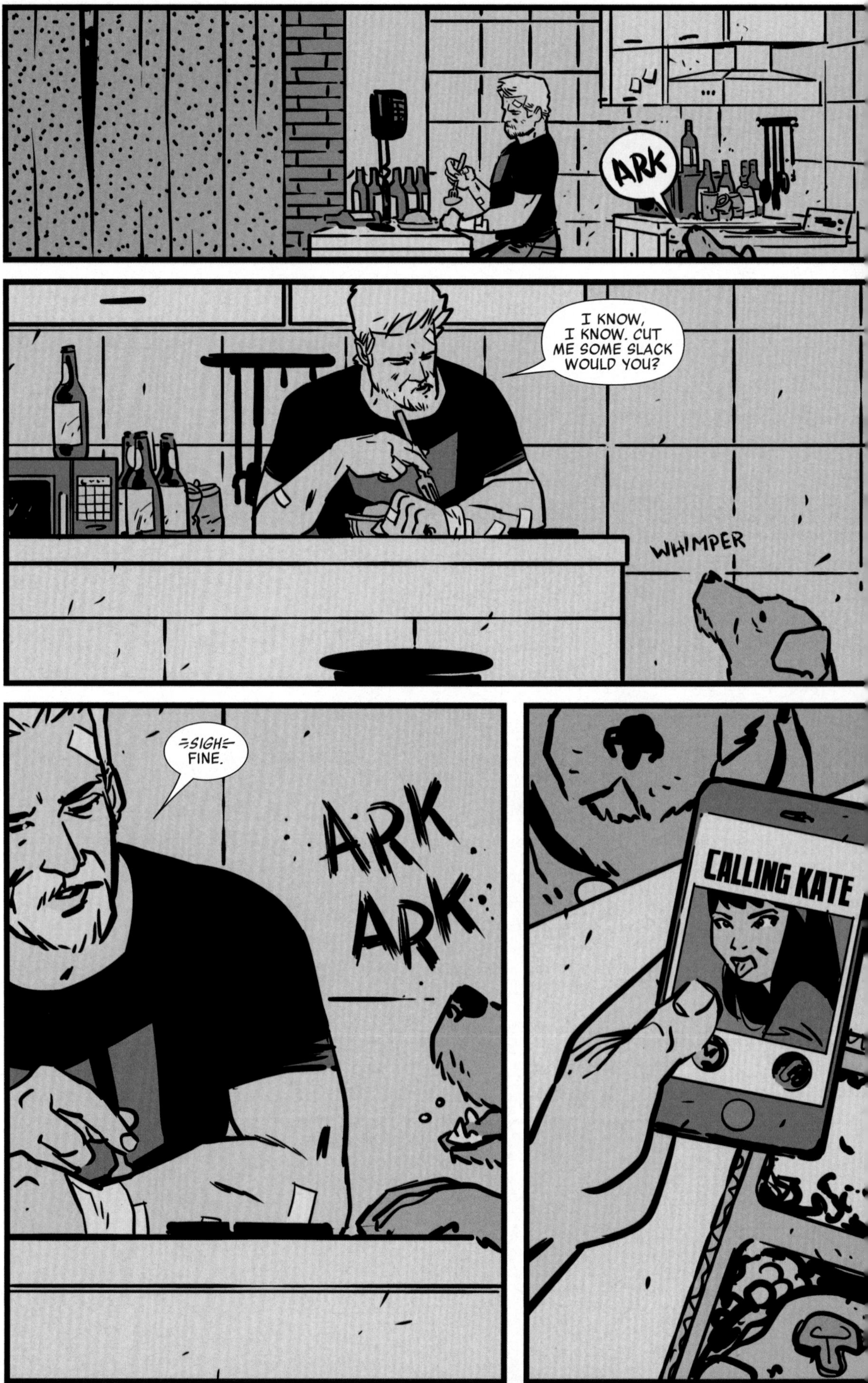
ARK
I KNOW, I KNOW. CUT ME SOME SLACK WOULD YOU?
WHIMPER
SIGH FINE.
ARK ARK
CALLING KATE

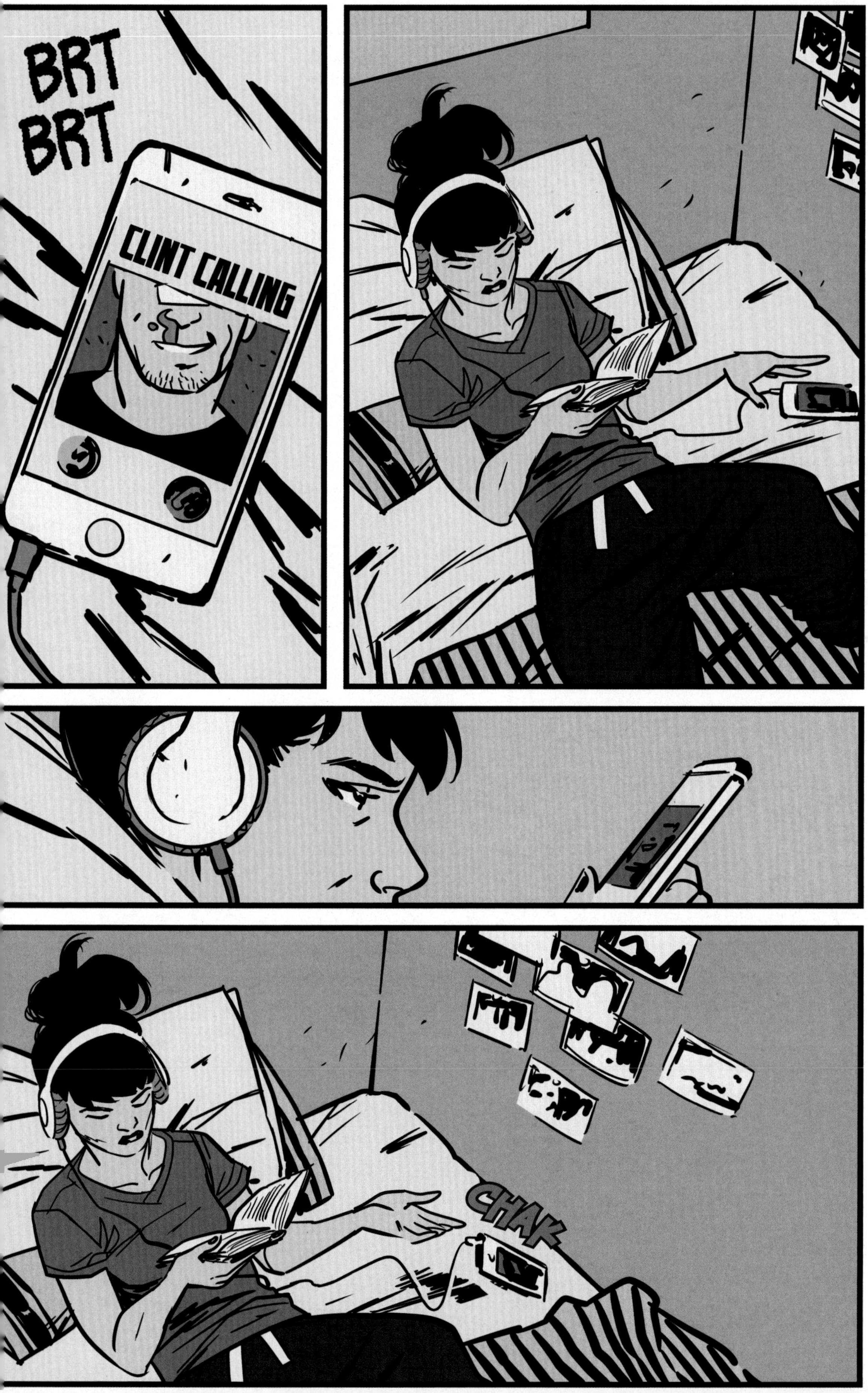
BRT
BRT
CLINT CALLING
CHAK

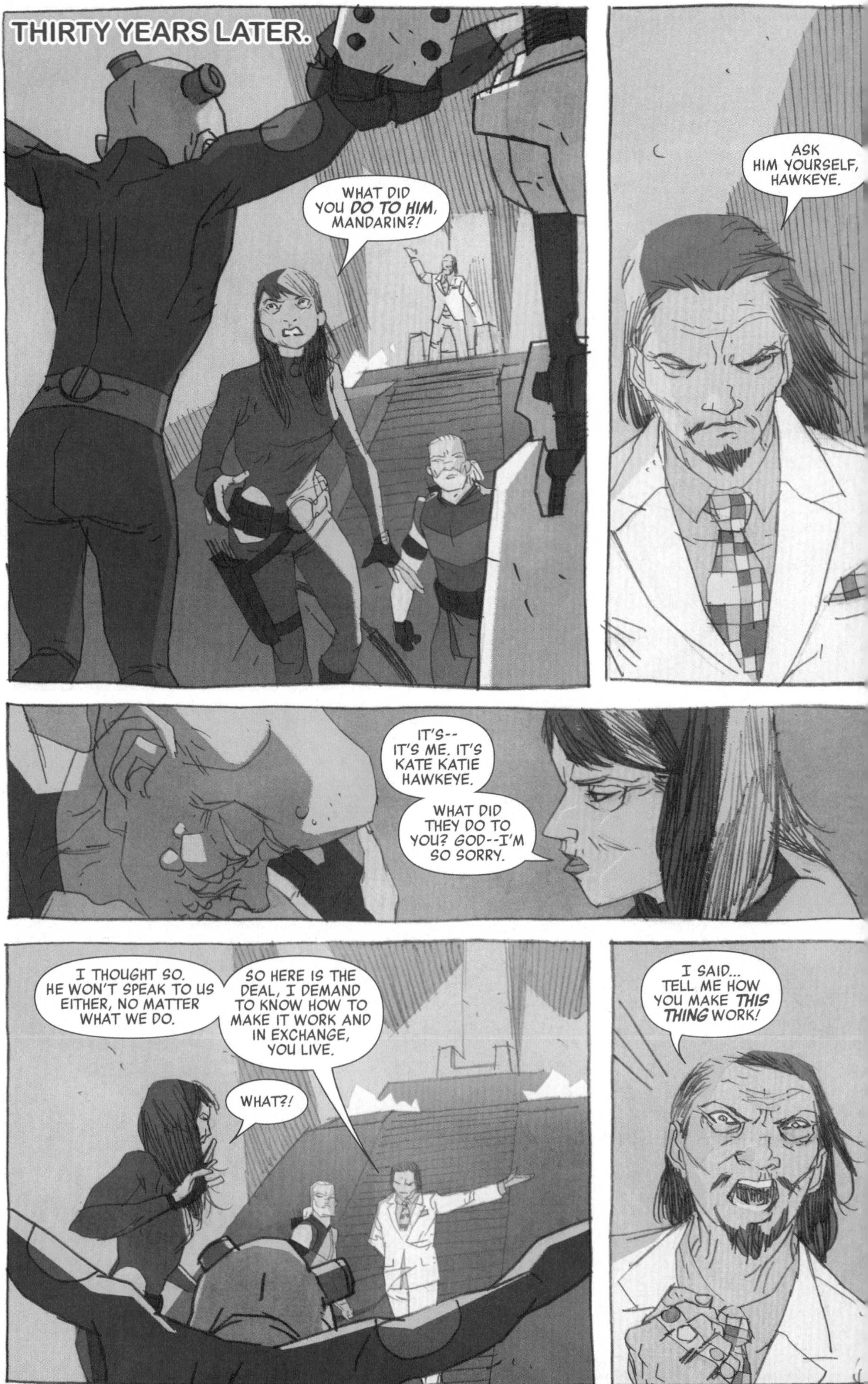
THIRTY YEARS LATER.
WHAT DID YOU DO TO HIM, MANDARIN?!
ASK HIM YOURSELF, HAWKEYE.
IT'S-- IT'S ME. IT'S KATE KATIE HAWKEYE.
WHAT DID THEY DO TO YOU? GOD--I'M SO SORRY.
I THOUGHT SO. HE WON'T SPEAK TO US EITHER, NO MATTER WHAT WE DO.
SO HERE IS THE DEAL, I DEMAND TO KNOW HOW TO MAKE IT WORK AND IN EXCHANGE, YOU LIVE.
WHAT?!
I SAID... TELL ME HOW YOU MAKE THIS THING WORK!

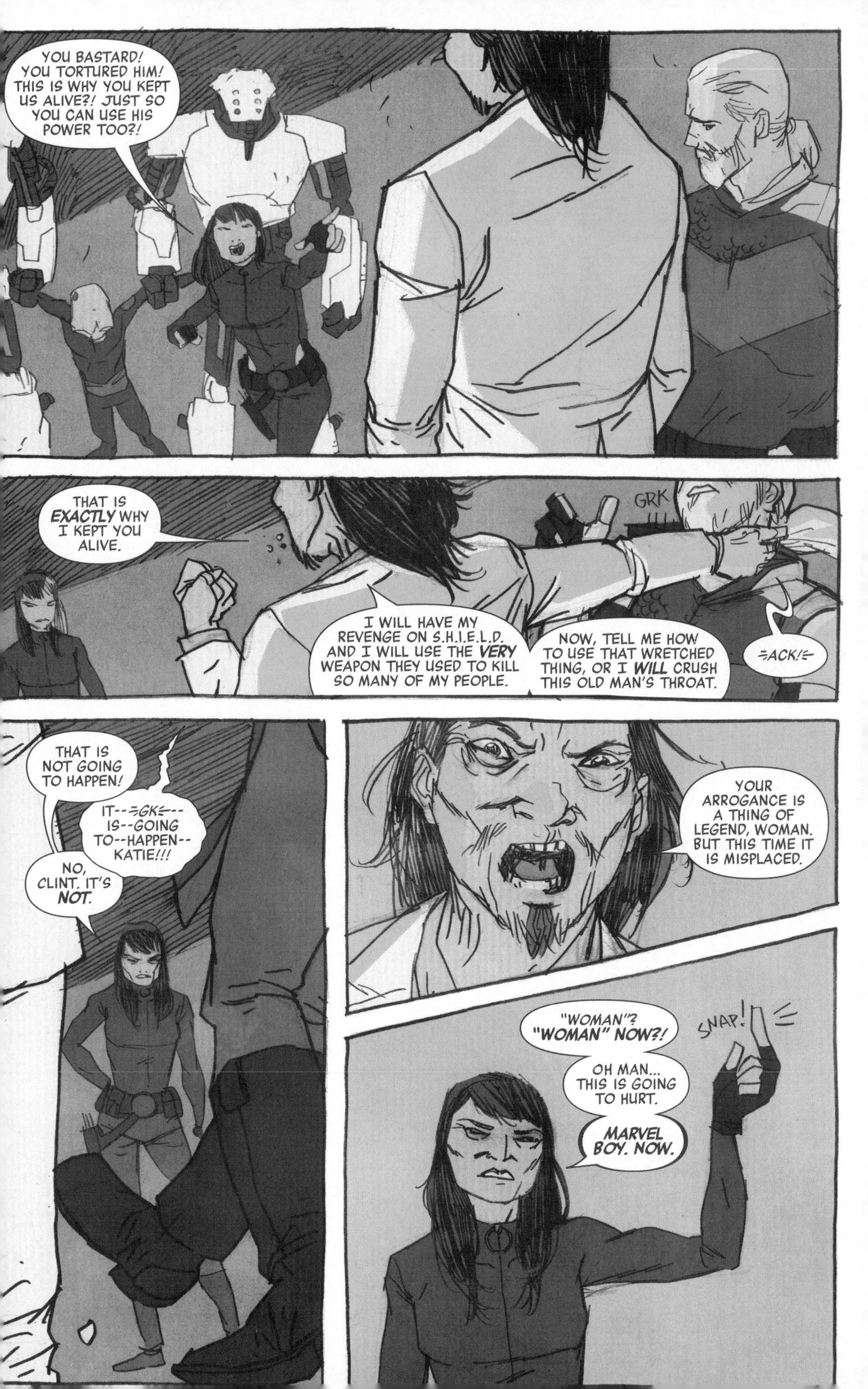
YOU BASTARD! YOU TORTURED HIM! THIS IS WHY YOU KEPT US ALIVE?! JUST SO YOU CAN USE HIS POWER TOO?!
THAT IS EXACTLY WHY I KEPT YOU ALIVE.
GRK
I WILL HAVE MY REVENGE ON S.H.I.E.L.D. AND I WILL USE THE VERY WEAPON THEY USED TO KILL SO MANY OF MY PEOPLE.
NOW, TELL ME HOW TO USE THAT WRETCHED THING, OR I WILL CRUSH THIS OLD MAN'S THROAT.
ACK!
THAT IS NOT GOING TO HAPPEN!
IT--GK--IS--GOING TO--HAPPEN--KATIE!!!
NO, CLINT. IT'S NOT.
YOUR ARROGANCE IS A THING OF LEGEND, WOMAN. BUT THIS TIME IT IS MISPLACED.
"WOMAN"? "WOMAN" NOW?!
SNAP!
OH MAN... THIS IS GOING TO HURT.
MARVEL BOY. NOW.

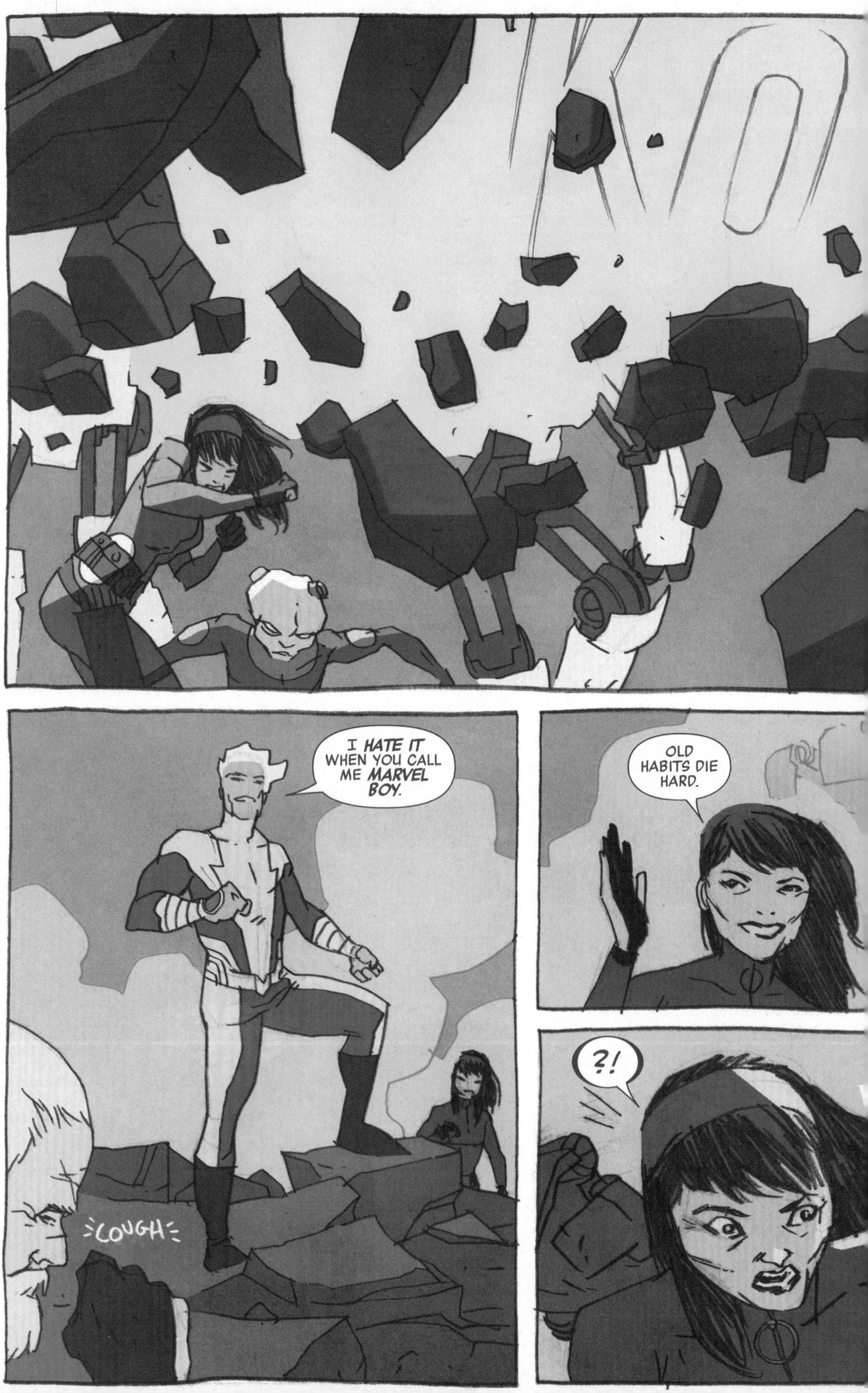

KO
I HATE IT WHEN YOU CALL ME MARVEL BOY.
COUGH
OLD HABITS DIE HARD.
?!

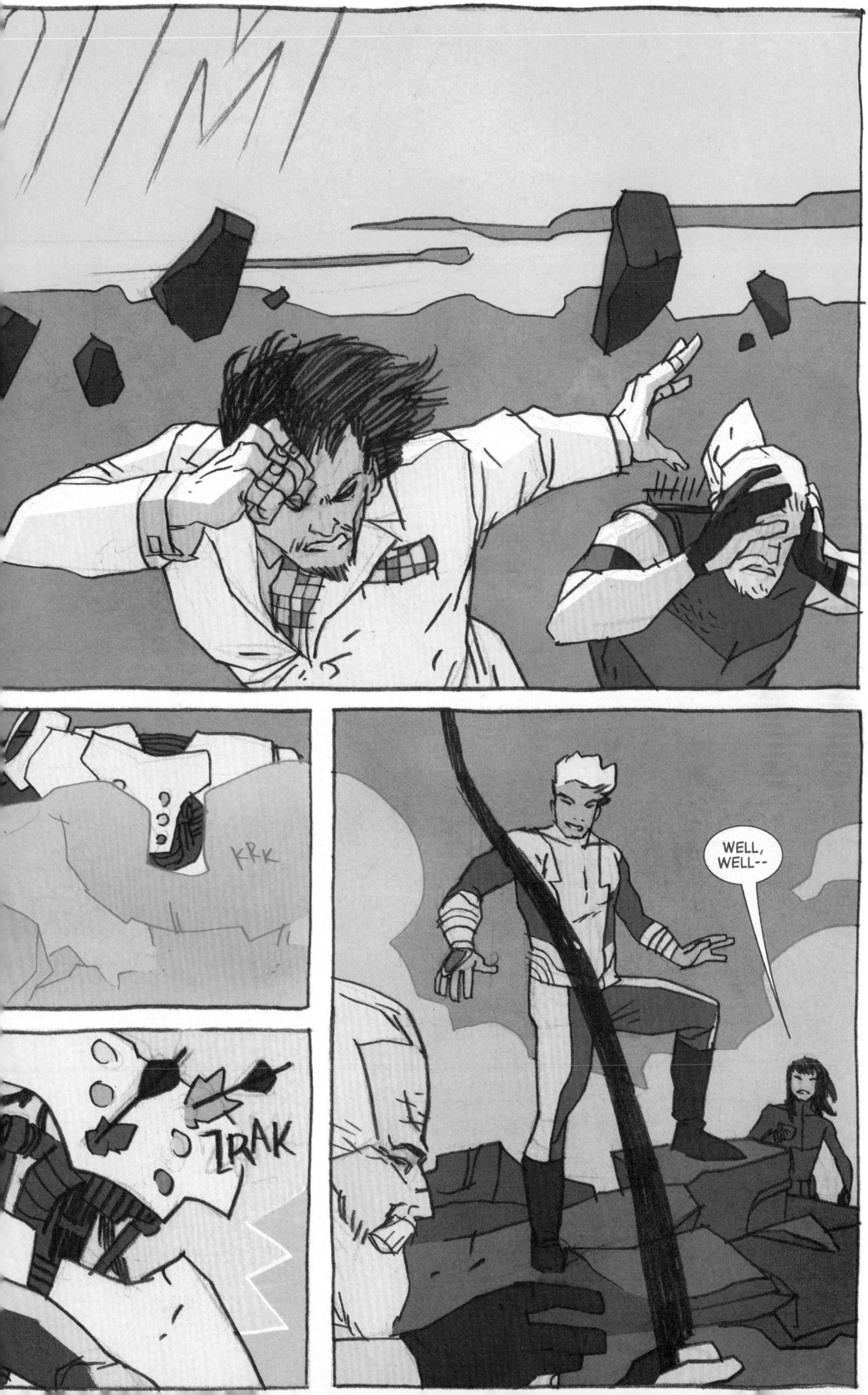
KRK
TRAK
WELL, WELL--

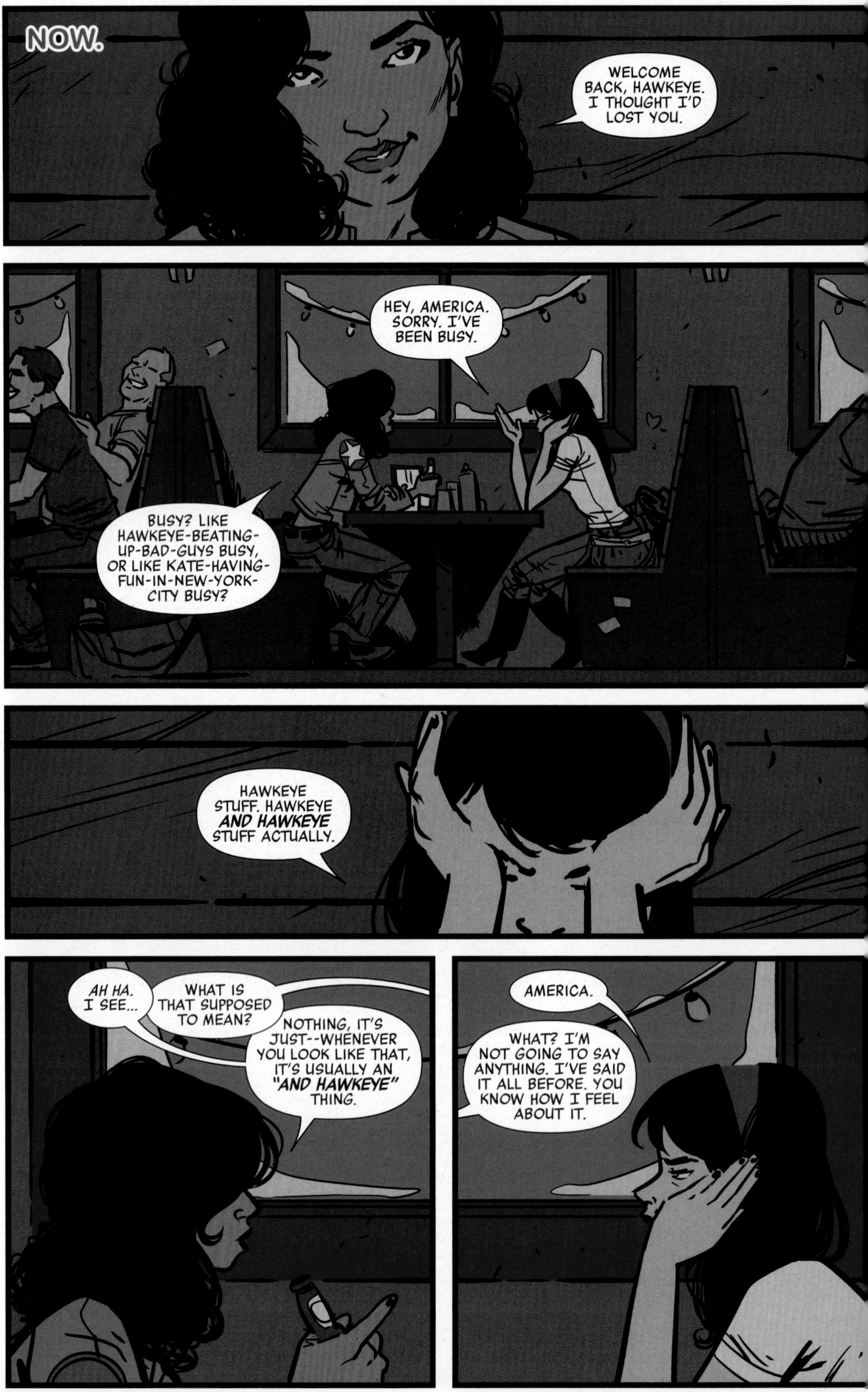
NOW.
WELCOME BACK, HAWKEYE. I THOUGHT I'D LOST YOU.
HEY, AMERICA. SORRY. I'VE BEEN BUSY.
BUSY? LIKE HAWKEYE-BEATING-UP-BAD-GUYS BUSY, OR LIKE KATE-HAVING-FUN-IN-NEW-YORK-CITY BUSY?
HAWKEYE STUFF. HAWKEYE *AND HAWKEYE* STUFF ACTUALLY.
AH HA. I SEE...
WHAT IS THAT SUPPOSED TO MEAN?
NOTHING, IT'S JUST--WHENEVER YOU LOOK LIKE THAT, IT'S USUALLY AN *"AND HAWKEYE"* THING.
AMERICA.
WHAT? I'M NOT GOING TO SAY ANYTHING. I'VE SAID IT ALL BEFORE. YOU KNOW HOW I FEEL ABOUT IT.

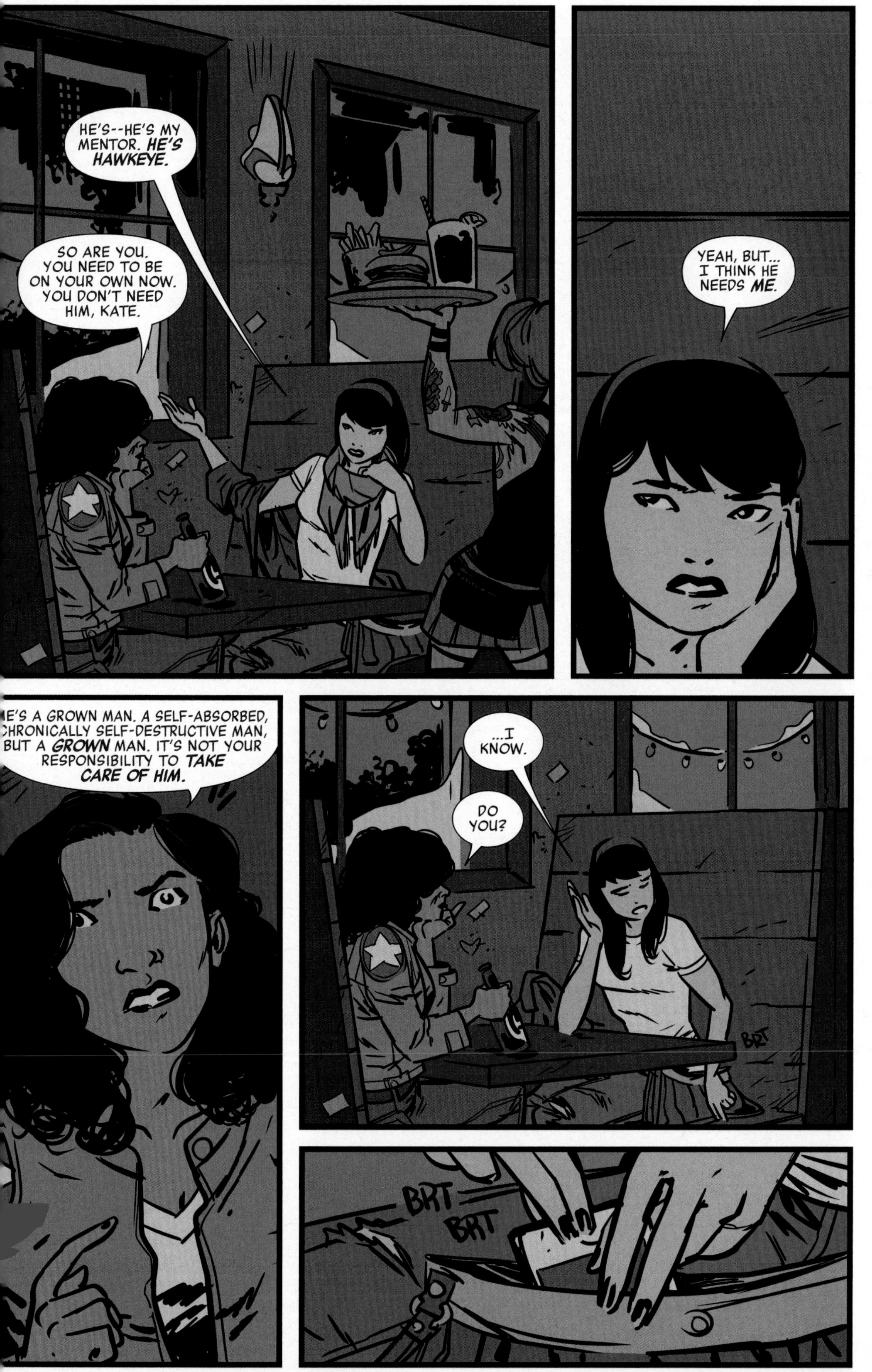

HE'S--HE'S MY MENTOR. HE'S HAWKEYE.
SO ARE YOU. YOU NEED TO BE ON YOUR OWN NOW. YOU DON'T NEED HIM, KATE.
YEAH, BUT... I THINK HE NEEDS ME.
E'S A GROWN MAN. A SELF-ABSORBED, CHRONICALLY SELF-DESTRUCTIVE MAN, BUT A GROWN MAN. IT'S NOT YOUR RESPONSIBILITY TO TAKE CARE OF HIM.
...I KNOW.
DO YOU?
BRT
BRT
BRT

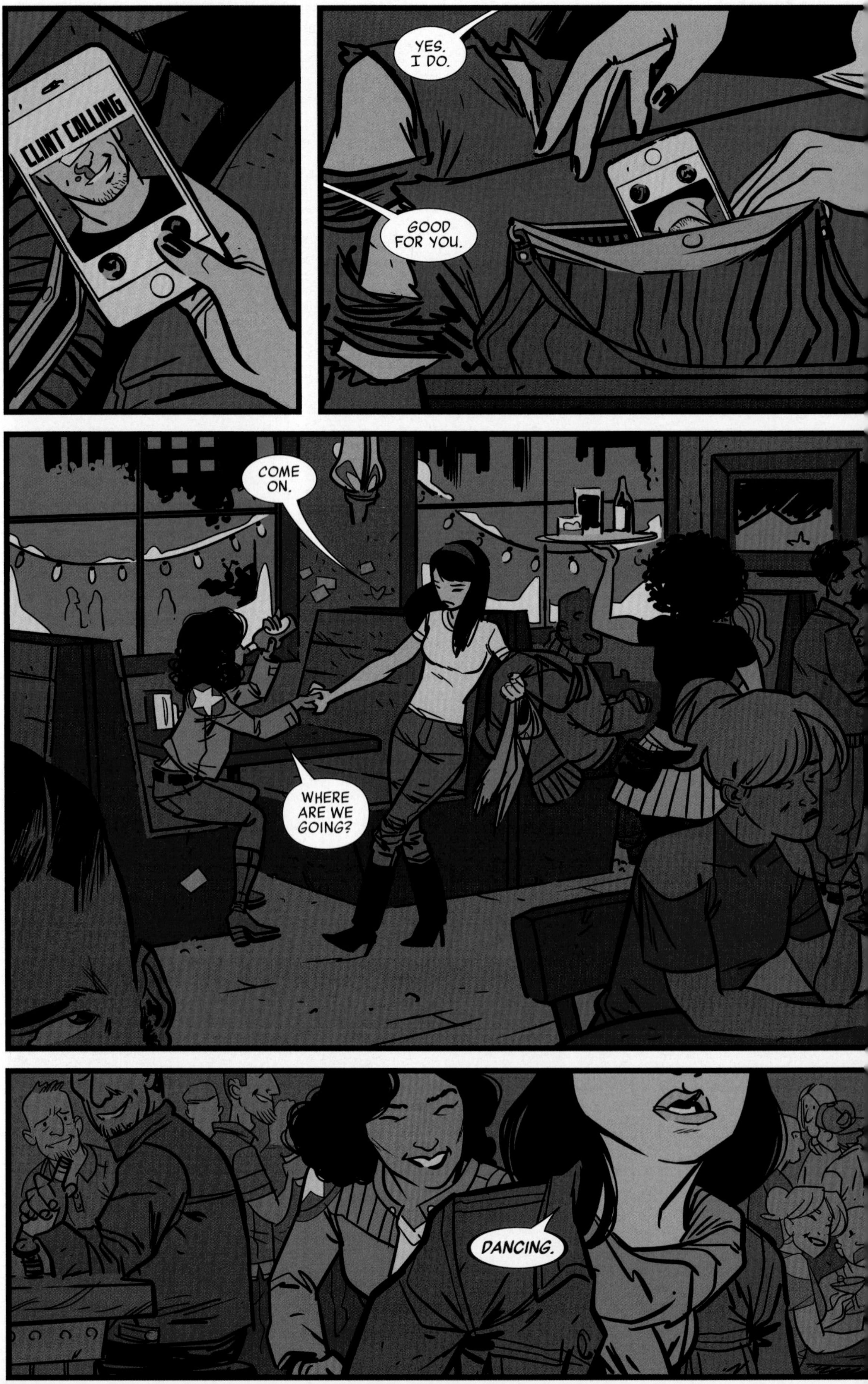
CLINT CALLING
YES. I DO.
GOOD FOR YOU.
COME ON.
WHERE ARE WE GOING?
DANCING.

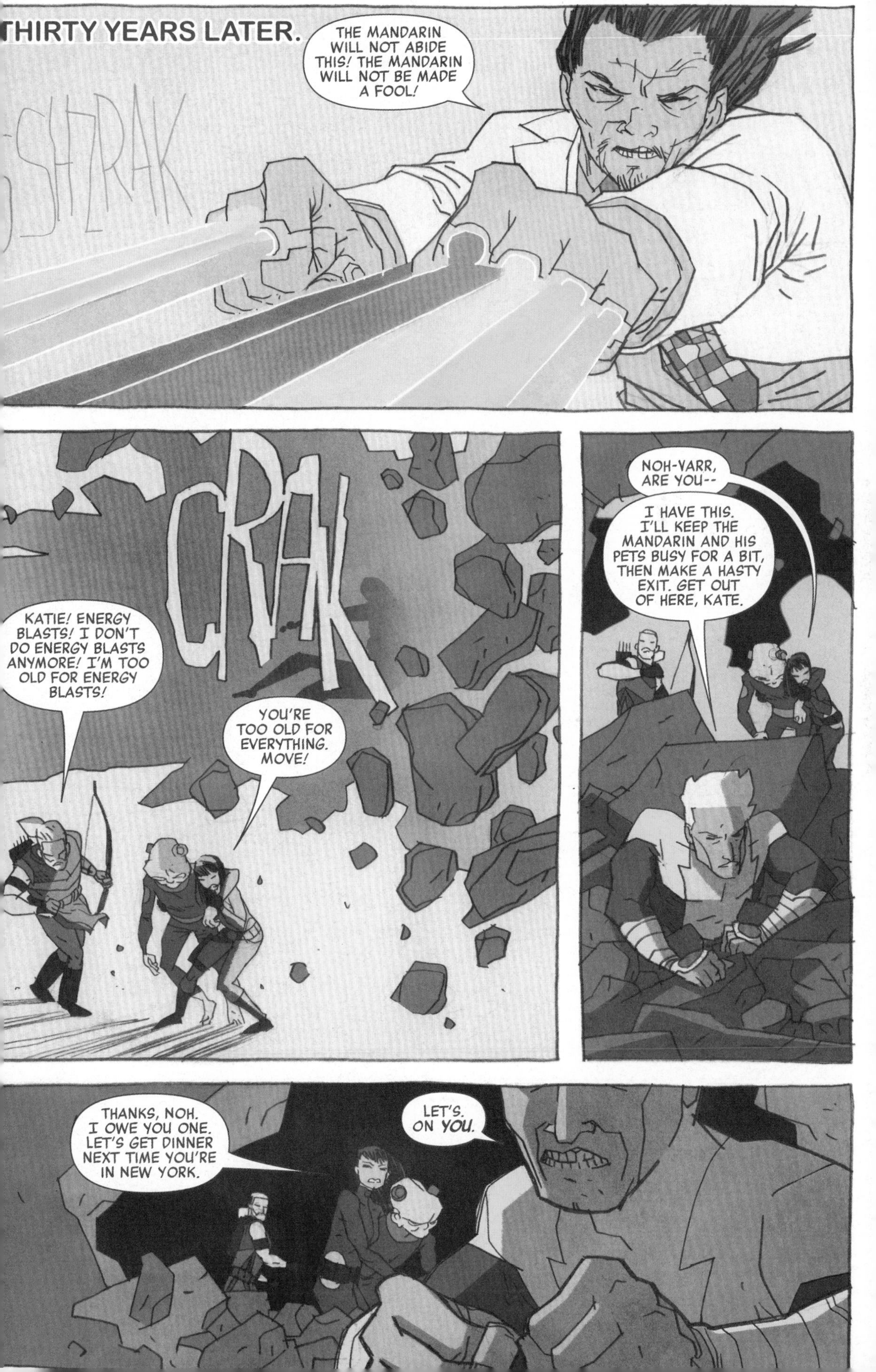
THIRTY YEARS LATER.
THE MANDARIN WILL NOT ABIDE THIS! THE MANDARIN WILL NOT BE MADE A FOOL!
SHZRAK
CRAK
KATIE! ENERGY BLASTS! I DON'T DO ENERGY BLASTS ANYMORE! I'M TOO OLD FOR ENERGY BLASTS!
YOU'RE TOO OLD FOR EVERYTHING. MOVE!
NOH-VARR, ARE YOU--
I HAVE THIS. I'LL KEEP THE MANDARIN AND HIS PETS BUSY FOR A BIT, THEN MAKE A HASTY EXIT. GET OUT OF HERE, KATE.
THANKS, NOH. I OWE YOU ONE. LET'S GET DINNER NEXT TIME YOU'RE IN NEW YORK.
LET'S. ON YOU.

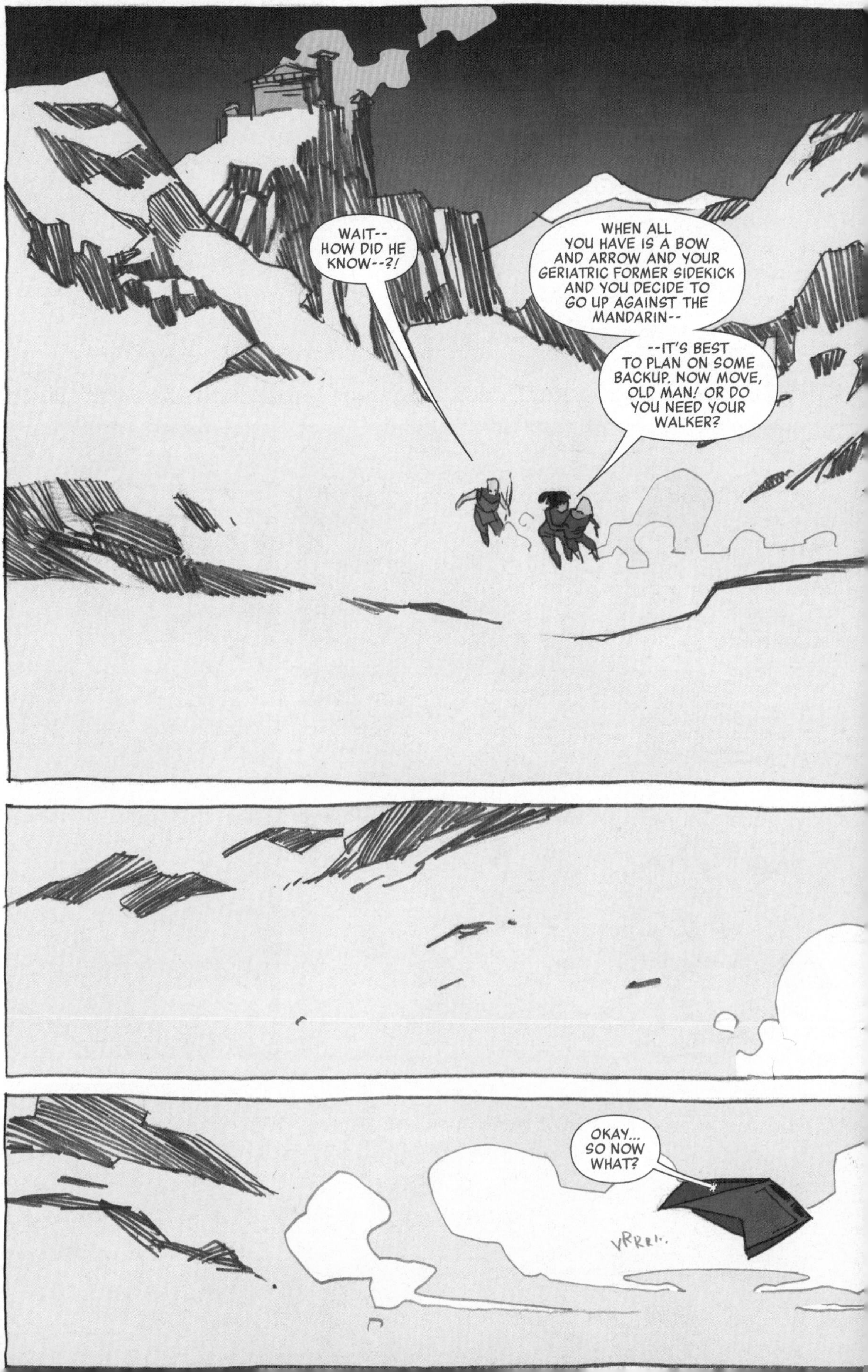
WAIT-- HOW DID HE KNOW--?!
WHEN ALL YOU HAVE IS A BOW AND ARROW AND YOUR GERIATRIC FORMER SIDEKICK AND YOU DECIDE TO GO UP AGAINST THE MANDARIN--
--IT'S BEST TO PLAN ON SOME BACKUP. NOW MOVE, OLD MAN! OR DO YOU NEED YOUR WALKER?
OKAY... SO NOW WHAT?
VRRR!..

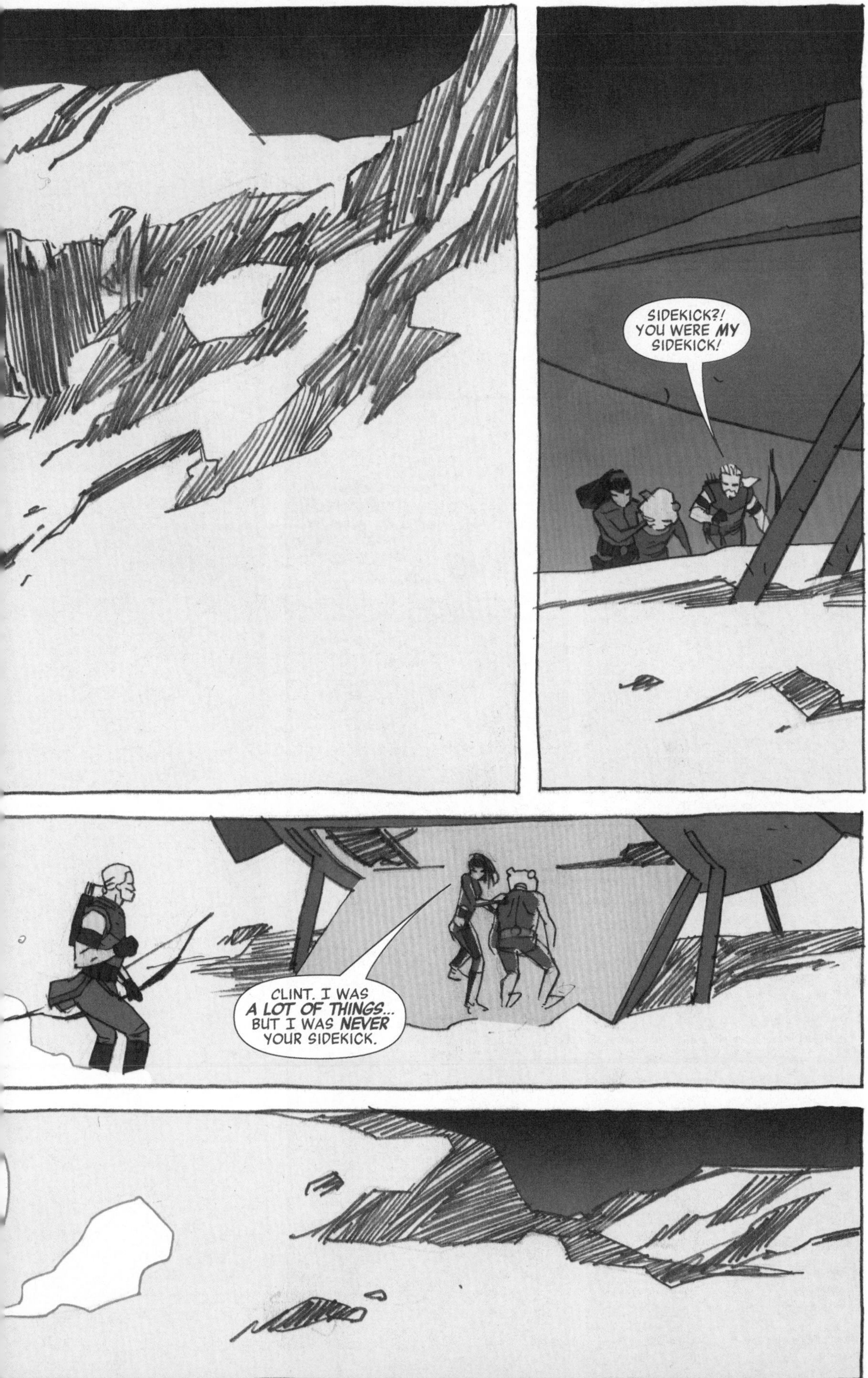
SIDEKICK?! YOU WERE MY SIDEKICK!
CLINT. I WAS A LOT OF THINGS... BUT I WAS NEVER YOUR SIDEKICK.

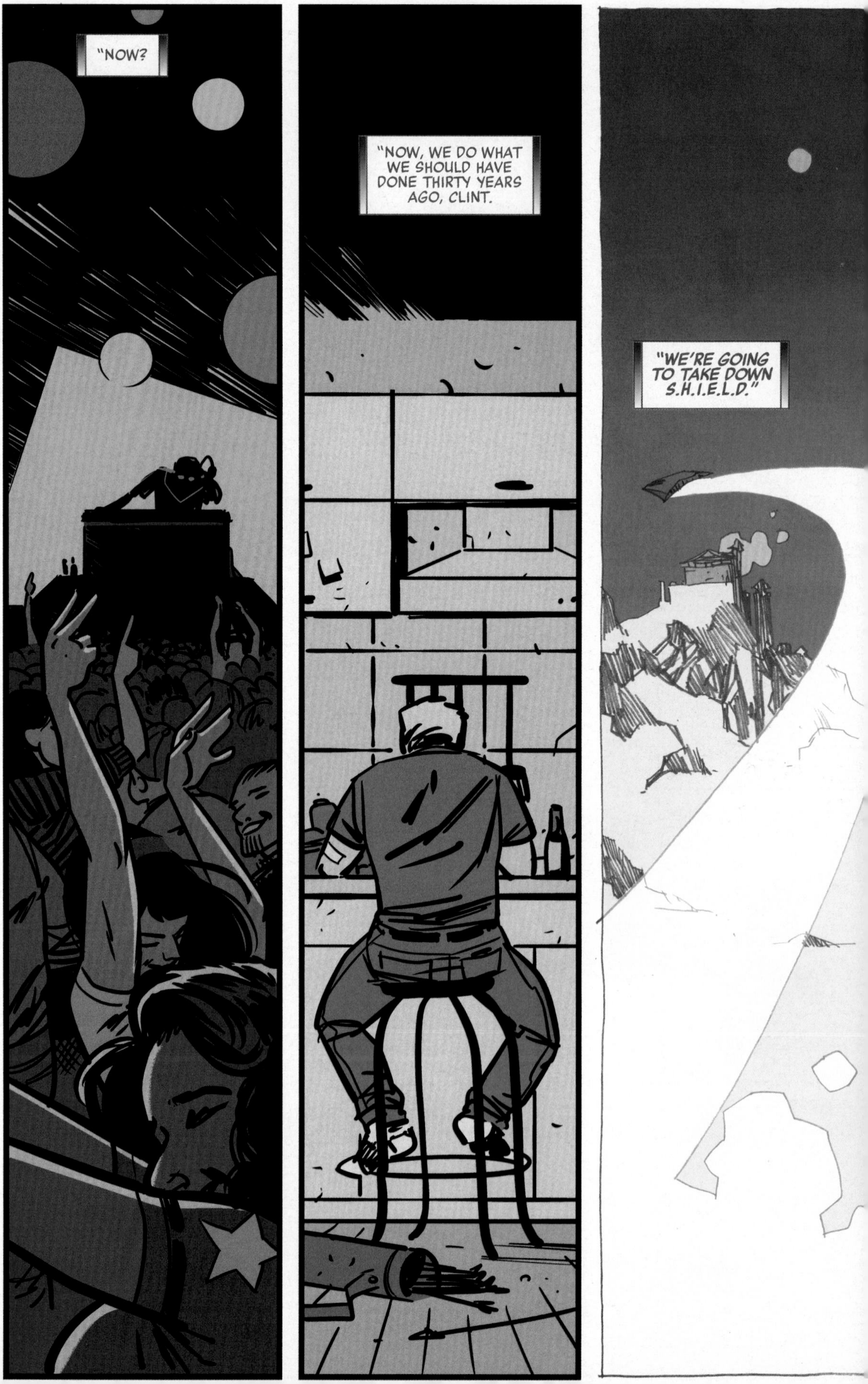
"NOW?
"NOW, WE DO WHAT WE SHOULD HAVE DONE THIRTY YEARS AGO, CLINT.
"WE'RE GOING TO TAKE DOWN S.H.I.E.L.D."

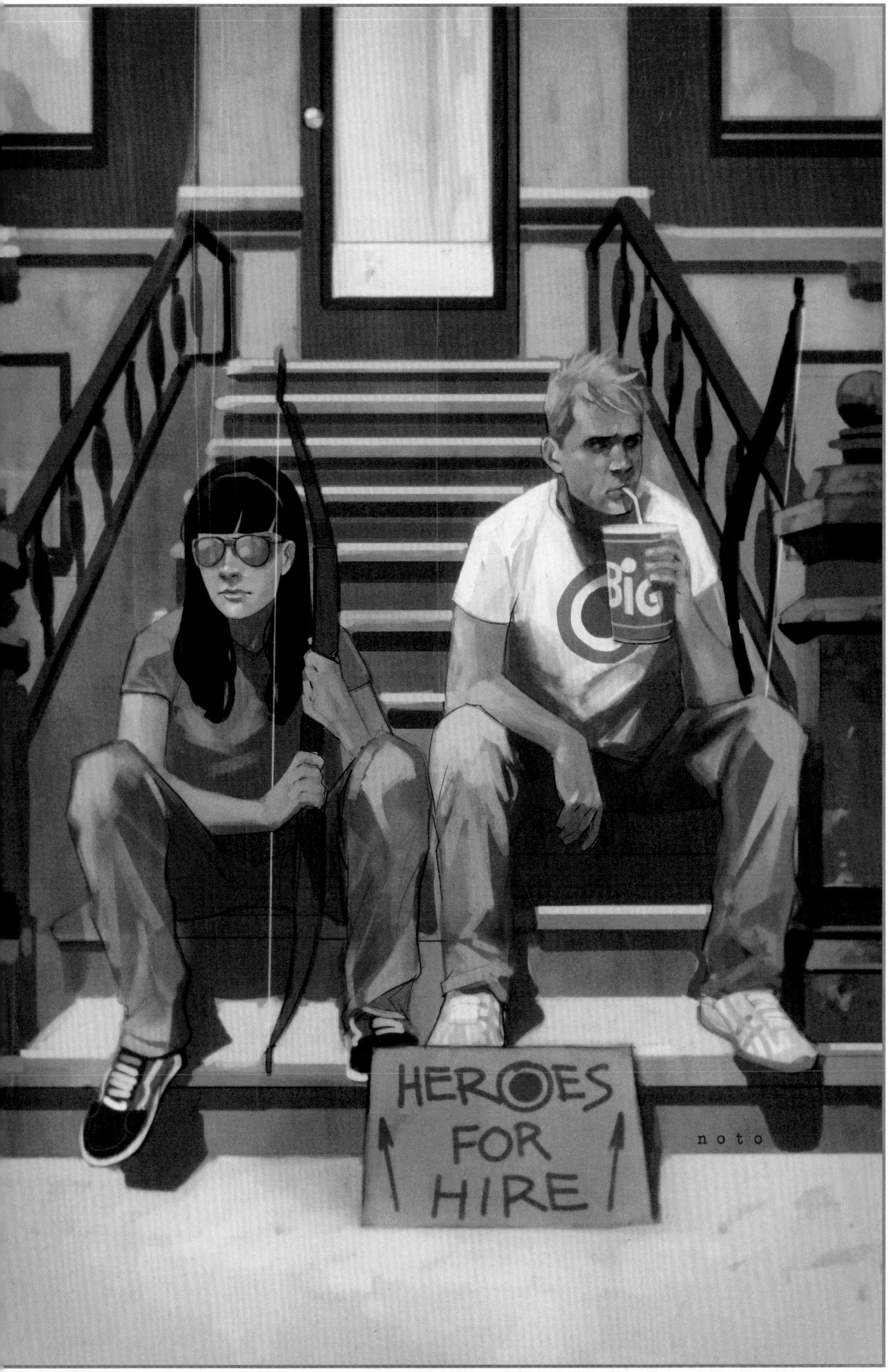
BIG
HEROES FOR HIRE
noto

ALL-NEW HAWKEYE **#2** VARIANT BY **PHIL NOTO**

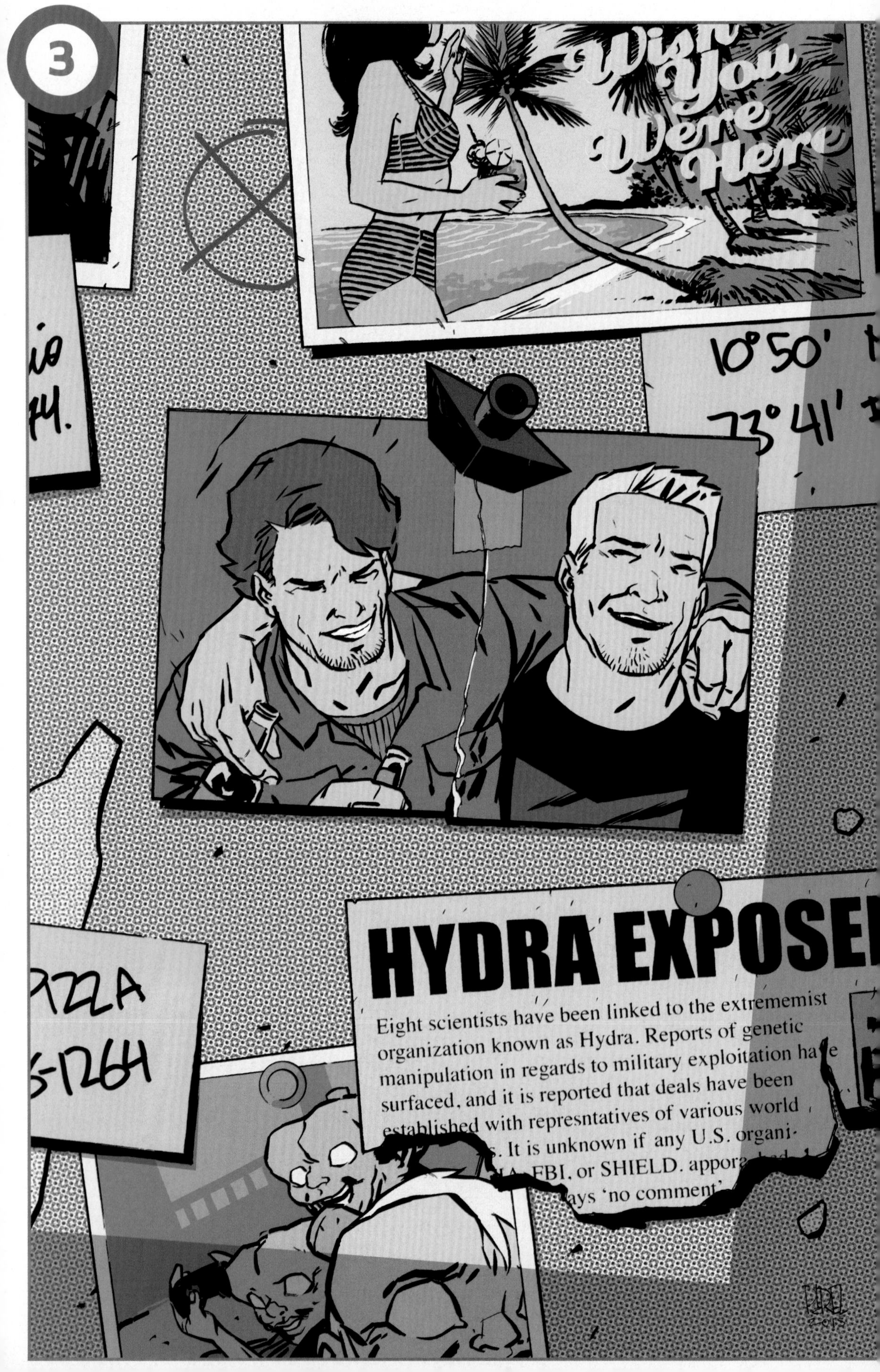
3
Wish You Were Here
10°50'
73°41'
io
74.
ZZA
5-1264
HYDRA EXPOSE
Eight scientists have been linked to the extrememist organization known as Hydra. Reports of genetic manipulation in regards to military exploitation ha e surfaced, and it is reported that deals have been established with represntatives of various world
s. It is unknown if any U.S. organi-
IA, FBI, or SHIELD. appora
ays 'no comment'

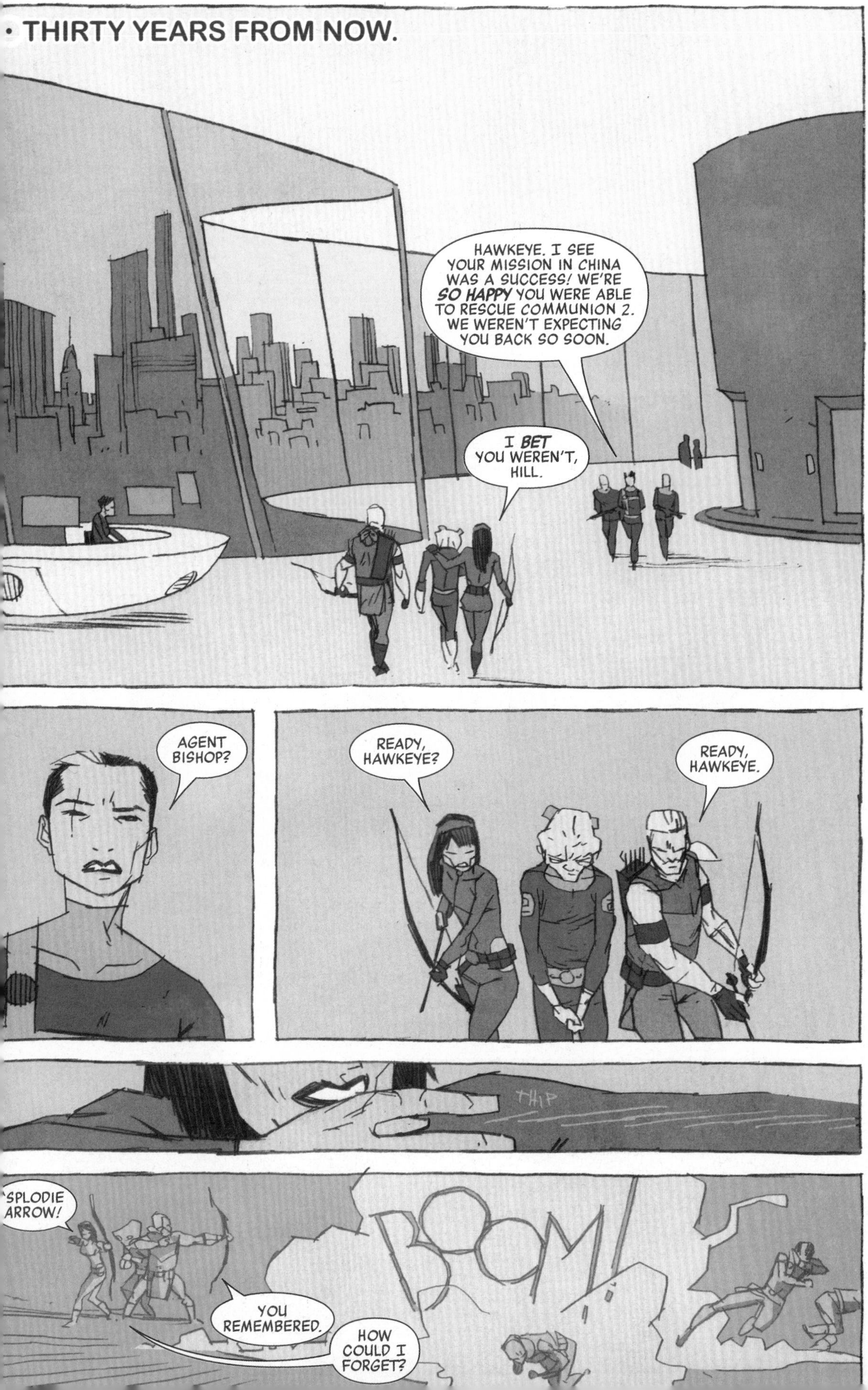
• THIRTY YEARS FROM NOW.
HAWKEYE. I SEE YOUR MISSION IN CHINA WAS A SUCCESS! WE'RE SO HAPPY YOU WERE ABLE TO RESCUE COMMUNION 2. WE WEREN'T EXPECTING YOU BACK SO SOON.
I BET YOU WEREN'T, HILL.
AGENT BISHOP?
READY, HAWKEYE?
READY, HAWKEYE.
THIP
'SPLODIE ARROW!
BOOM!
YOU REMEMBERED.
HOW COULD I FORGET?

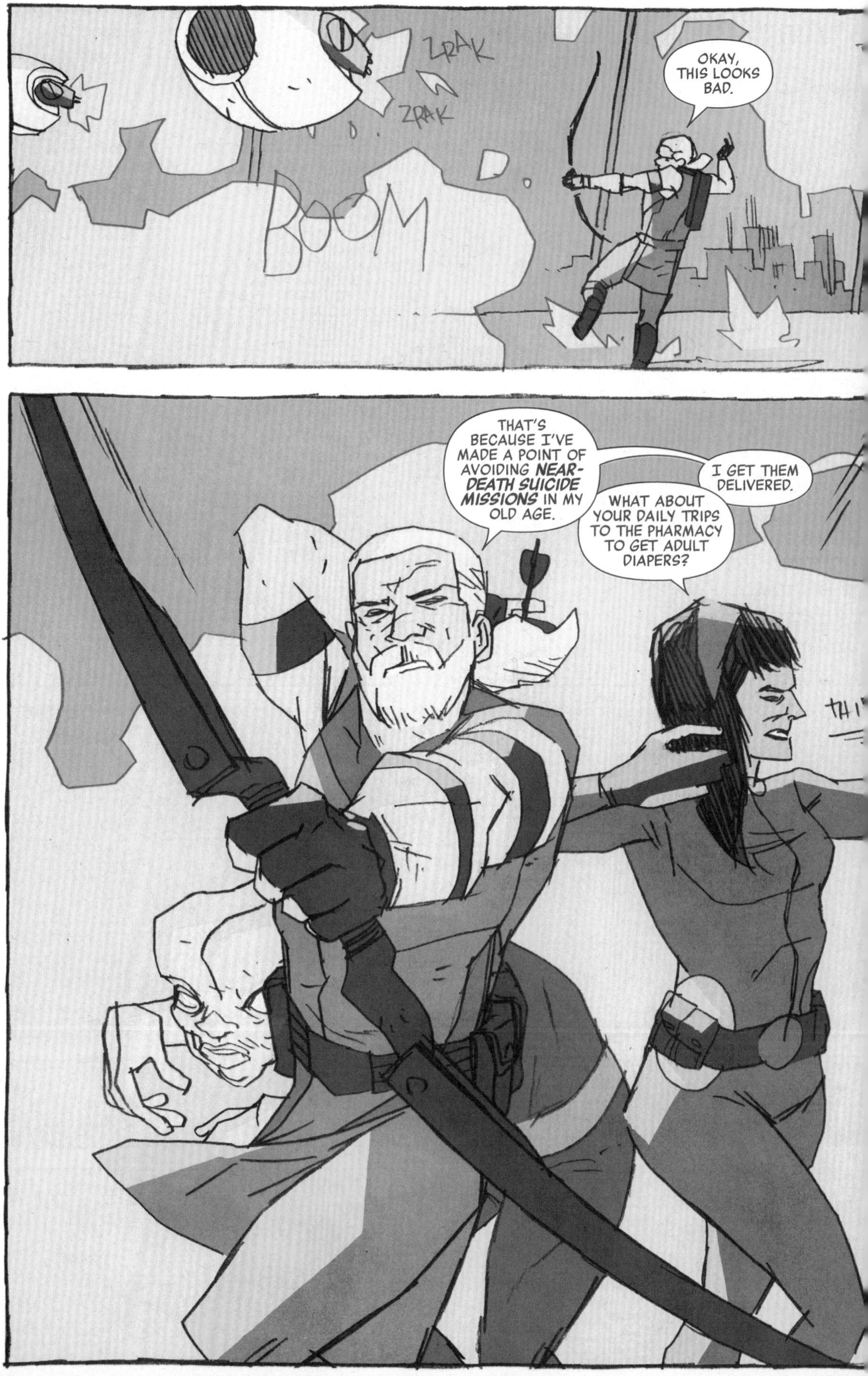
ZRAK
ZRAK
BOOM
OKAY, THIS LOOKS BAD.
THAT'S BECAUSE I'VE MADE A POINT OF AVOIDING **NEAR-DEATH SUICIDE MISSIONS** IN MY OLD AGE.
WHAT ABOUT YOUR DAILY TRIPS TO THE PHARMACY TO GET ADULT DIAPERS?
I GET THEM DELIVERED.

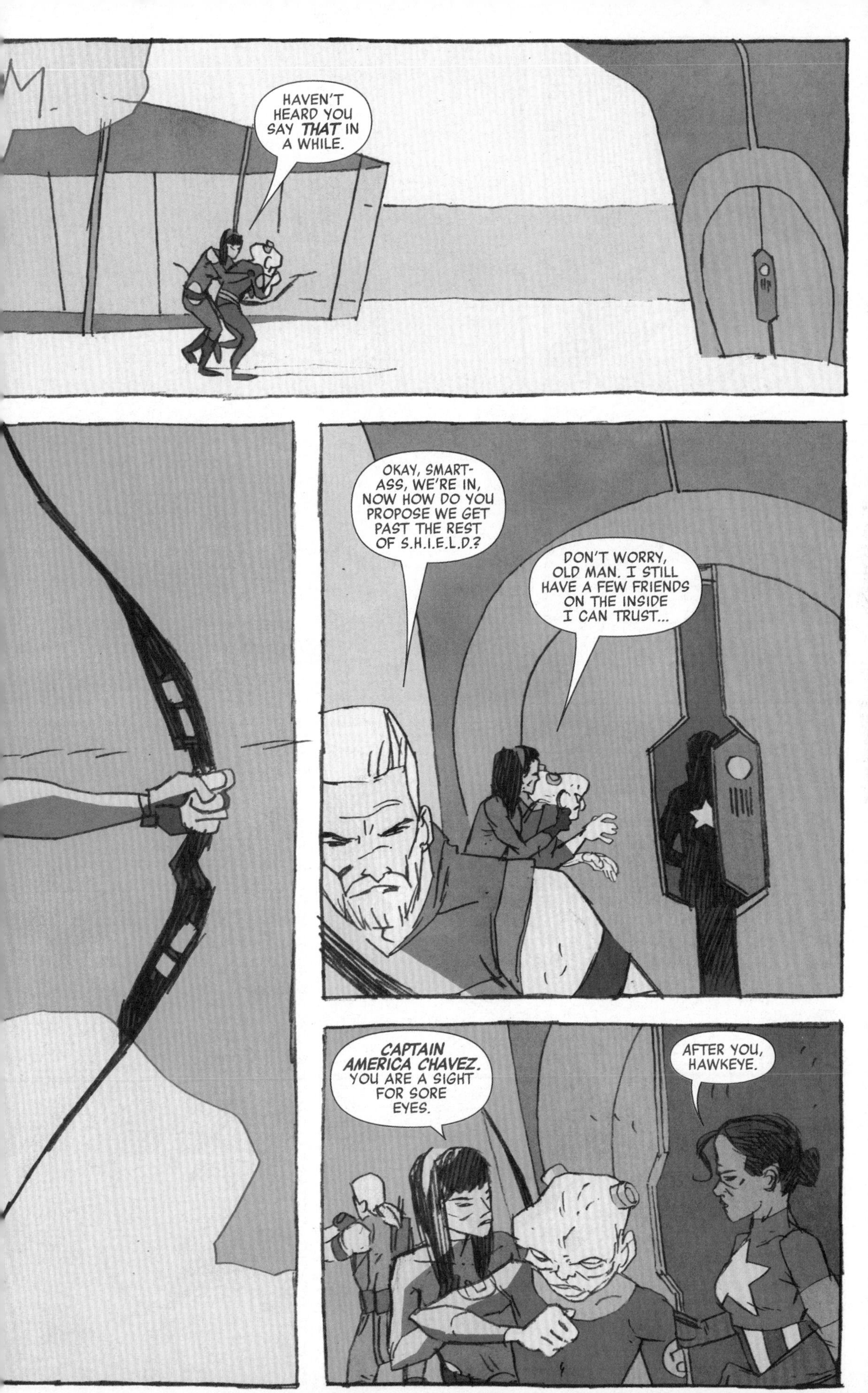
M-
HAVEN'T HEARD YOU SAY THAT IN A WHILE.
OKAY, SMART-ASS, WE'RE IN, NOW HOW DO YOU PROPOSE WE GET PAST THE REST OF S.H.I.E.L.D.?
DON'T WORRY, OLD MAN. I STILL HAVE A FEW FRIENDS ON THE INSIDE I CAN TRUST...
CAPTAIN AMERICA CHAVEZ. YOU ARE A SIGHT FOR SORE EYES.
AFTER YOU, HAWKEYE.

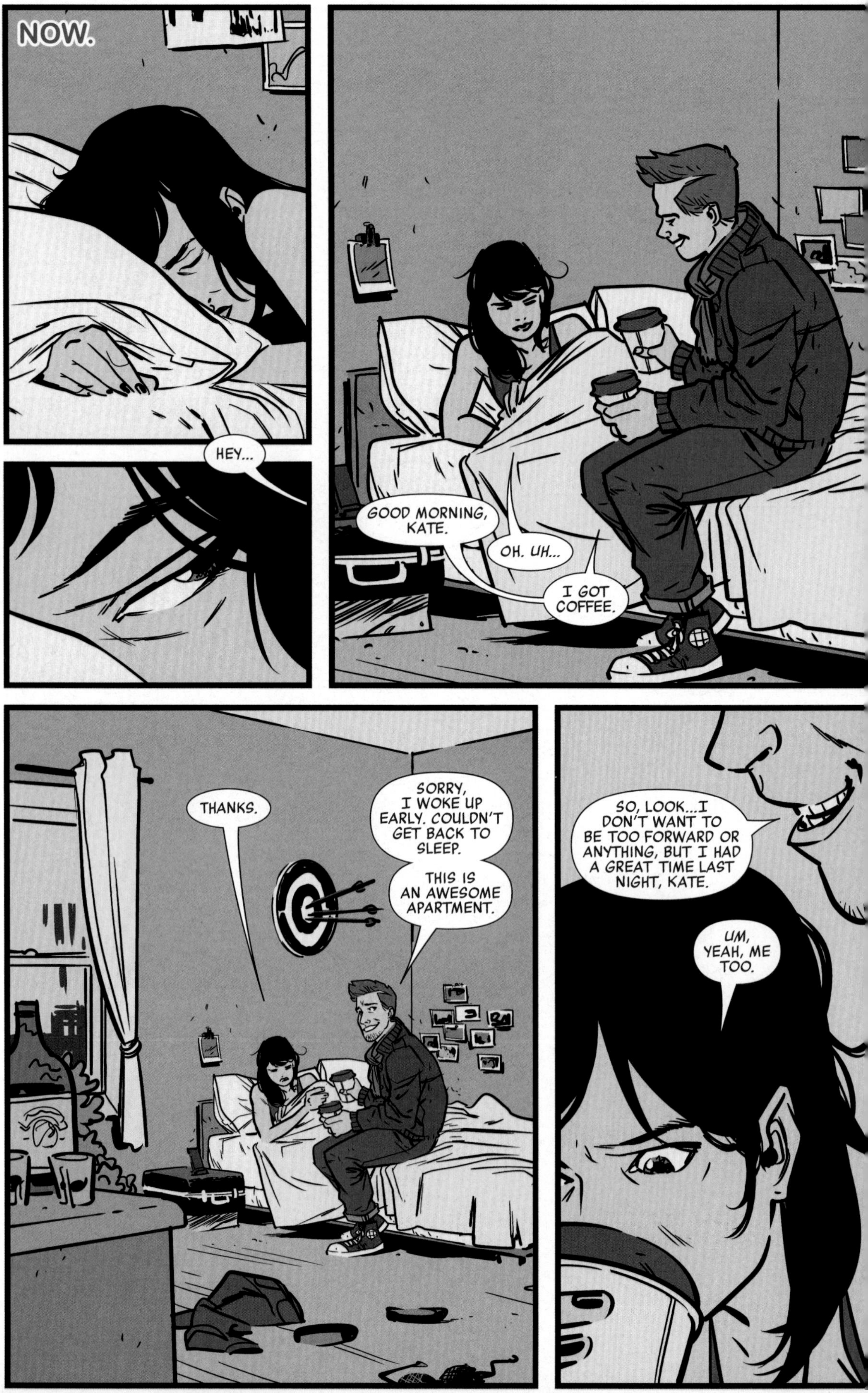
NOW.
HEY...
GOOD MORNING, KATE.
OH. UH...
I GOT COFFEE.
THANKS.
SORRY, I WOKE UP EARLY. COULDN'T GET BACK TO SLEEP.
THIS IS AN AWESOME APARTMENT.
SO, LOOK...I DON'T WANT TO BE TOO FORWARD OR ANYTHING, BUT I HAD A GREAT TIME LAST NIGHT, KATE.
UM, YEAH, ME TOO.

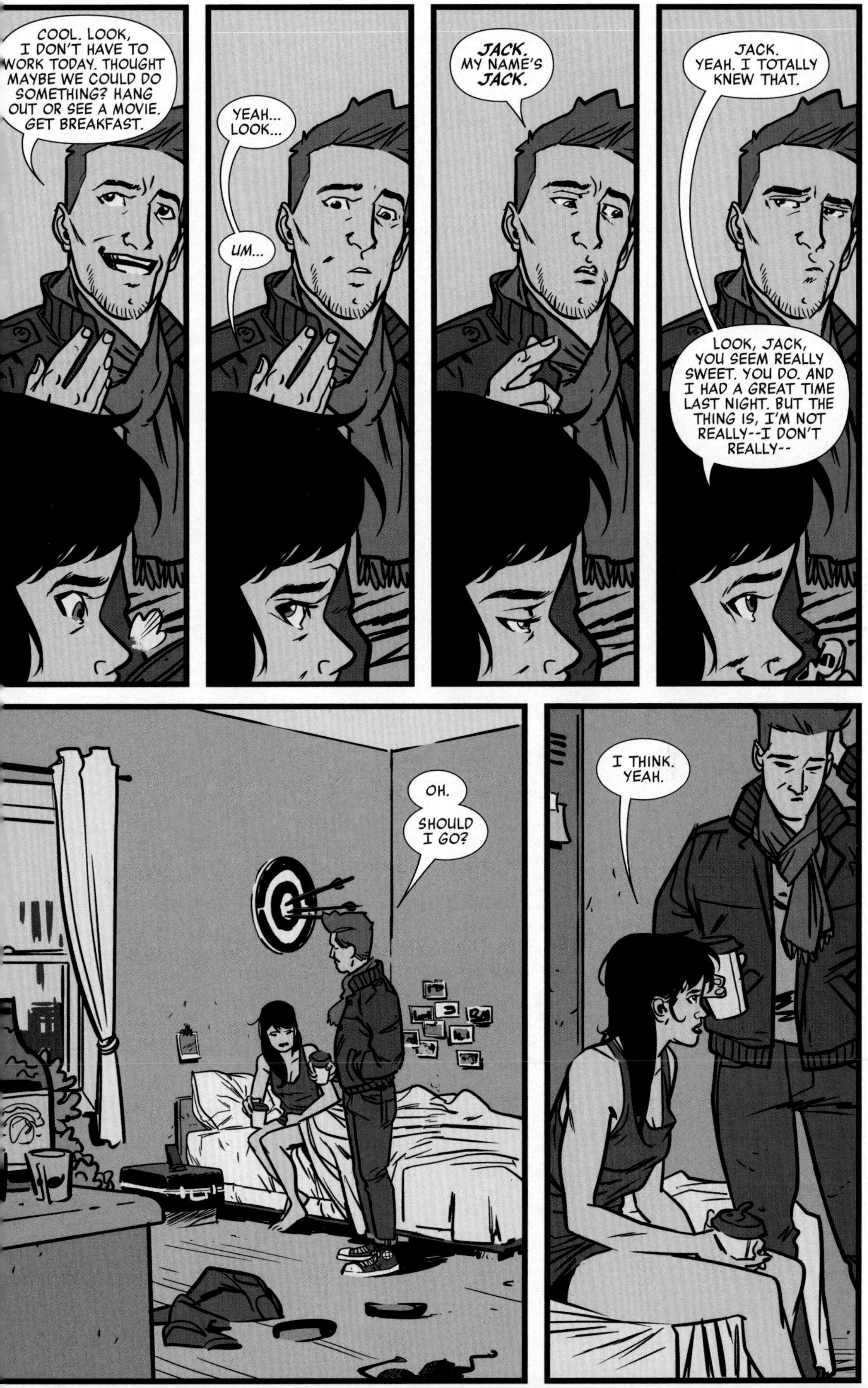
COOL. LOOK, I DON'T HAVE TO WORK TODAY. THOUGHT MAYBE WE COULD DO SOMETHING? HANG OUT OR SEE A MOVIE. GET BREAKFAST.
YEAH... LOOK...
UM...
JACK. MY NAME'S JACK.
JACK. YEAH. I TOTALLY KNEW THAT.
LOOK, JACK, YOU SEEM REALLY SWEET. YOU DO. AND I HAD A GREAT TIME LAST NIGHT. BUT THE THING IS, I'M NOT REALLY--I DON'T REALLY--
OH.
SHOULD I GO?
I THINK. YEAH.

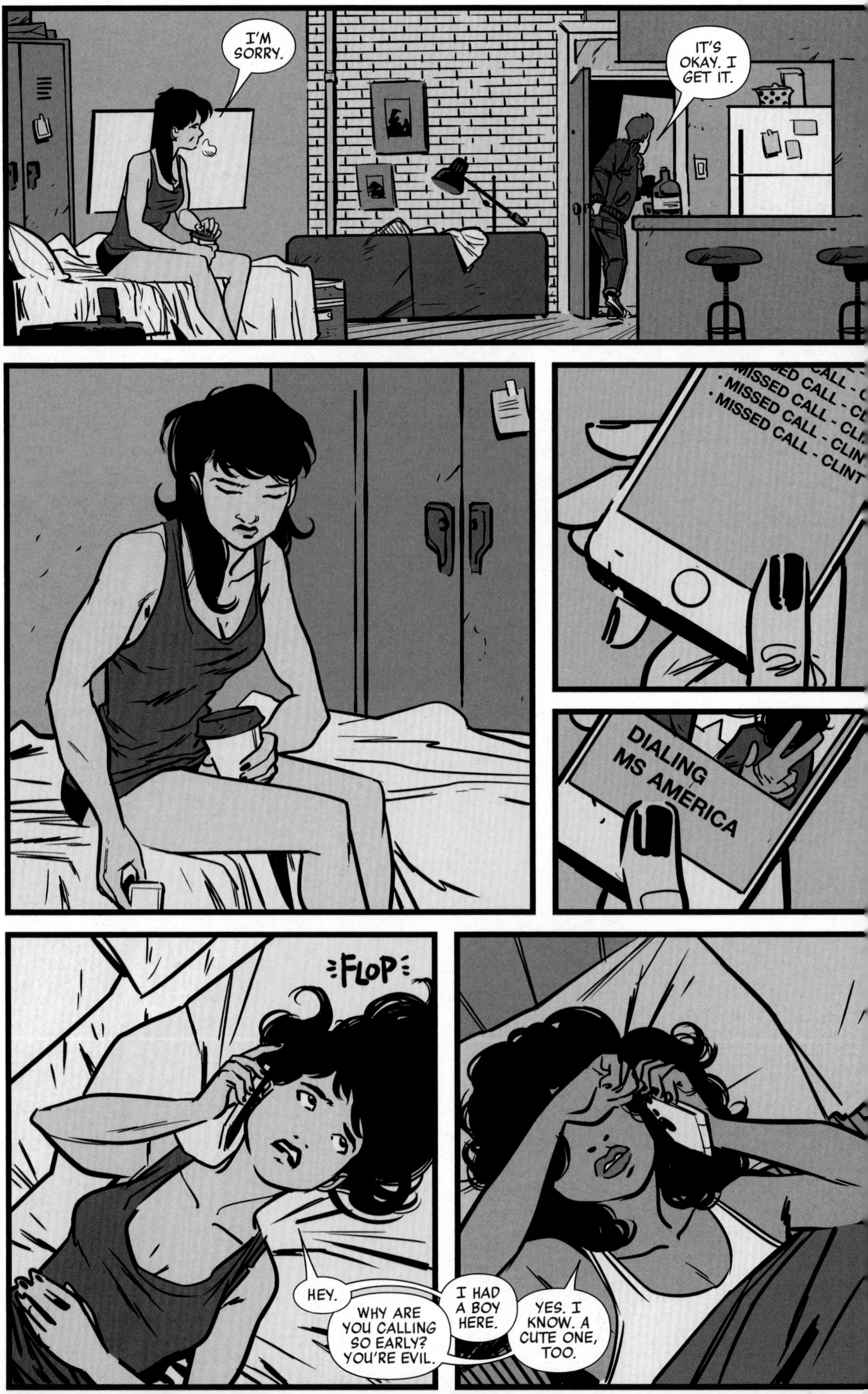
I'M SORRY.
IT'S OKAY. I GET IT.
• MISSED CALL - CLINT
• MISSED CALL - CLINT
• MISSED CALL - CLINT
DIALING MS AMERICA
FLOP
HEY.
WHY ARE YOU CALLING SO EARLY? YOU'RE EVIL.
I HAD A BOY HERE.
YES. I KNOW. A CUTE ONE, TOO.

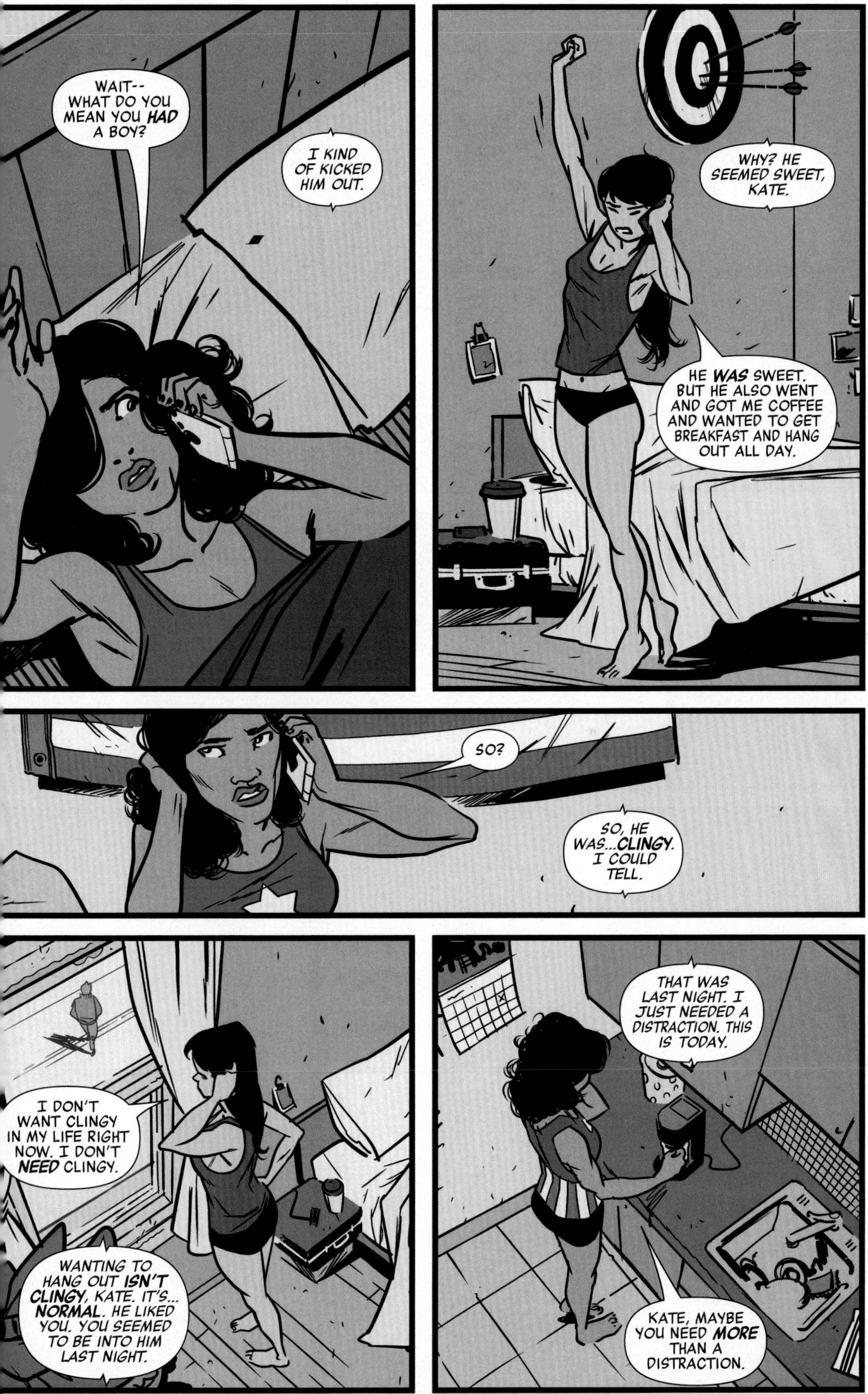
WAIT-- WHAT DO YOU MEAN YOU HAD A BOY?
I KIND OF KICKED HIM OUT.
WHY? HE SEEMED SWEET, KATE.
HE WAS SWEET. BUT HE ALSO WENT AND GOT ME COFFEE AND WANTED TO GET BREAKFAST AND HANG OUT ALL DAY.
SO?
SO, HE WAS...CLINGY. I COULD TELL.
I DON'T WANT CLINGY IN MY LIFE RIGHT NOW. I DON'T NEED CLINGY.
WANTING TO HANG OUT ISN'T CLINGY, KATE. IT'S... NORMAL. HE LIKED YOU. YOU SEEMED TO BE INTO HIM LAST NIGHT.
THAT WAS LAST NIGHT. I JUST NEEDED A DISTRACTION. THIS IS TODAY.
KATE, MAYBE YOU NEED MORE THAN A DISTRACTION.

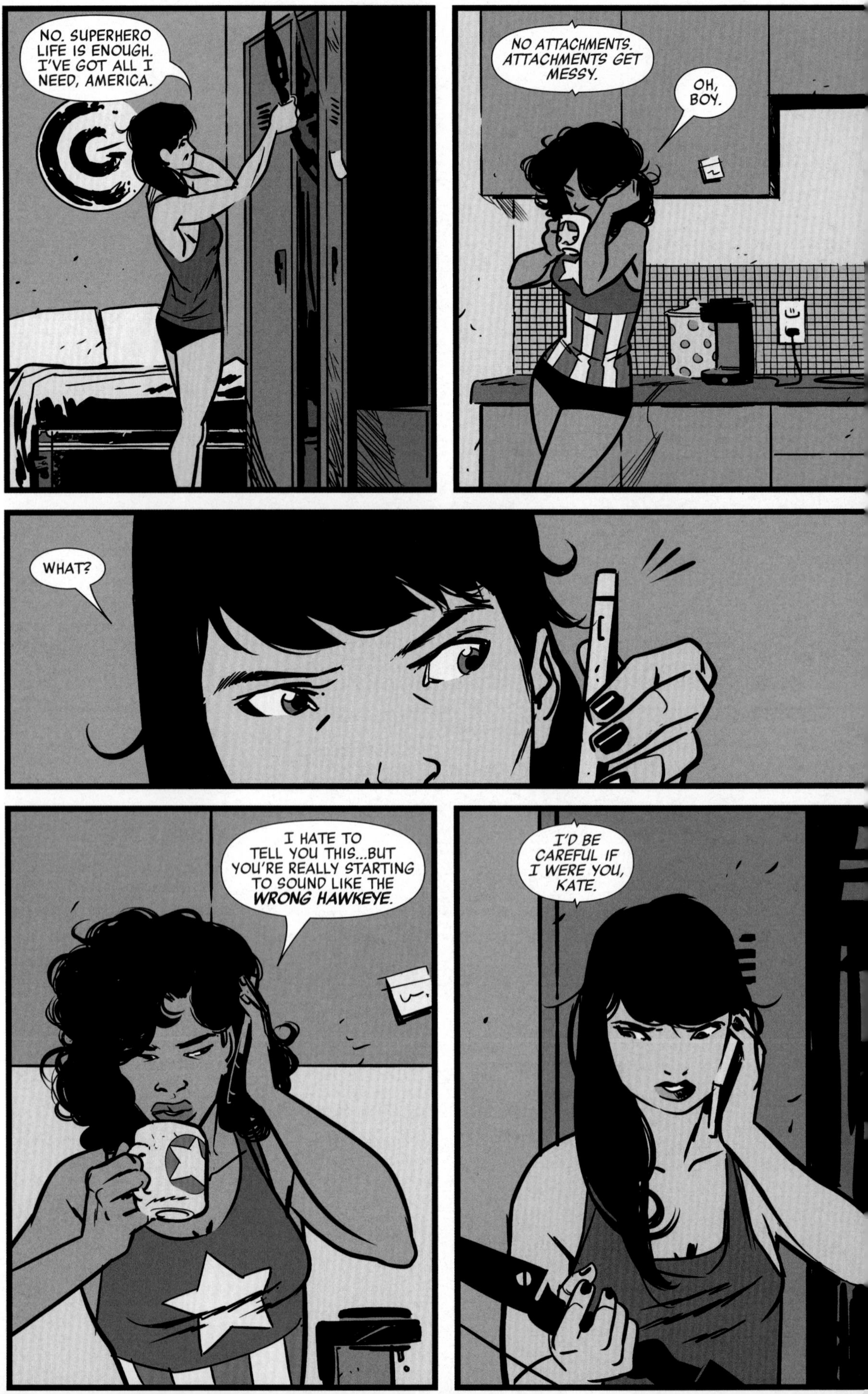
NO. SUPERHERO LIFE IS ENOUGH. I'VE GOT ALL I NEED, AMERICA.
NO ATTACHMENTS. ATTACHMENTS GET MESSY.
OH, BOY.
WHAT?
I HATE TO TELL YOU THIS...BUT YOU'RE REALLY STARTING TO SOUND LIKE THE **WRONG HAWKEYE**.
I'D BE CAREFUL IF I WERE YOU, KATE.

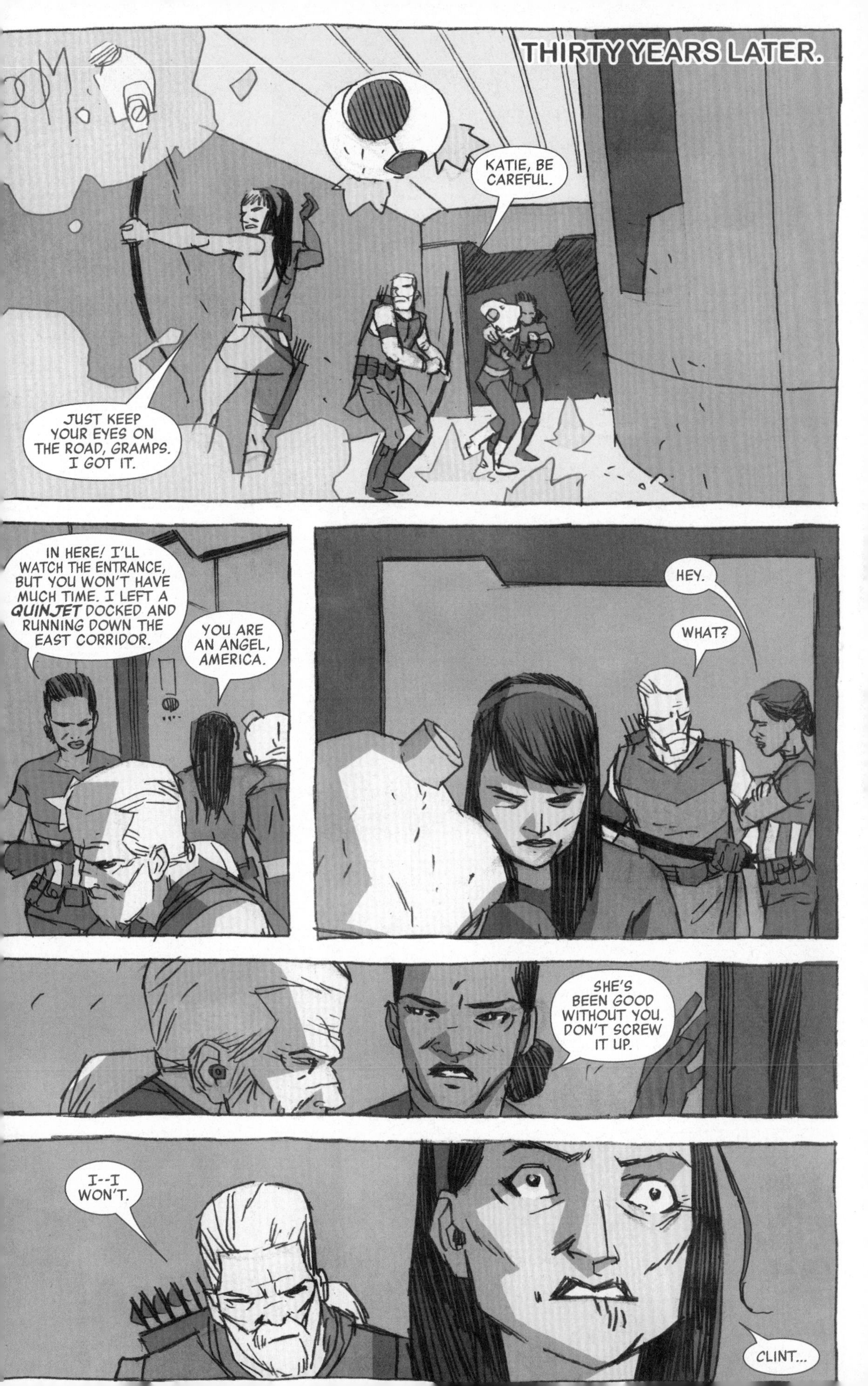
THIRTY YEARS LATER.
KATIE, BE CAREFUL.
JUST KEEP YOUR EYES ON THE ROAD, GRAMPS. I GOT IT.
IN HERE! I'LL WATCH THE ENTRANCE, BUT YOU WON'T HAVE MUCH TIME. I LEFT A QUINJET DOCKED AND RUNNING DOWN THE EAST CORRIDOR.
YOU ARE AN ANGEL, AMERICA.
HEY.
WHAT?
SHE'S BEEN GOOD WITHOUT YOU. DON'T SCREW IT UP.
I--I WON'T.
CLINT...

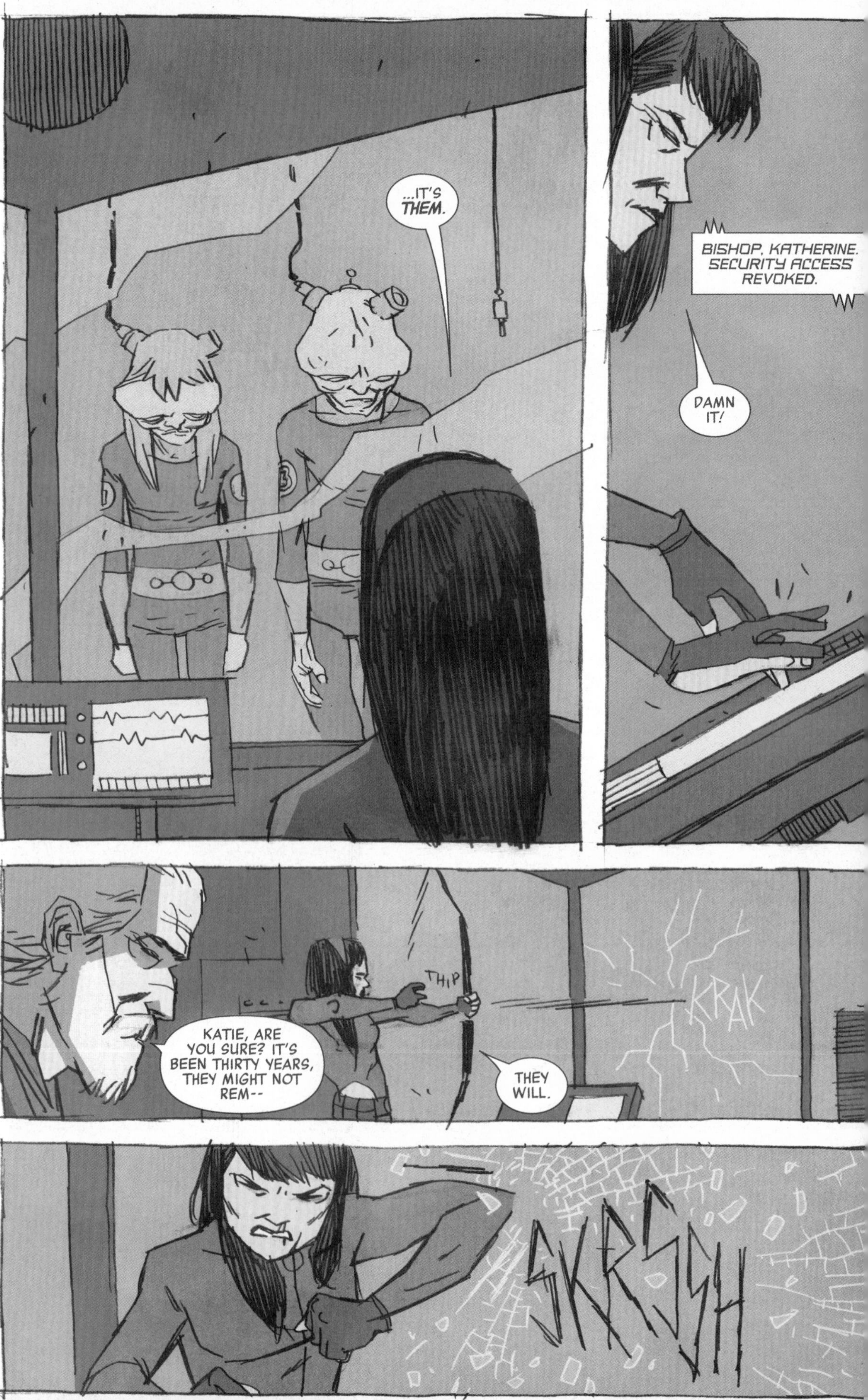
...IT'S THEM.
BISHOP, KATHERINE. SECURITY ACCESS REVOKED.
DAMN IT!
THIP
KRAK
KATIE, ARE YOU SURE? IT'S BEEN THIRTY YEARS, THEY MIGHT NOT REM--
THEY WILL.
SKRSSH

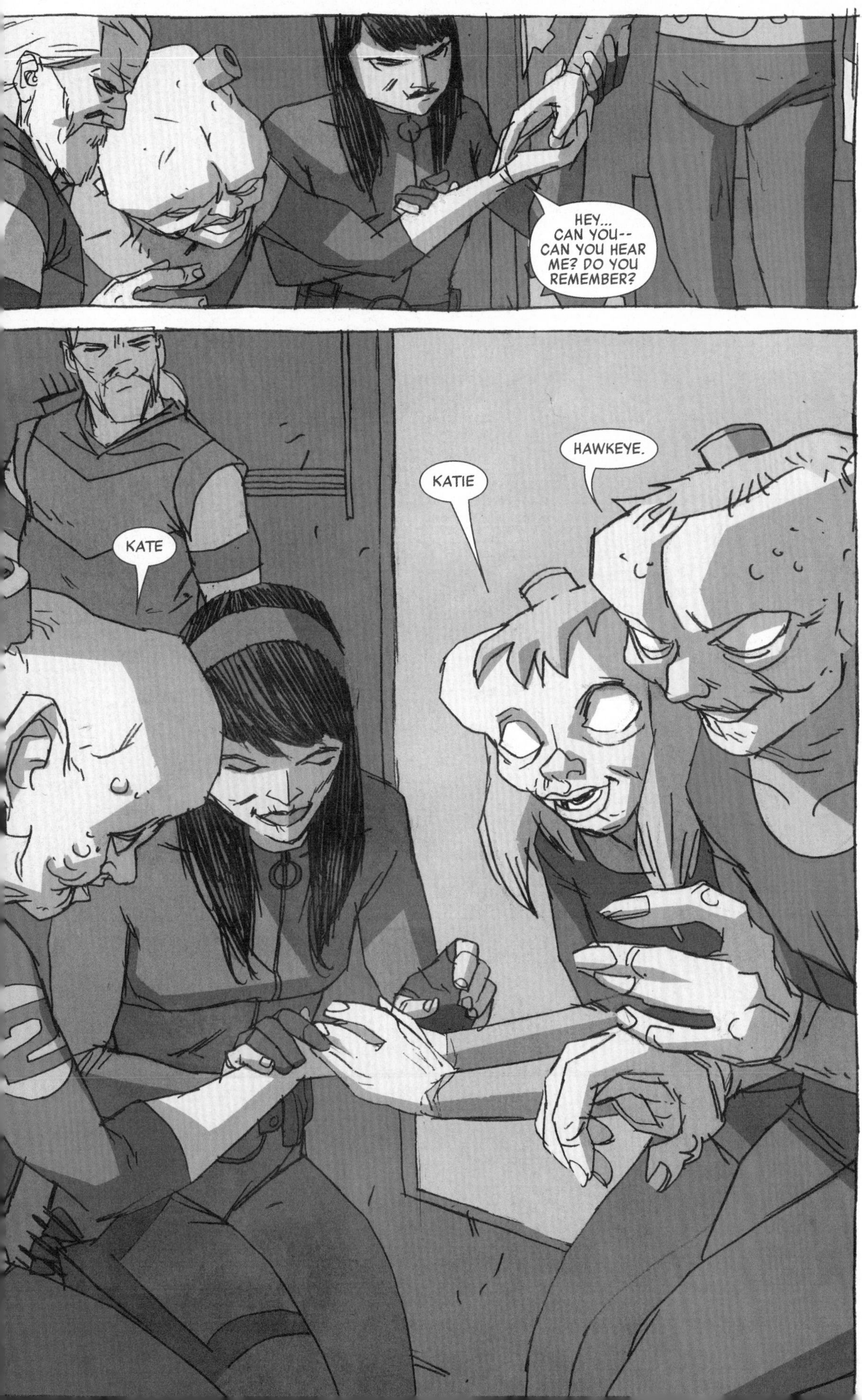
HEY... CAN YOU-- CAN YOU HEAR ME? DO YOU REMEMBER?
KATE
KATIE
HAWKEYE.

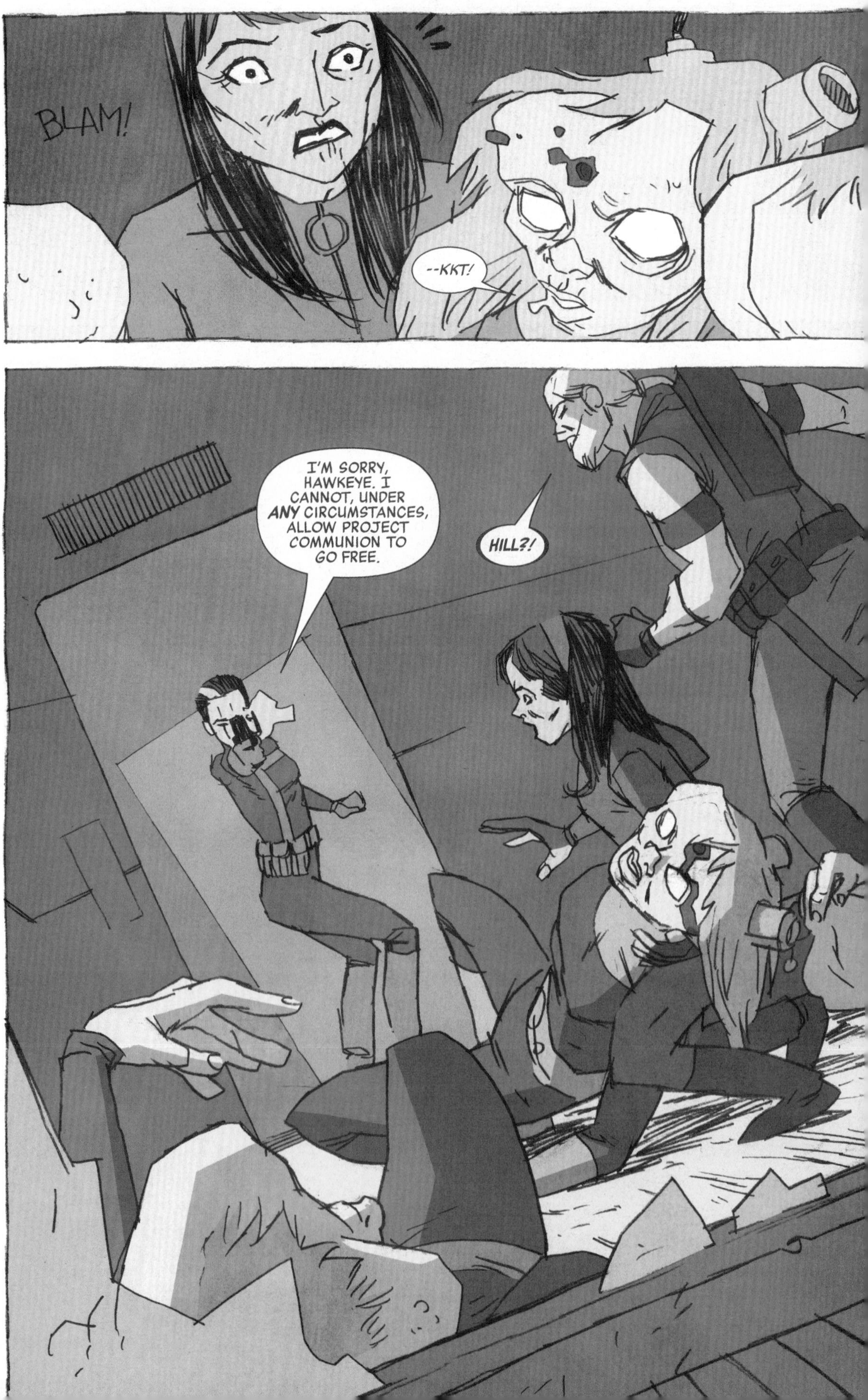
BLAM!
--KKT!
I'M SORRY, HAWKEYE. I CANNOT, UNDER ANY CIRCUMSTANCES, ALLOW PROJECT COMMUNION TO GO FREE.
HILL?!

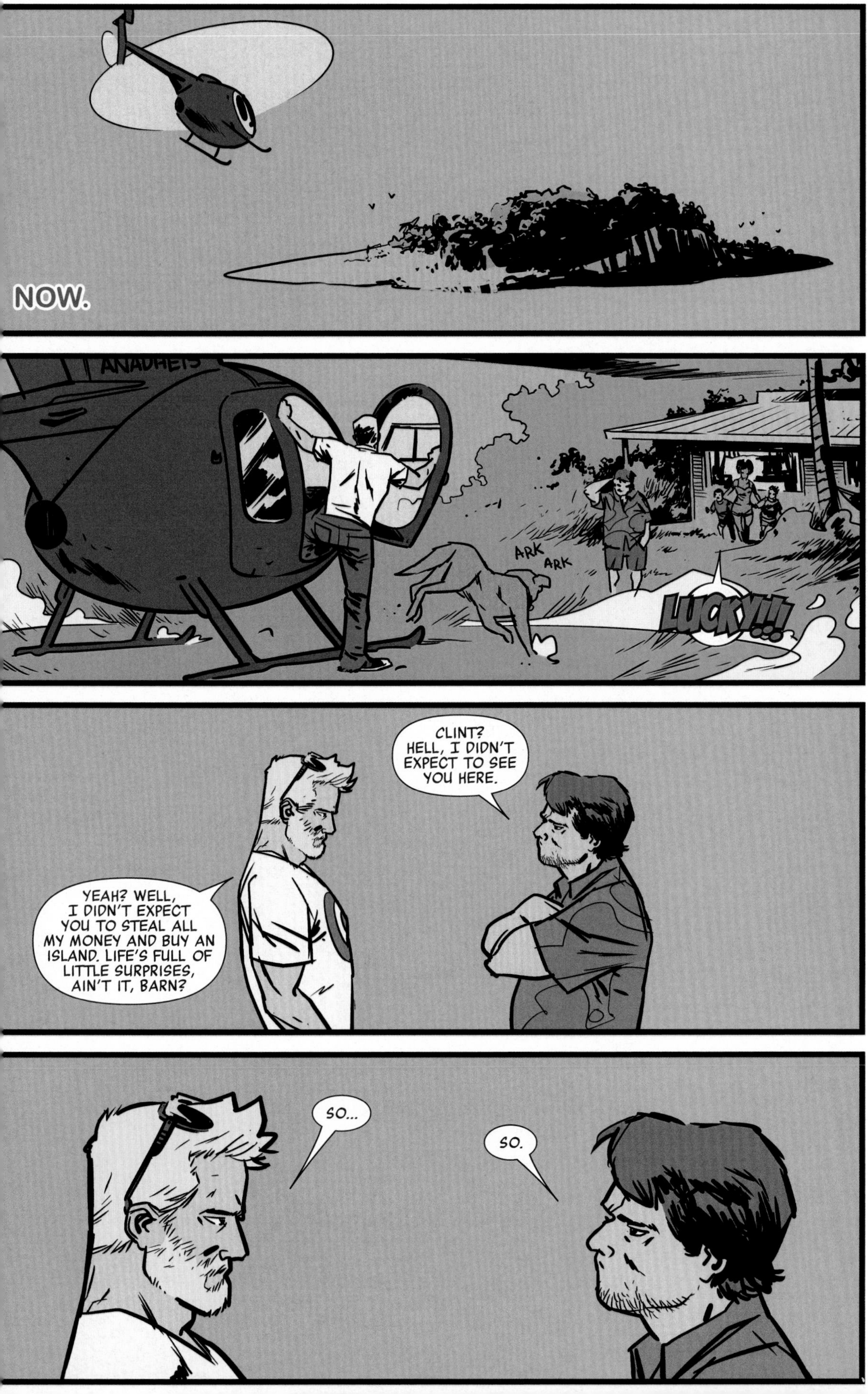
NOW.
ARK
ARK
LUCKY!!!
CLINT? HELL, I DIDN'T EXPECT TO SEE YOU HERE.
YEAH? WELL, I DIDN'T EXPECT YOU TO STEAL ALL MY MONEY AND BUY AN ISLAND. LIFE'S FULL OF LITTLE SURPRISES, AIN'T IT, BARN?
SO...
SO.

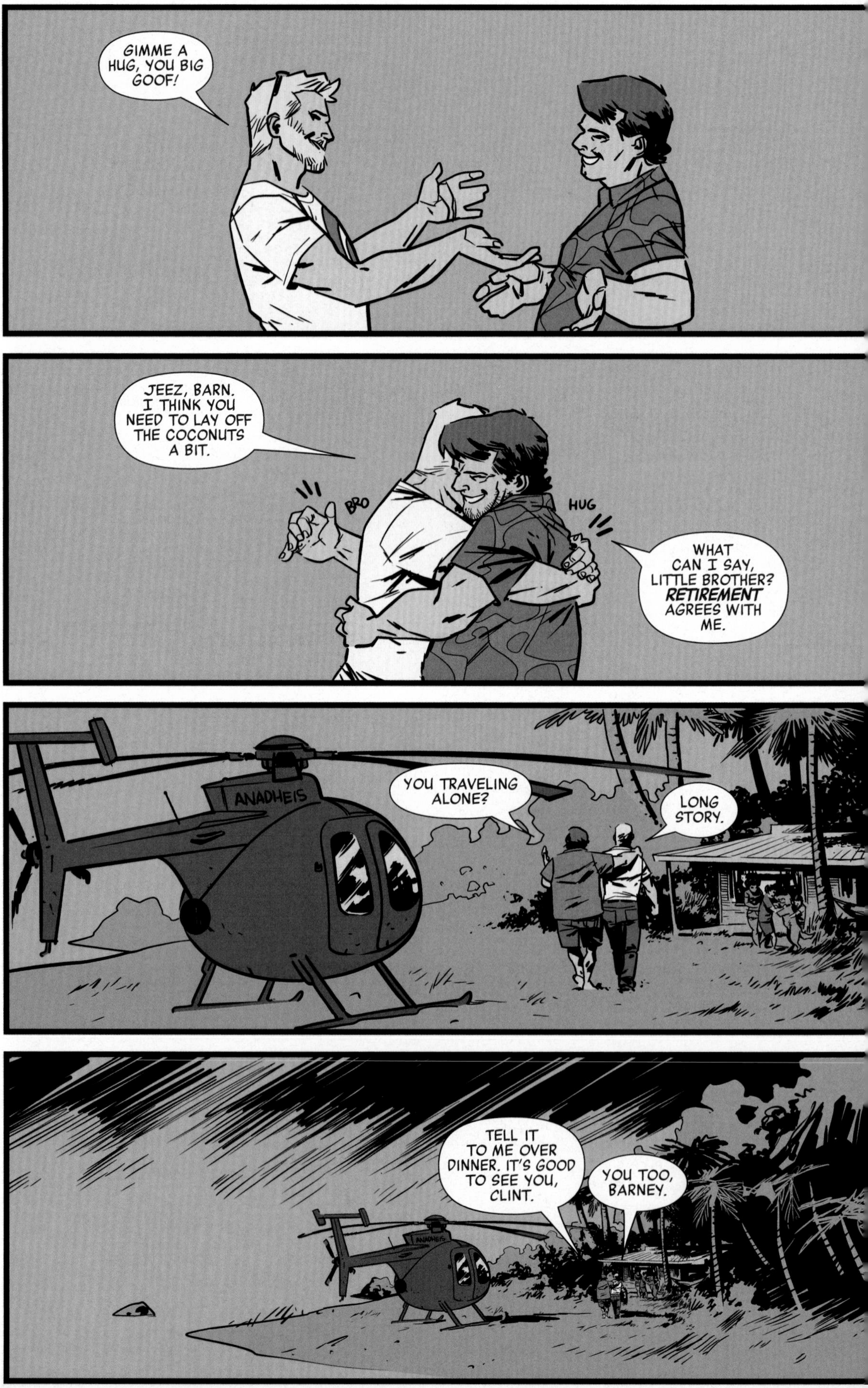
GIMME A HUG, YOU BIG GOOF!
JEEZ, BARN. I THINK YOU NEED TO LAY OFF THE COCONUTS A BIT.
BRO
HUG
WHAT CAN I SAY, LITTLE BROTHER? *RETIREMENT* AGREES WITH ME.
ANADHEIS
YOU TRAVELING ALONE?
LONG STORY.
TELL IT TO ME OVER DINNER. IT'S GOOD TO SEE YOU, CLINT.
YOU TOO, BARNEY.

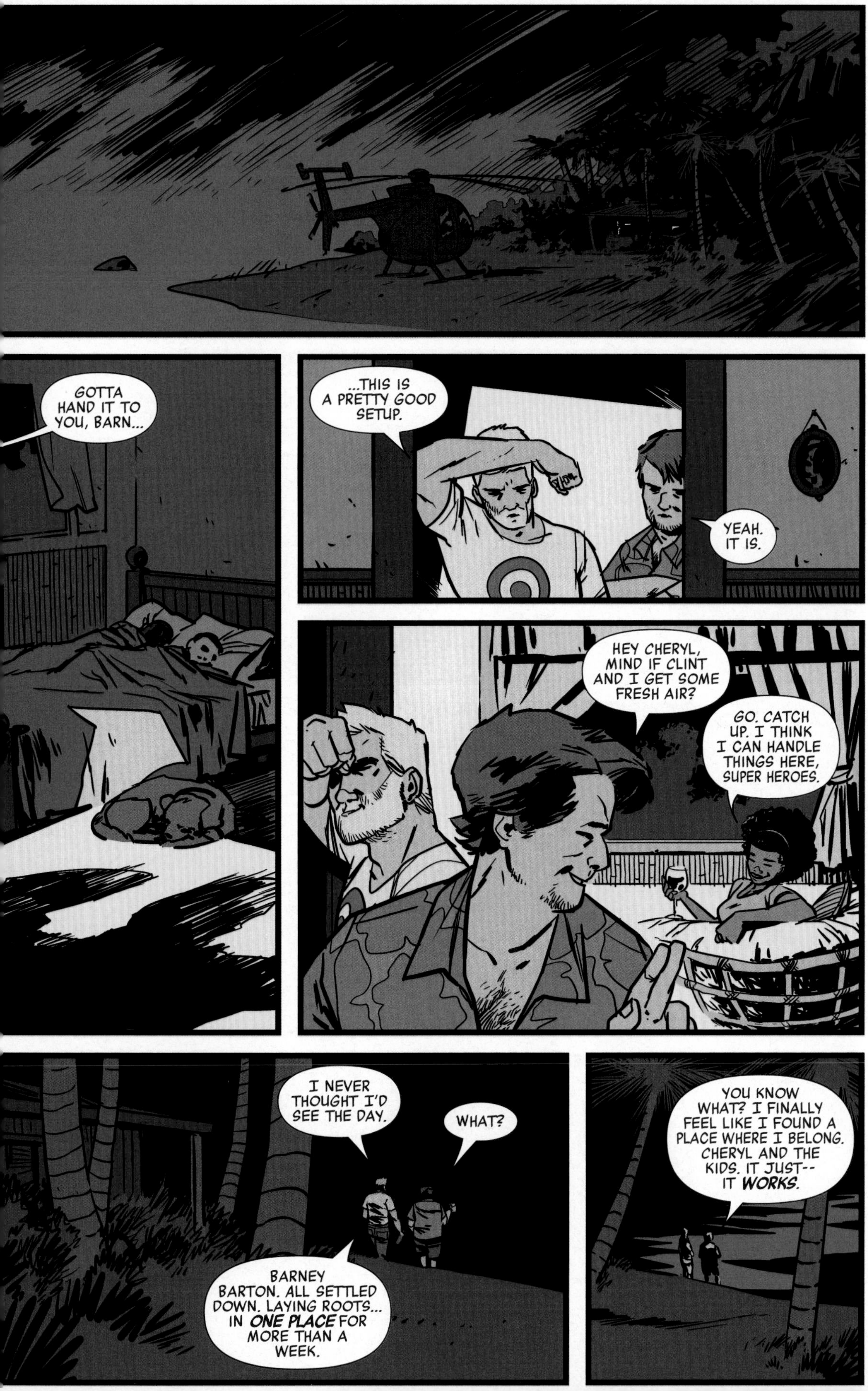
GOTTA HAND IT TO YOU, BARN...
...THIS IS A PRETTY GOOD SETUP.
YEAH. IT IS.
HEY CHERYL, MIND IF CLINT AND I GET SOME FRESH AIR?
GO. CATCH UP. I THINK I CAN HANDLE THINGS HERE, SUPER HEROES.
I NEVER THOUGHT I'D SEE THE DAY.
WHAT?
BARNEY BARTON. ALL SETTLED DOWN. LAYING ROOTS... IN ONE PLACE FOR MORE THAN A WEEK.
YOU KNOW WHAT? I FINALLY FEEL LIKE I FOUND A PLACE WHERE I BELONG. CHERYL AND THE KIDS. IT JUST-- IT WORKS.

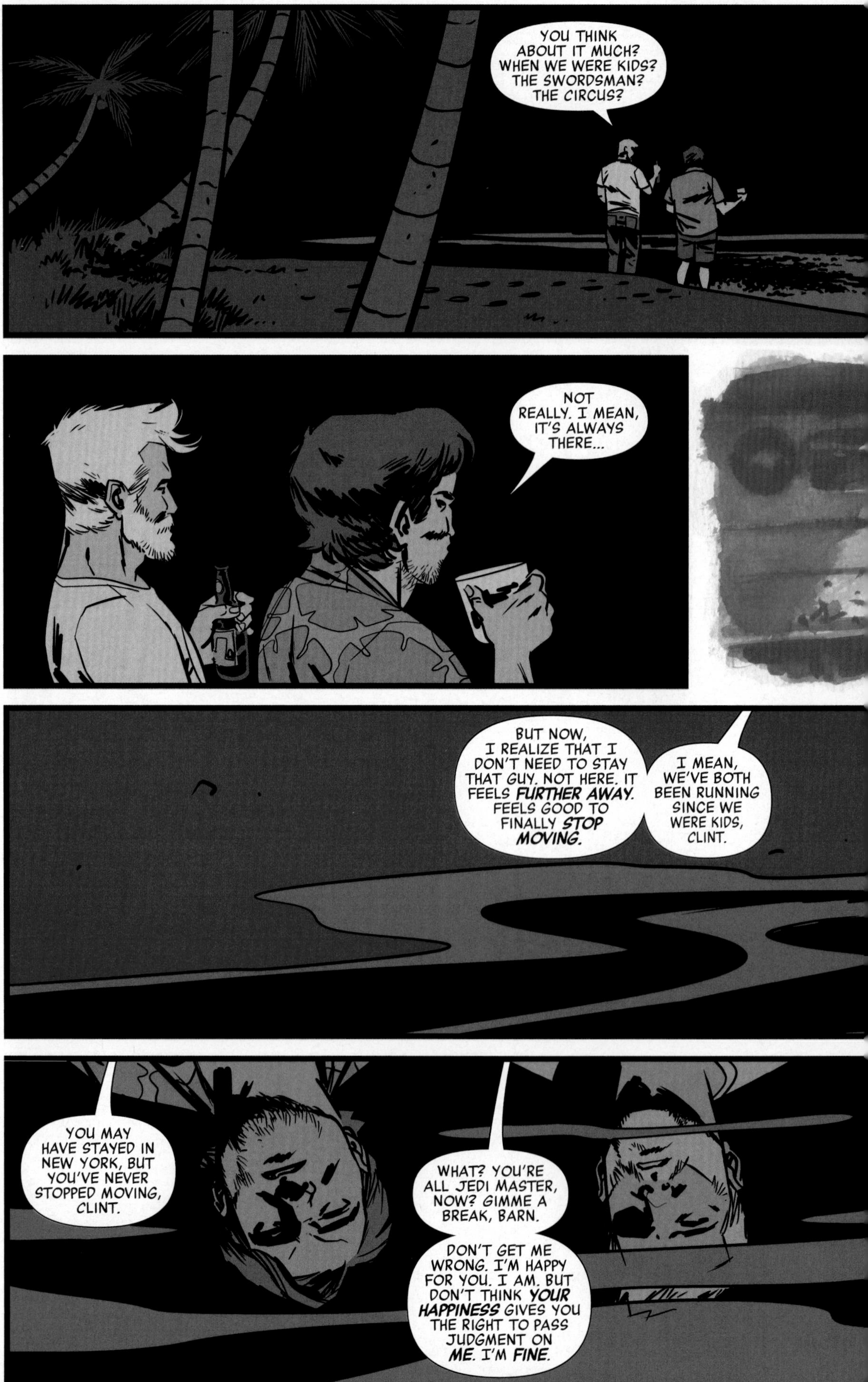
YOU THINK ABOUT IT MUCH? WHEN WE WERE KIDS? THE SWORDSMAN? THE CIRCUS?
NOT REALLY. I MEAN, IT'S ALWAYS THERE...
BUT NOW, I REALIZE THAT I DON'T NEED TO STAY THAT GUY. NOT HERE. IT FEELS FURTHER AWAY. FEELS GOOD TO FINALLY STOP MOVING.
I MEAN, WE'VE BOTH BEEN RUNNING SINCE WE WERE KIDS, CLINT.
YOU MAY HAVE STAYED IN NEW YORK, BUT YOU'VE NEVER STOPPED MOVING, CLINT.
WHAT? YOU'RE ALL JEDI MASTER, NOW? GIMME A BREAK, BARN.
DON'T GET ME WRONG. I'M HAPPY FOR YOU. I AM. BUT DON'T THINK YOUR HAPPINESS GIVES YOU THE RIGHT TO PASS JUDGMENT ON ME. I'M FINE.

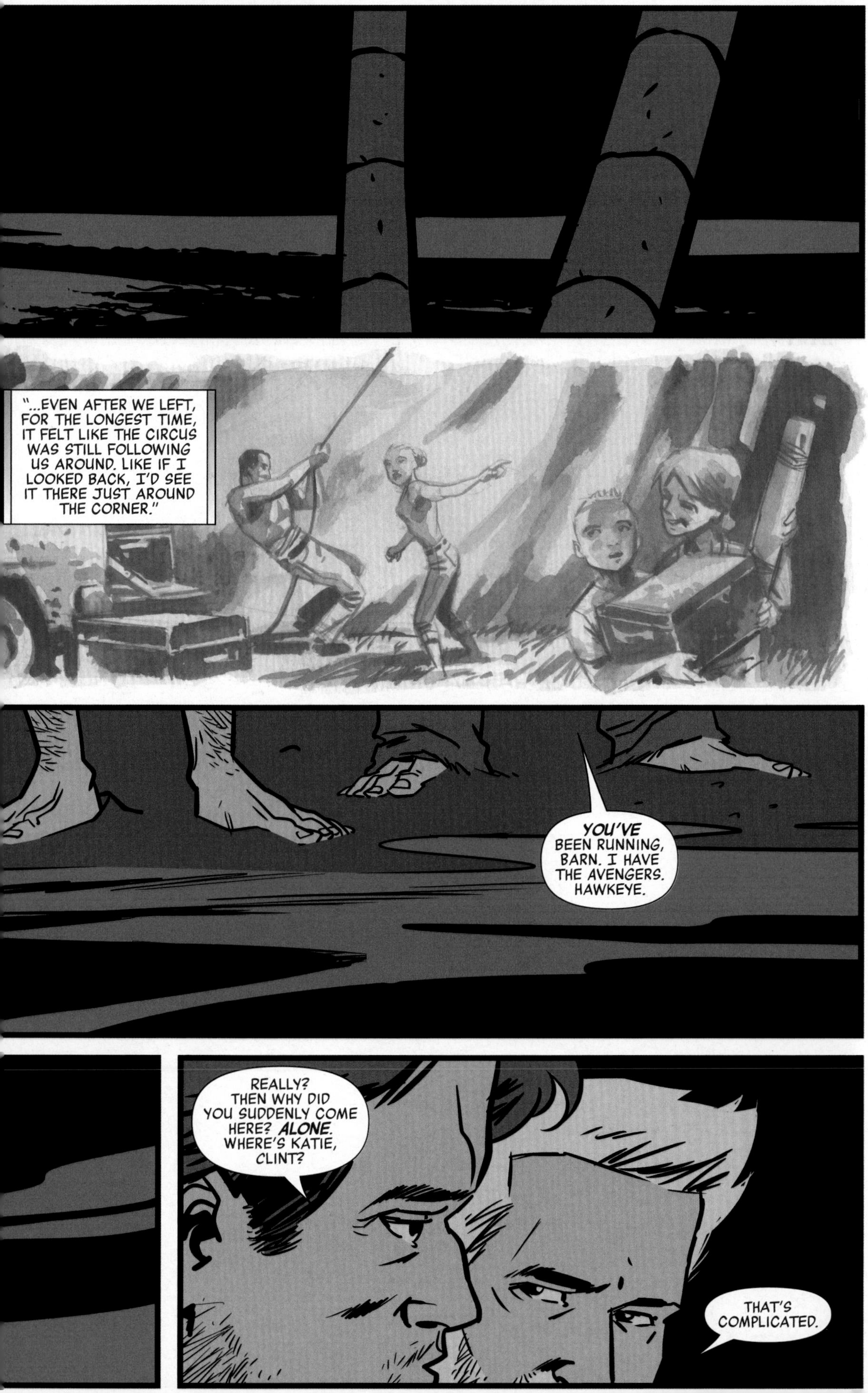
"...EVEN AFTER WE LEFT, FOR THE LONGEST TIME, IT FELT LIKE THE CIRCUS WAS STILL FOLLOWING US AROUND. LIKE IF I LOOKED BACK, I'D SEE IT THERE JUST AROUND THE CORNER."
YOU'VE BEEN RUNNING, BARN. I HAVE THE AVENGERS. HAWKEYE.
REALLY? THEN WHY DID YOU SUDDENLY COME HERE? ALONE. WHERE'S KATIE, CLINT?
THAT'S COMPLICATED.

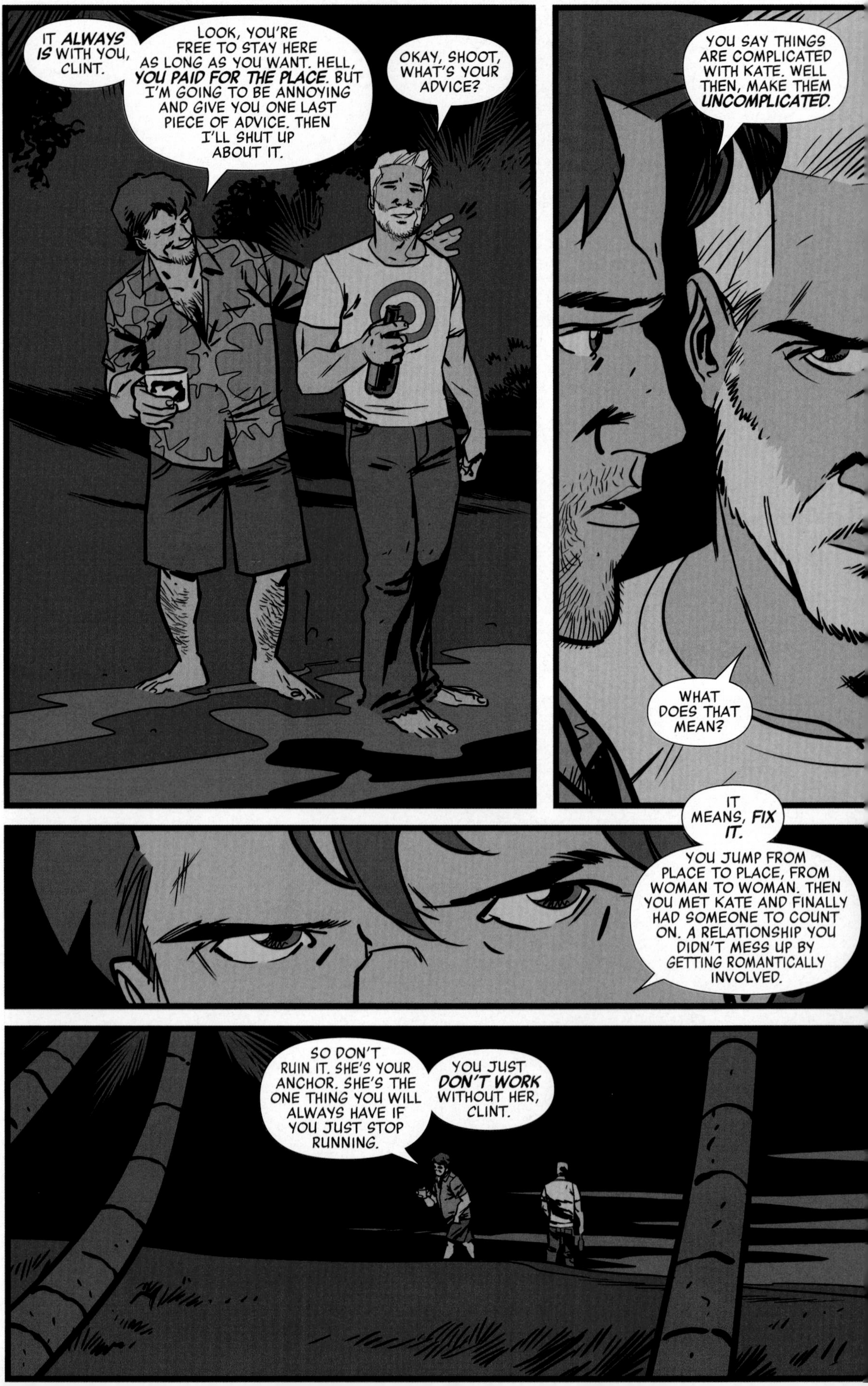
IT ALWAYS IS WITH YOU, CLINT.
LOOK, YOU'RE FREE TO STAY HERE AS LONG AS YOU WANT. HELL, YOU PAID FOR THE PLACE. BUT I'M GOING TO BE ANNOYING AND GIVE YOU ONE LAST PIECE OF ADVICE. THEN I'LL SHUT UP ABOUT IT.
OKAY, SHOOT, WHAT'S YOUR ADVICE?
YOU SAY THINGS ARE COMPLICATED WITH KATE. WELL THEN, MAKE THEM UNCOMPLICATED.
WHAT DOES THAT MEAN?
IT MEANS, FIX IT.
YOU JUMP FROM PLACE TO PLACE, FROM WOMAN TO WOMAN. THEN YOU MET KATE AND FINALLY HAD SOMEONE TO COUNT ON. A RELATIONSHIP YOU DIDN'T MESS UP BY GETTING ROMANTICALLY INVOLVED.
SO DON'T RUIN IT. SHE'S YOUR ANCHOR. SHE'S THE ONE THING YOU WILL ALWAYS HAVE IF YOU JUST STOP RUNNING.
YOU JUST DON'T WORK WITHOUT HER, CLINT.

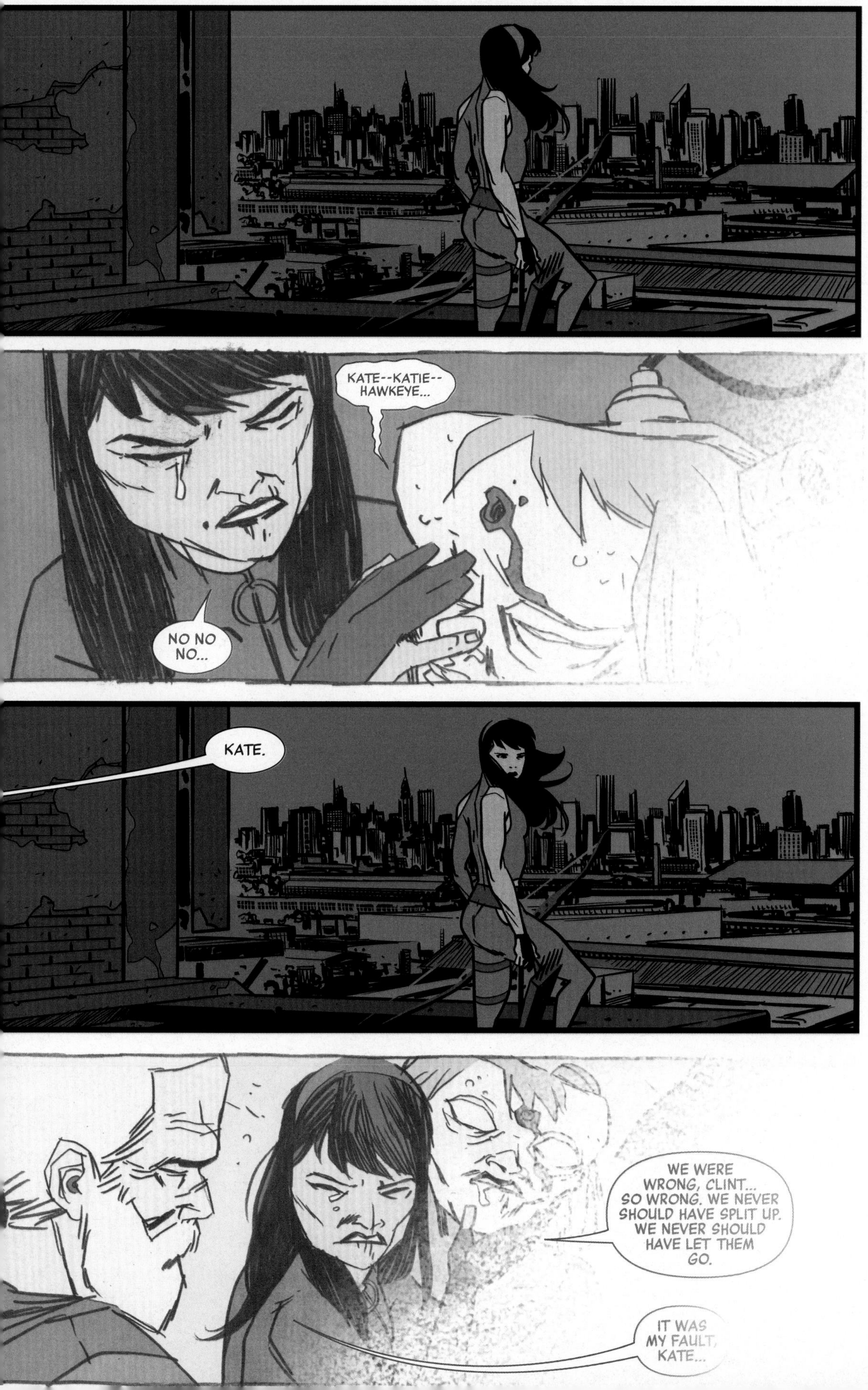
KATE--KATIE--
HAWKEYE...
NO NO
NO...
KATE.
WE WERE
WRONG, CLINT...
SO WRONG. WE NEVER
SHOULD HAVE SPLIT UP.
WE NEVER SHOULD
HAVE LET THEM
GO.
IT WAS
MY FAULT,
KATE...

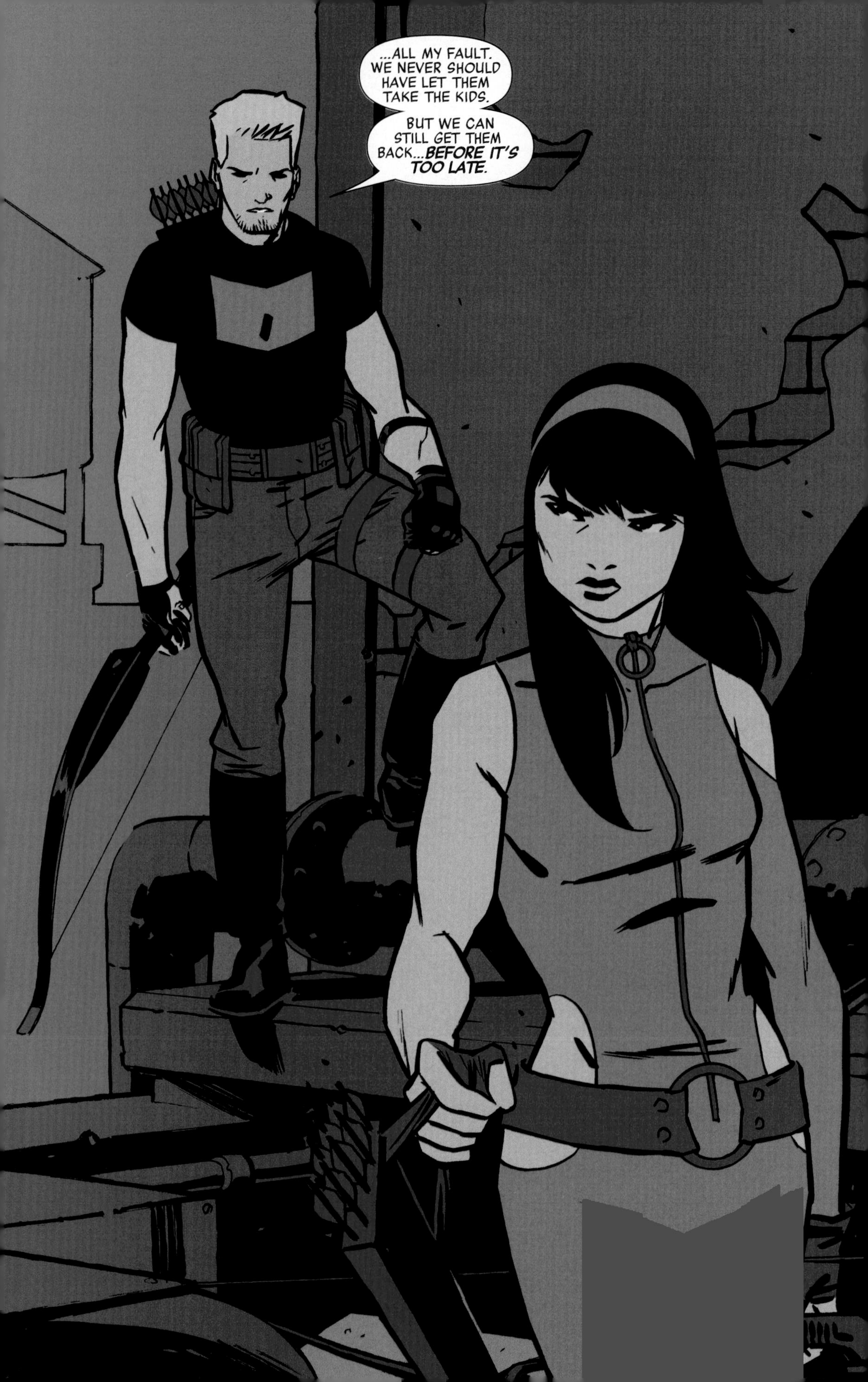
...ALL MY FAULT. WE NEVER SHOULD HAVE LET THEM TAKE THE KIDS.
BUT WE CAN STILL GET THEM BACK...*BEFORE IT'S TOO LATE.*

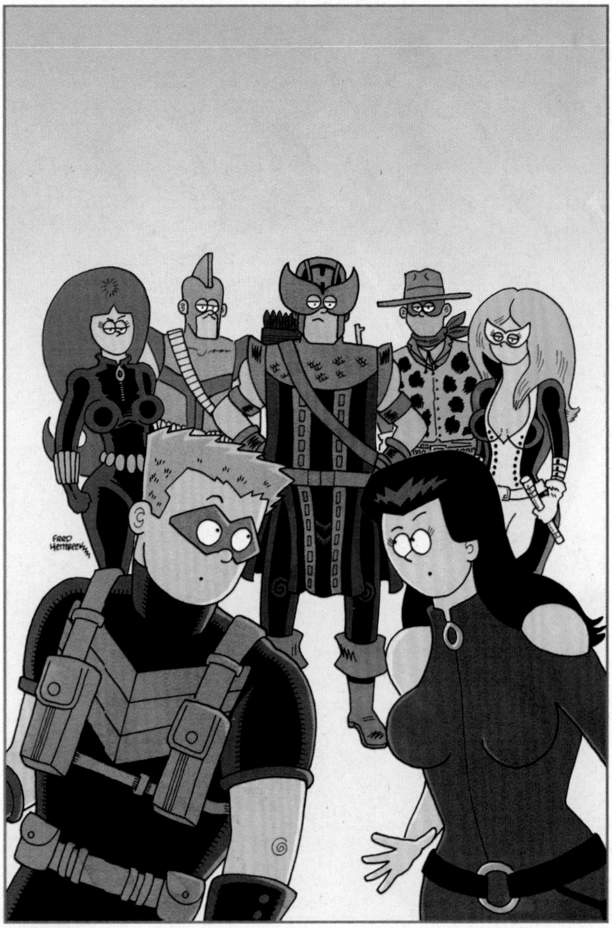
FRED HEMBECK

ALL-NEW HAWKEYE #2
VARIANT BY **FRED HEMBECK**
& **ANDY TROY**

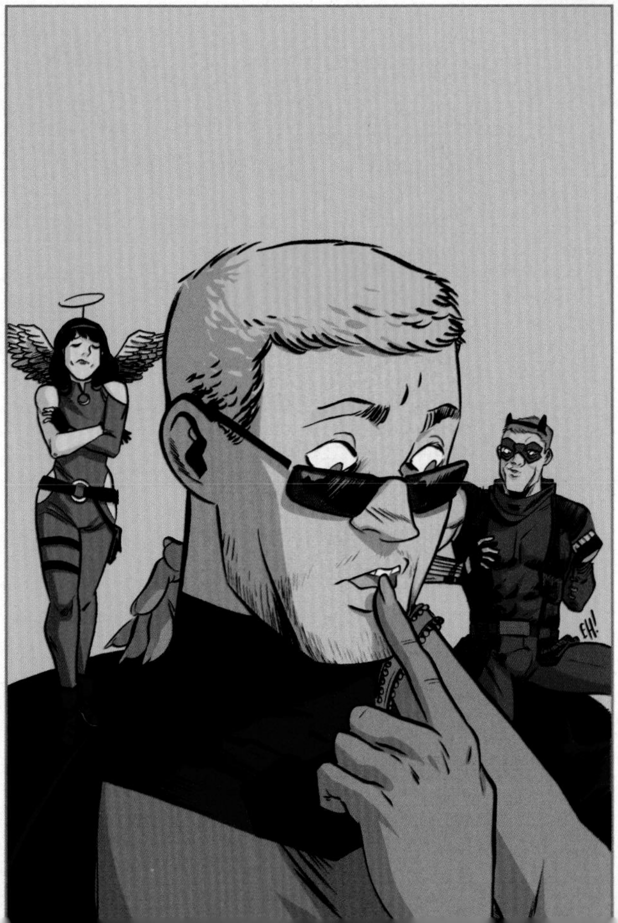
EH!

ALL-NEW HAWKEYE #3
VARIANT BY **ERICA HENDERSON**

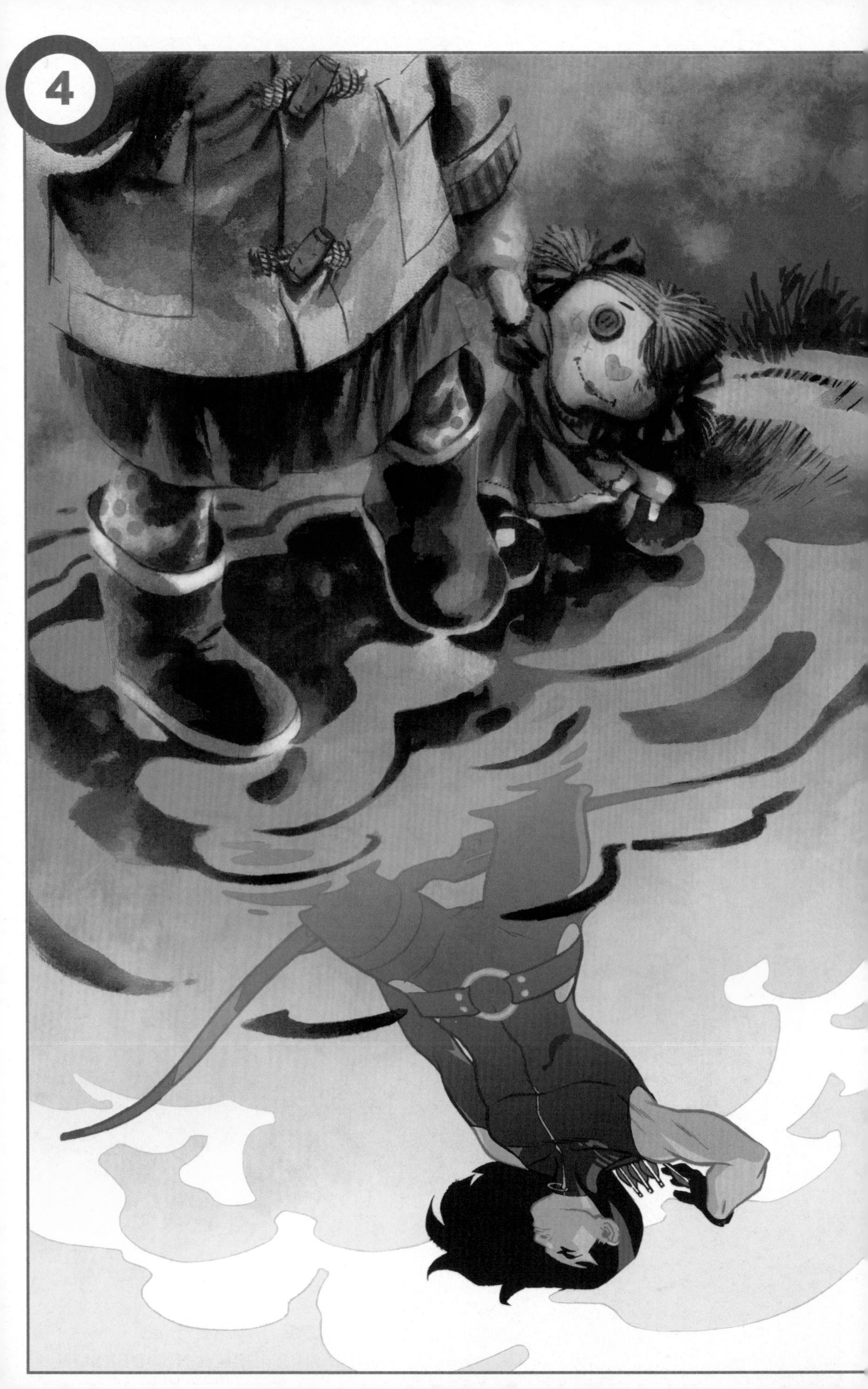
4

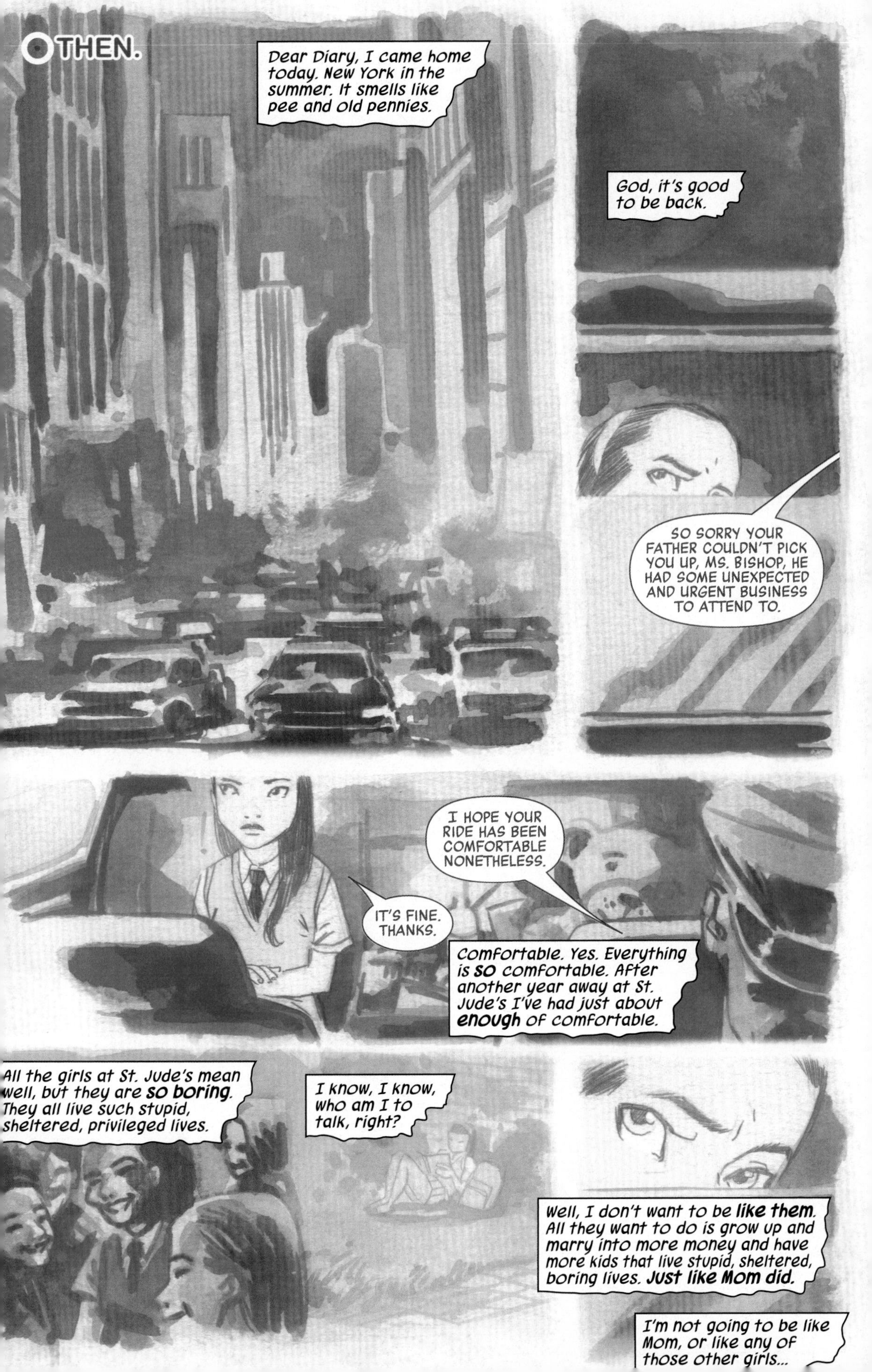
THEN.
Dear Diary, I came home today. New York in the summer. It smells like pee and old pennies.
God, it's good to be back.
SO SORRY YOUR FATHER COULDN'T PICK YOU UP, MS. BISHOP. HE HAD SOME UNEXPECTED AND URGENT BUSINESS TO ATTEND TO.
I HOPE YOUR RIDE HAS BEEN COMFORTABLE NONETHELESS.
IT'S FINE. THANKS.
Comfortable. Yes. Everything is **so** comfortable. After another year away at St. Jude's I've had just about **enough** of comfortable.
All the girls at St. Jude's mean well, but they are **so boring**. They all live such stupid, sheltered, privileged lives.
I know, I know, who am I to talk, right?
Well, I don't want to be **like them**. All they want to do is grow up and marry into more money and have more kids that live stupid, sheltered, boring lives. **Just like Mom did.**
I'm not going to be like Mom, or like any of those other girls...

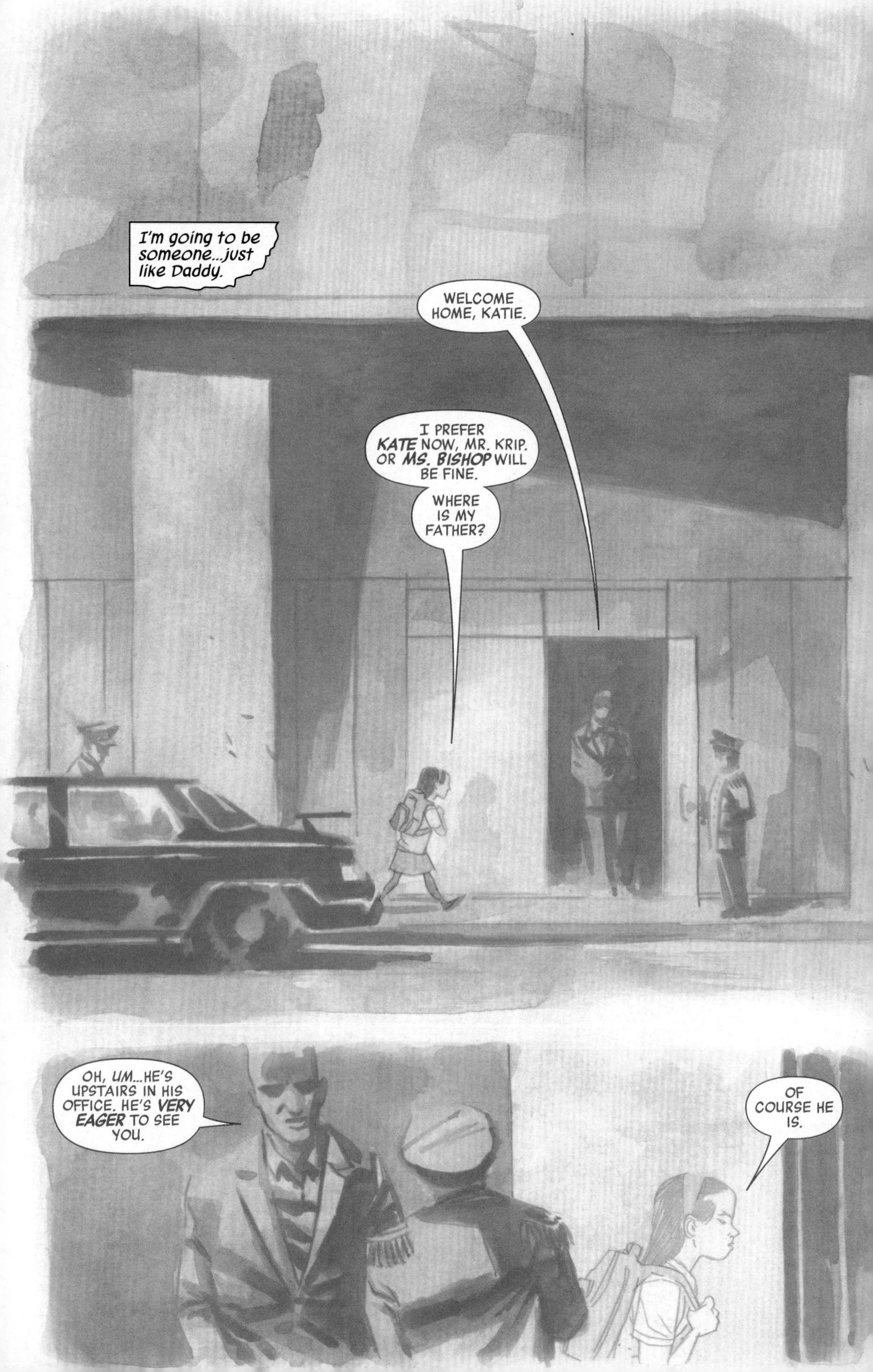
I'm going to be someone...just like Daddy.
WELCOME HOME, KATIE.
I PREFER KATE NOW, MR. KRIP. OR MS. BISHOP WILL BE FINE.
WHERE IS MY FATHER?
OH, UM...HE'S UPSTAIRS IN HIS OFFICE. HE'S VERY EAGER TO SEE YOU.
OF COURSE HE IS.

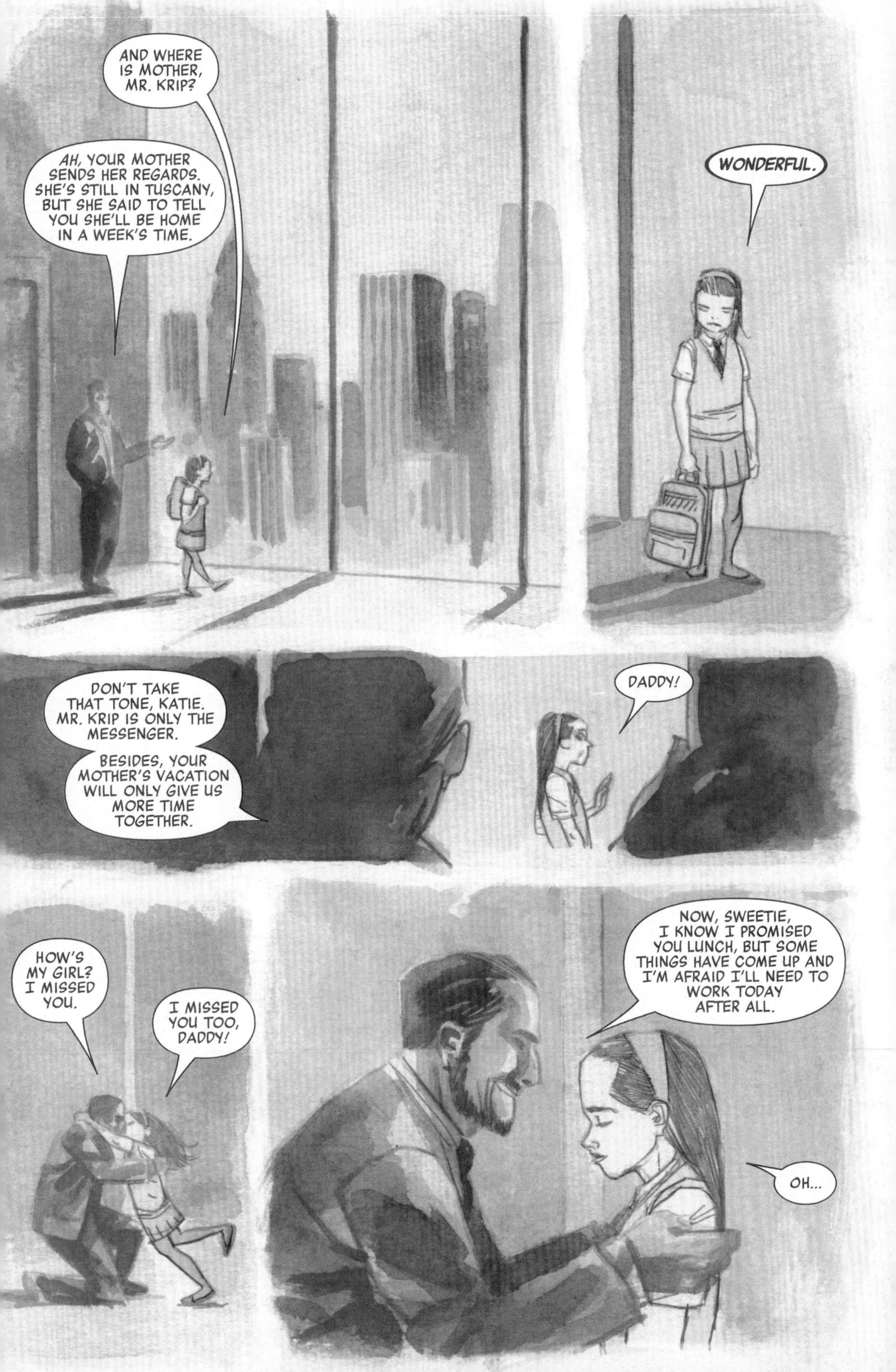
AND WHERE IS MOTHER, MR. KRIP?
AH, YOUR MOTHER SENDS HER REGARDS. SHE'S STILL IN TUSCANY, BUT SHE SAID TO TELL YOU SHE'LL BE HOME IN A WEEK'S TIME.
WONDERFUL.
DON'T TAKE THAT TONE, KATIE. MR. KRIP IS ONLY THE MESSENGER.
BESIDES, YOUR MOTHER'S VACATION WILL ONLY GIVE US MORE TIME TOGETHER.
DADDY!
HOW'S MY GIRL? I MISSED YOU.
I MISSED YOU TOO, DADDY!
NOW, SWEETIE, I KNOW I PROMISED YOU LUNCH, BUT SOME THINGS HAVE COME UP AND I'M AFRAID I'LL NEED TO WORK TODAY AFTER ALL.
OH...

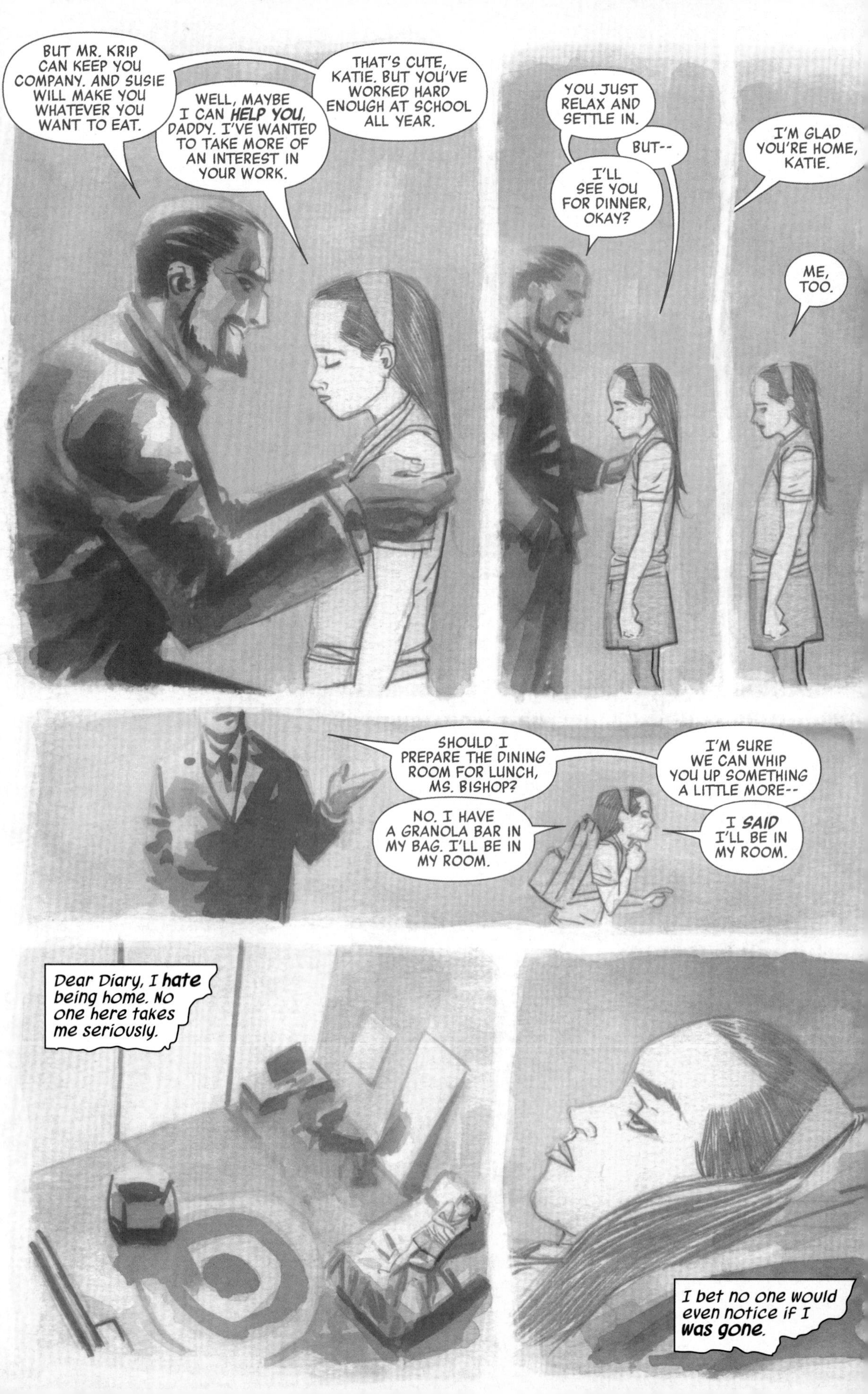

BUT MR. KRIP CAN KEEP YOU COMPANY. AND SUSIE WILL MAKE YOU WHATEVER YOU WANT TO EAT.
WELL, MAYBE I CAN **HELP YOU**, DADDY. I'VE WANTED TO TAKE MORE OF AN INTEREST IN YOUR WORK.
THAT'S CUTE, KATIE. BUT YOU'VE WORKED HARD ENOUGH AT SCHOOL ALL YEAR.
YOU JUST RELAX AND SETTLE IN.
BUT--
I'LL SEE YOU FOR DINNER, OKAY?
I'M GLAD YOU'RE HOME, KATIE.
ME, TOO.
SHOULD I PREPARE THE DINING ROOM FOR LUNCH, MS. BISHOP?
NO. I HAVE A GRANOLA BAR IN MY BAG. I'LL BE IN MY ROOM.
I'M SURE WE CAN WHIP YOU UP SOMETHING A LITTLE MORE--
I **SAID** I'LL BE IN MY ROOM.
*Dear Diary, I **hate** being home. No one here takes me seriously.*
*I bet no one would even notice if I **was gone**.*

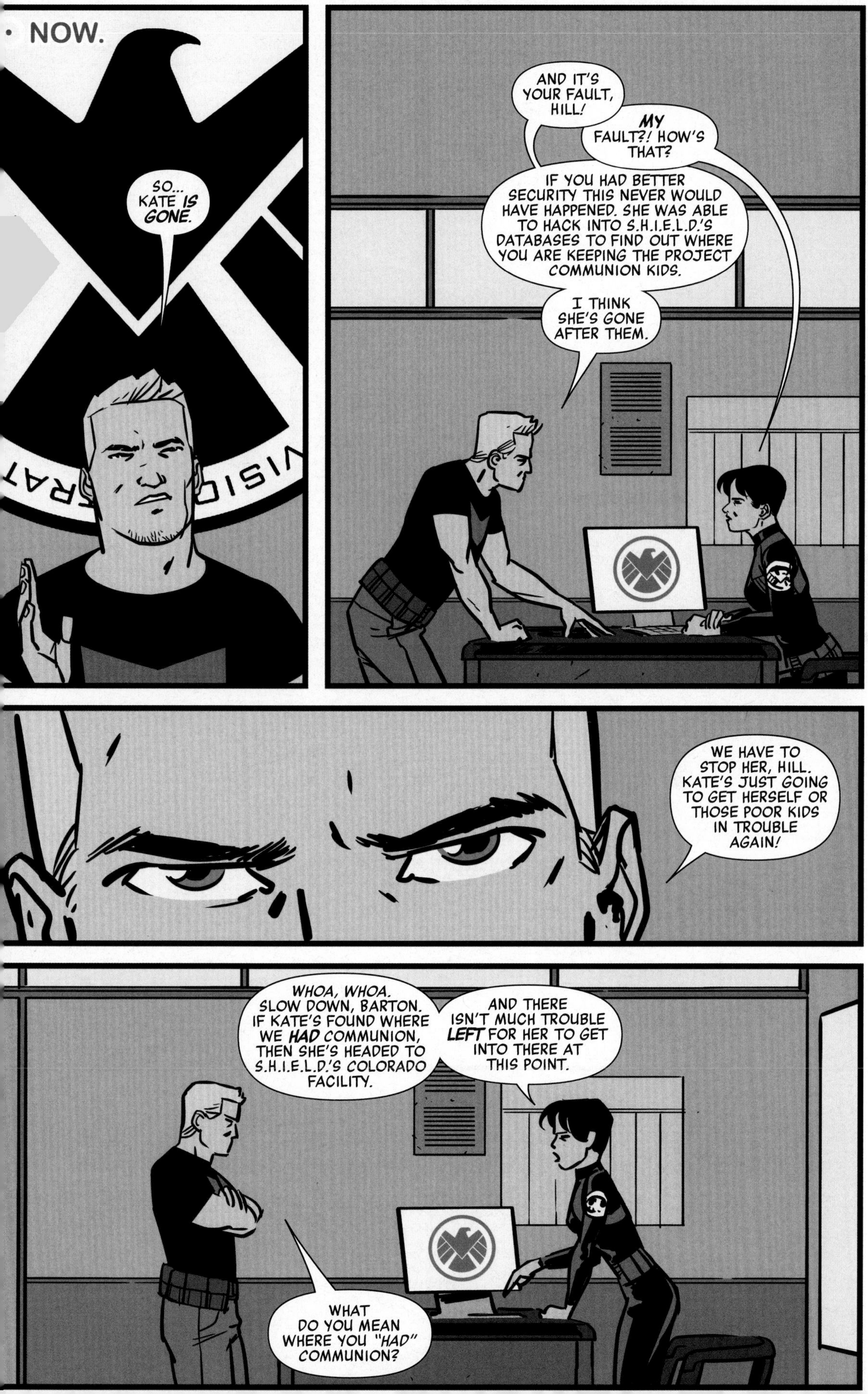
NOW.
SO... KATE IS GONE.
AND IT'S YOUR FAULT, HILL!
MY FAULT?! HOW'S THAT?
IF YOU HAD BETTER SECURITY THIS NEVER WOULD HAVE HAPPENED. SHE WAS ABLE TO HACK INTO S.H.I.E.L.D.'S DATABASES TO FIND OUT WHERE YOU ARE KEEPING THE PROJECT COMMUNION KIDS.
I THINK SHE'S GONE AFTER THEM.
WE HAVE TO STOP HER, HILL. KATE'S JUST GOING TO GET HERSELF OR THOSE POOR KIDS IN TROUBLE AGAIN!
WHOA, WHOA. SLOW DOWN, BARTON. IF KATE'S FOUND WHERE WE HAD COMMUNION, THEN SHE'S HEADED TO S.H.I.E.L.D.'S COLORADO FACILITY.
AND THERE ISN'T MUCH TROUBLE LEFT FOR HER TO GET INTO THERE AT THIS POINT.
WHAT DO YOU MEAN WHERE YOU "HAD" COMMUNION?

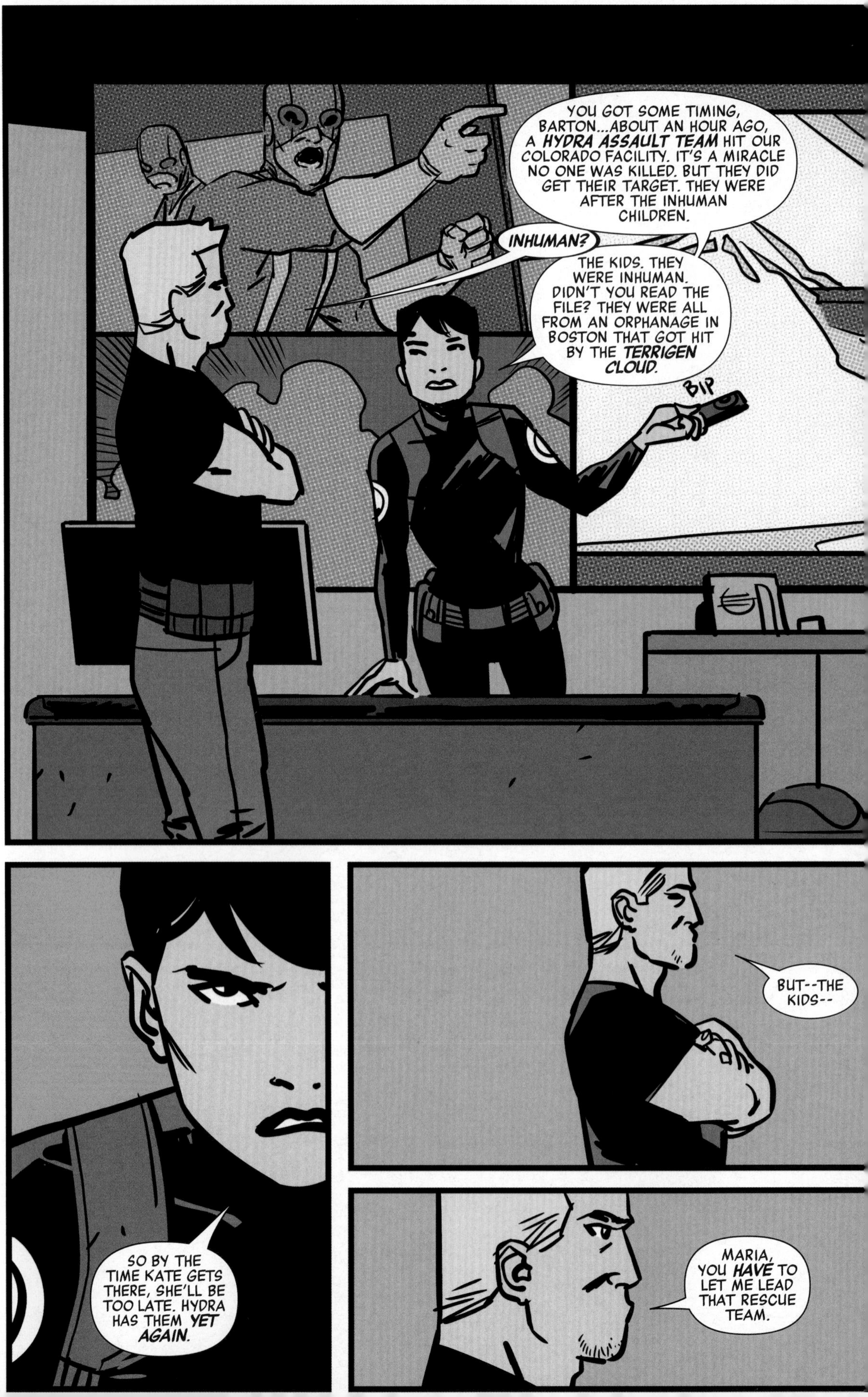

YOU GOT SOME TIMING, BARTON...ABOUT AN HOUR AGO, A **HYDRA ASSAULT TEAM** HIT OUR COLORADO FACILITY. IT'S A MIRACLE NO ONE WAS KILLED. BUT THEY DID GET THEIR TARGET. THEY WERE AFTER THE INHUMAN CHILDREN.
INHUMAN?
THE KIDS. THEY WERE INHUMAN. DIDN'T YOU READ THE FILE? THEY WERE ALL FROM AN ORPHANAGE IN BOSTON THAT GOT HIT BY THE **TERRIGEN CLOUD**.
BIP
BUT--THE KIDS--
SO BY THE TIME KATE GETS THERE, SHE'LL BE TOO LATE. HYDRA HAS THEM **YET AGAIN**.
MARIA, YOU **HAVE** TO LET ME LEAD THAT RESCUE TEAM.

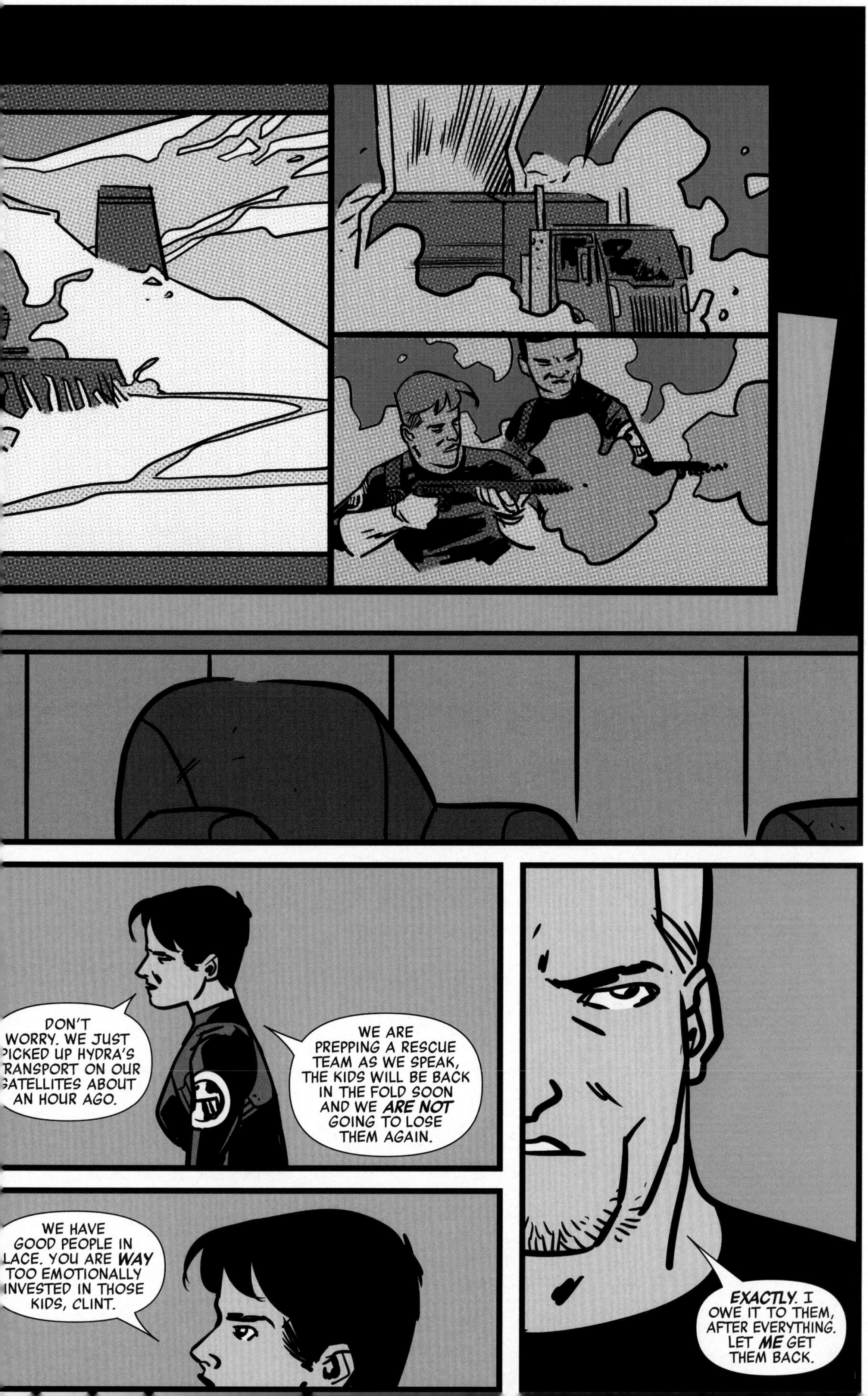
DON'T WORRY. WE JUST ICKED UP HYDRA'S RANSPORT ON OUR ATELLITES ABOUT AN HOUR AGO.
WE ARE PREPPING A RESCUE TEAM AS WE SPEAK, THE KIDS WILL BE BACK IN THE FOLD SOON AND WE ***ARE NOT*** GOING TO LOSE THEM AGAIN.
WE HAVE GOOD PEOPLE IN LACE. YOU ARE ***WAY*** TOO EMOTIONALLY INVESTED IN THOSE KIDS, CLINT.
EXACTLY. I OWE IT TO THEM, AFTER EVERYTHING. LET ***ME*** GET THEM BACK.

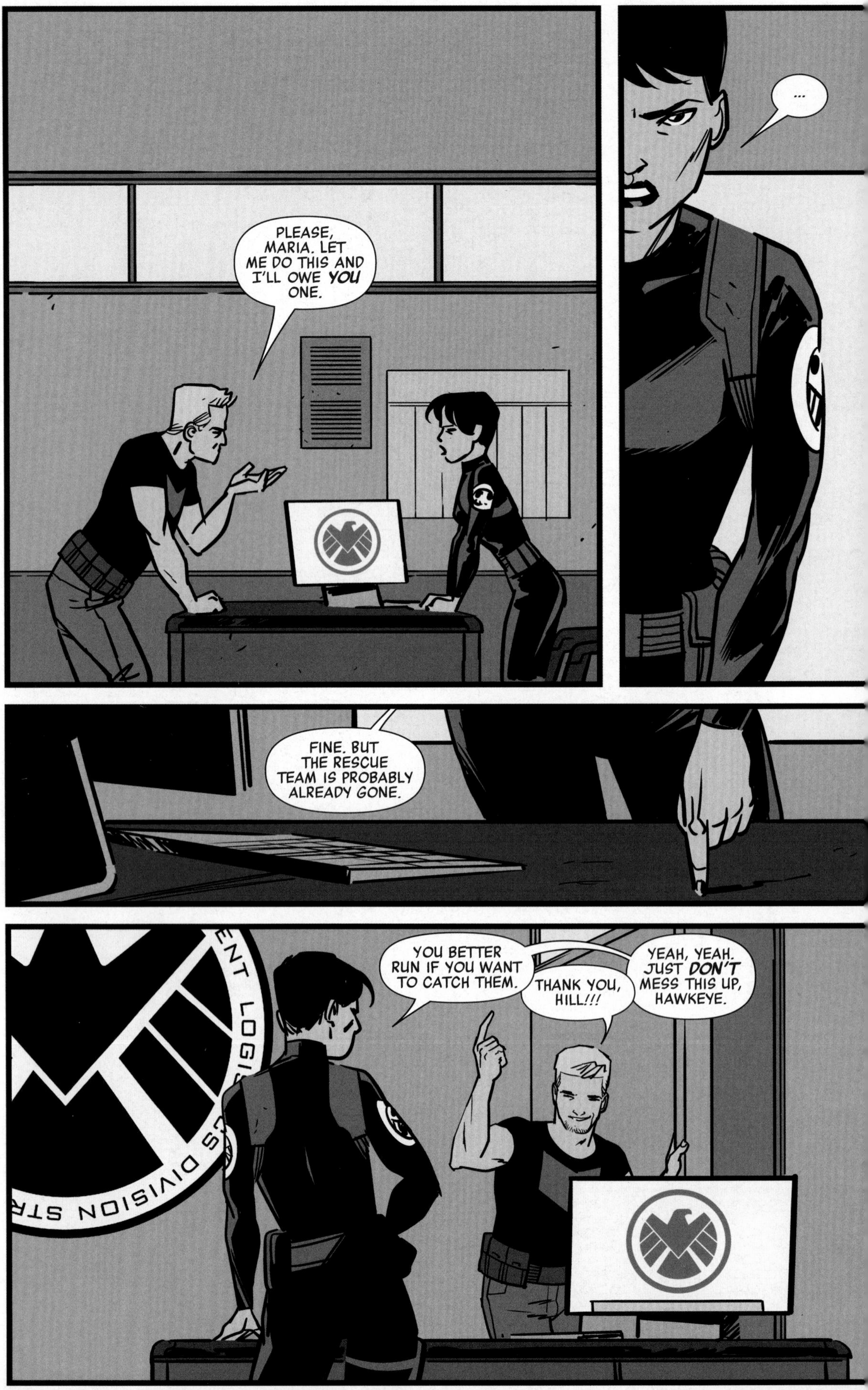
PLEASE, MARIA. LET ME DO THIS AND I'LL OWE YOU ONE.
...
FINE. BUT THE RESCUE TEAM IS PROBABLY ALREADY GONE.
YOU BETTER RUN IF YOU WANT TO CATCH THEM.
THANK YOU, HILL!!!
YEAH, YEAH. JUST DON'T MESS THIS UP, HAWKEYE.

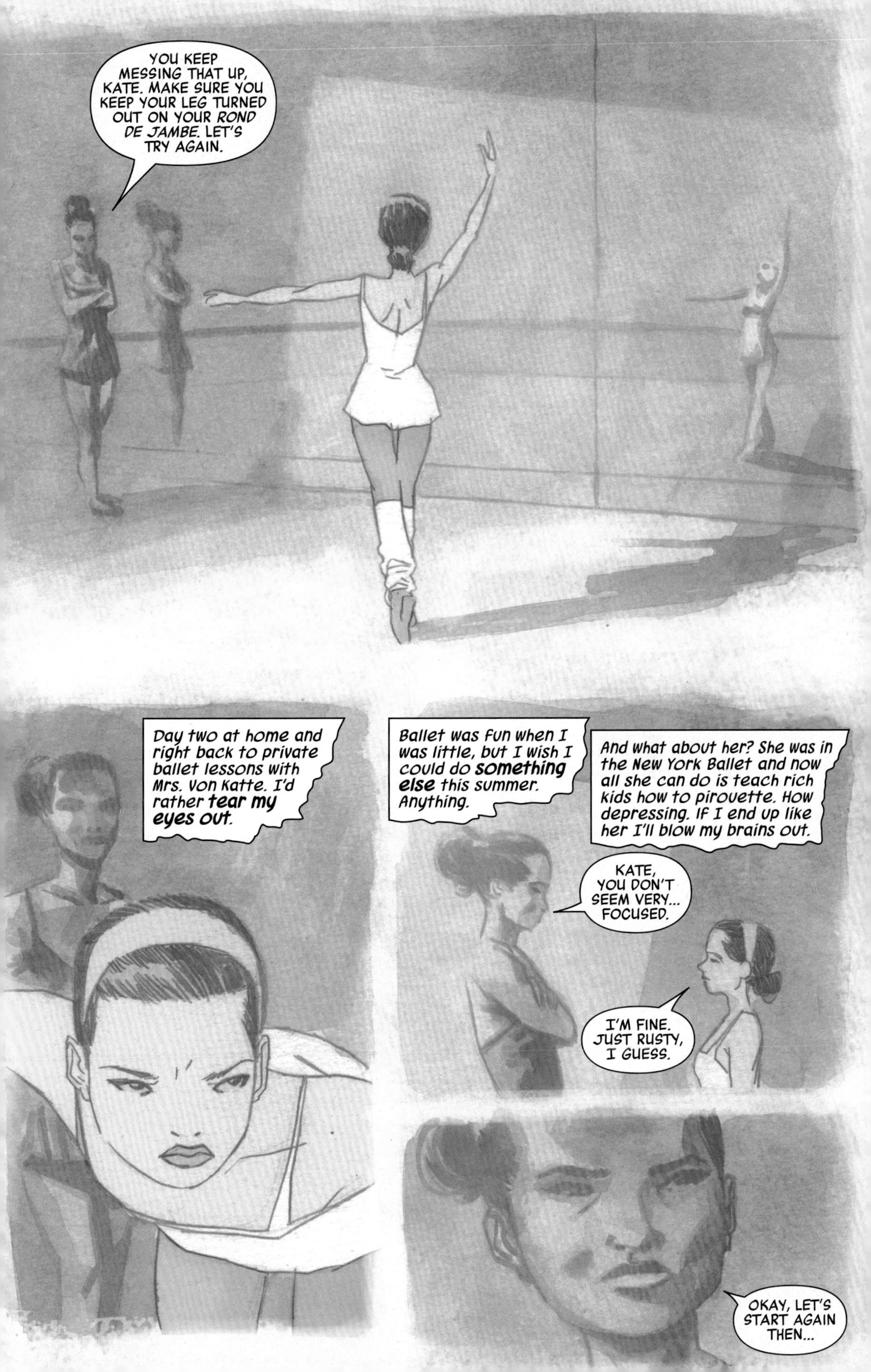

YOU KEEP MESSING THAT UP, KATE. MAKE SURE YOU KEEP YOUR LEG TURNED OUT ON YOUR *RONDE DE JAMBE*. LET'S TRY AGAIN.
Day two at home and right back to private ballet lessons with Mrs. Von Katte. I'd rather **tear my eyes out**.
Ballet was fun when I was little, but I wish I could do **something else** this summer. Anything.
And what about her? She was in the New York Ballet and now all she can do is teach rich kids how to pirouette. How depressing. If I end up like her I'll blow my brains out.
KATE, YOU DON'T SEEM VERY... FOCUSED.
I'M FINE. JUST RUSTY, I GUESS.
OKAY, LET'S START AGAIN THEN...

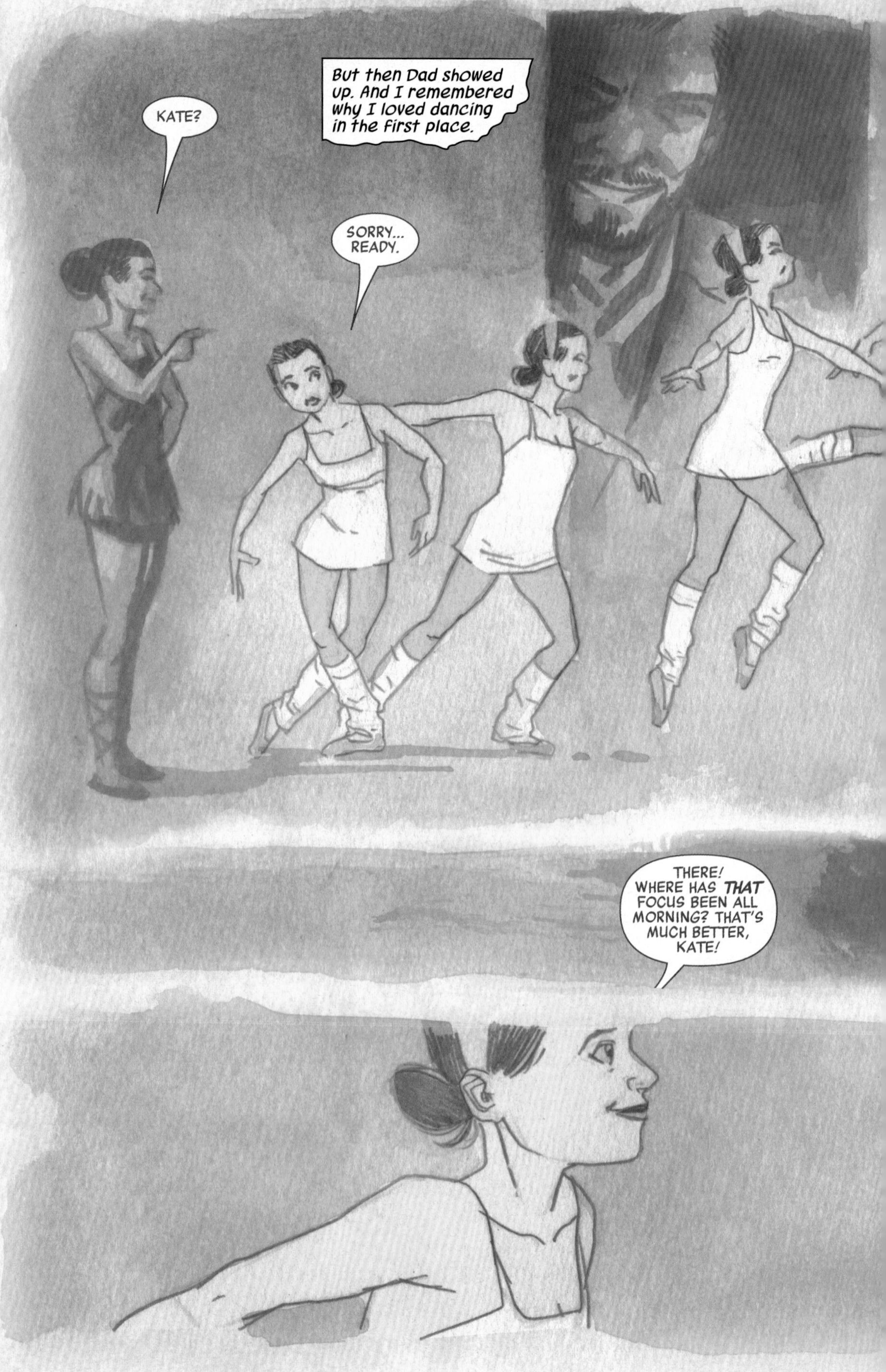
KATE?
But then Dad showed up. And I remembered why I loved dancing in the first place.
SORRY... READY.
THERE! WHERE HAS *THAT* FOCUS BEEN ALL MORNING? THAT'S MUCH BETTER, KATE!

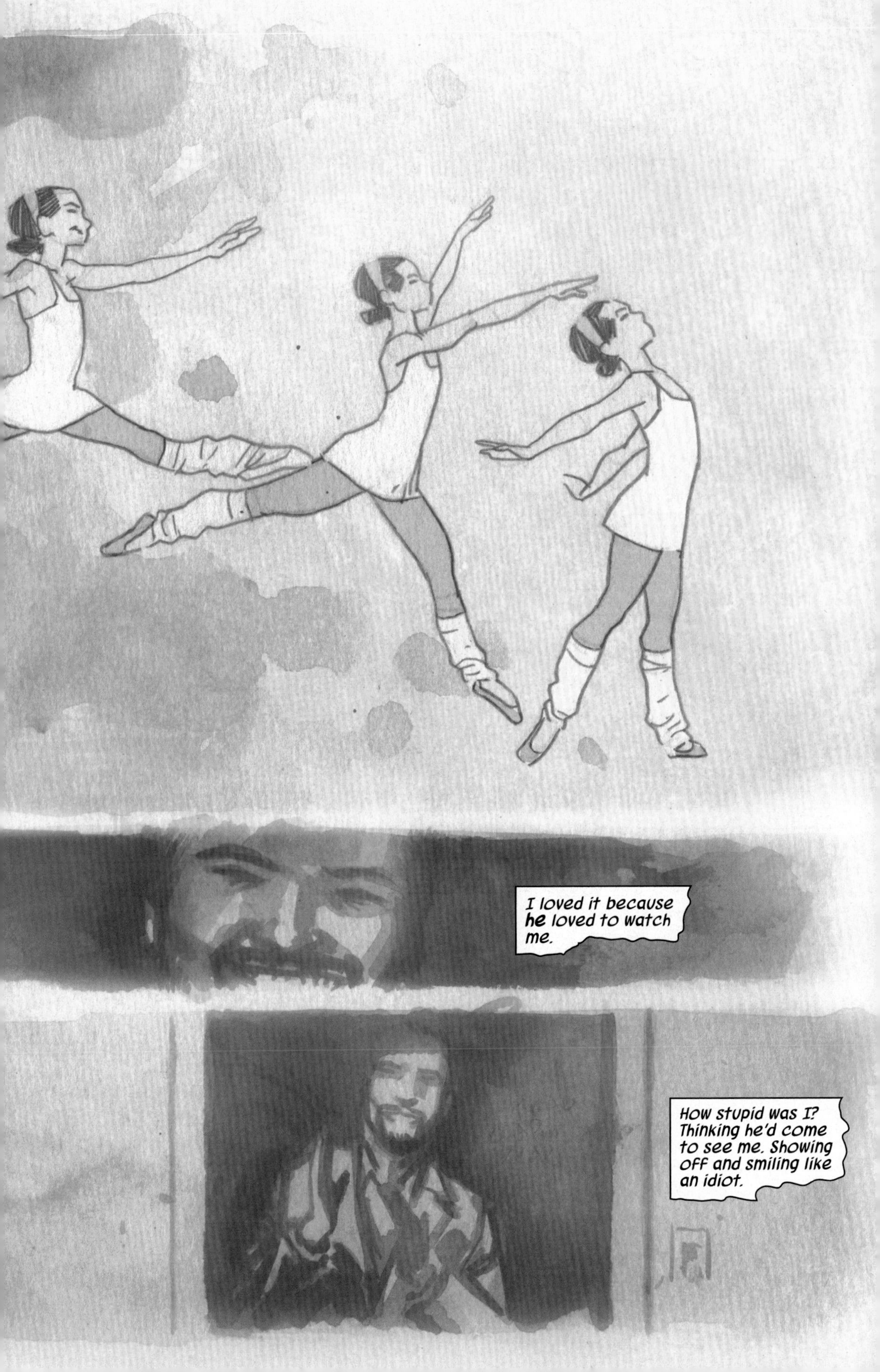
I loved it because **he** loved to watch me.
How stupid was I? Thinking he'd come to see me. Showing off and smiling like an idiot.

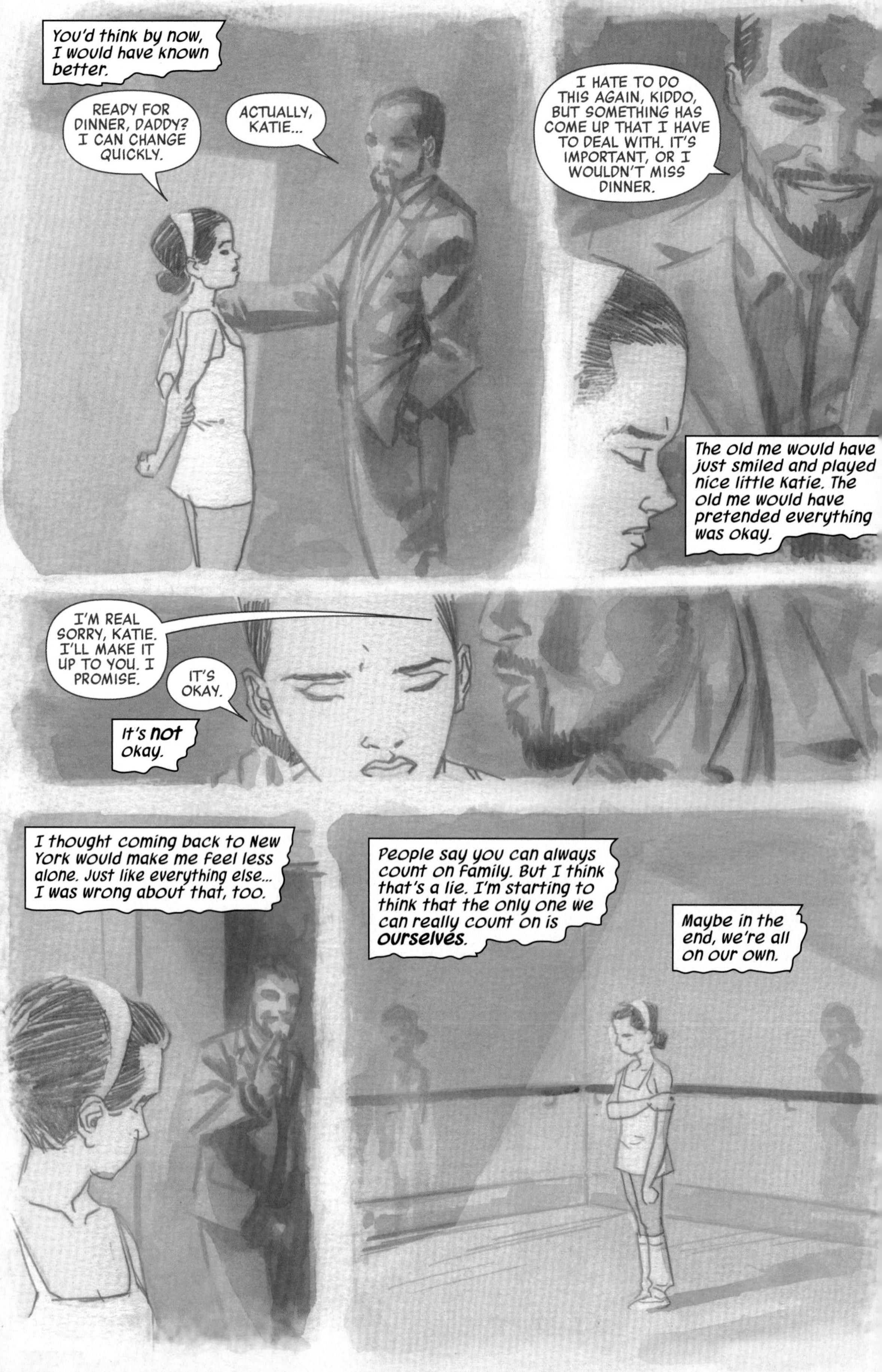
You'd think by now, I would have known better.
READY FOR DINNER, DADDY? I CAN CHANGE QUICKLY.
ACTUALLY, KATIE...
I HATE TO DO THIS AGAIN, KIDDO, BUT SOMETHING HAS COME UP THAT I HAVE TO DEAL WITH. IT'S IMPORTANT, OR I WOULDN'T MISS DINNER.
The old me would have just smiled and played nice little Katie. The old me would have pretended everything was okay.
I'M REAL SORRY, KATIE. I'LL MAKE IT UP TO YOU. I PROMISE.
IT'S OKAY.
It's **not** okay.
I thought coming back to New York would make me feel less alone. Just like everything else... I was wrong about that, too.
People say you can always count on family. But I think that's a lie. I'm starting to think that the only one we can really count on is **ourselves**.
Maybe in the end, we're all on our own.

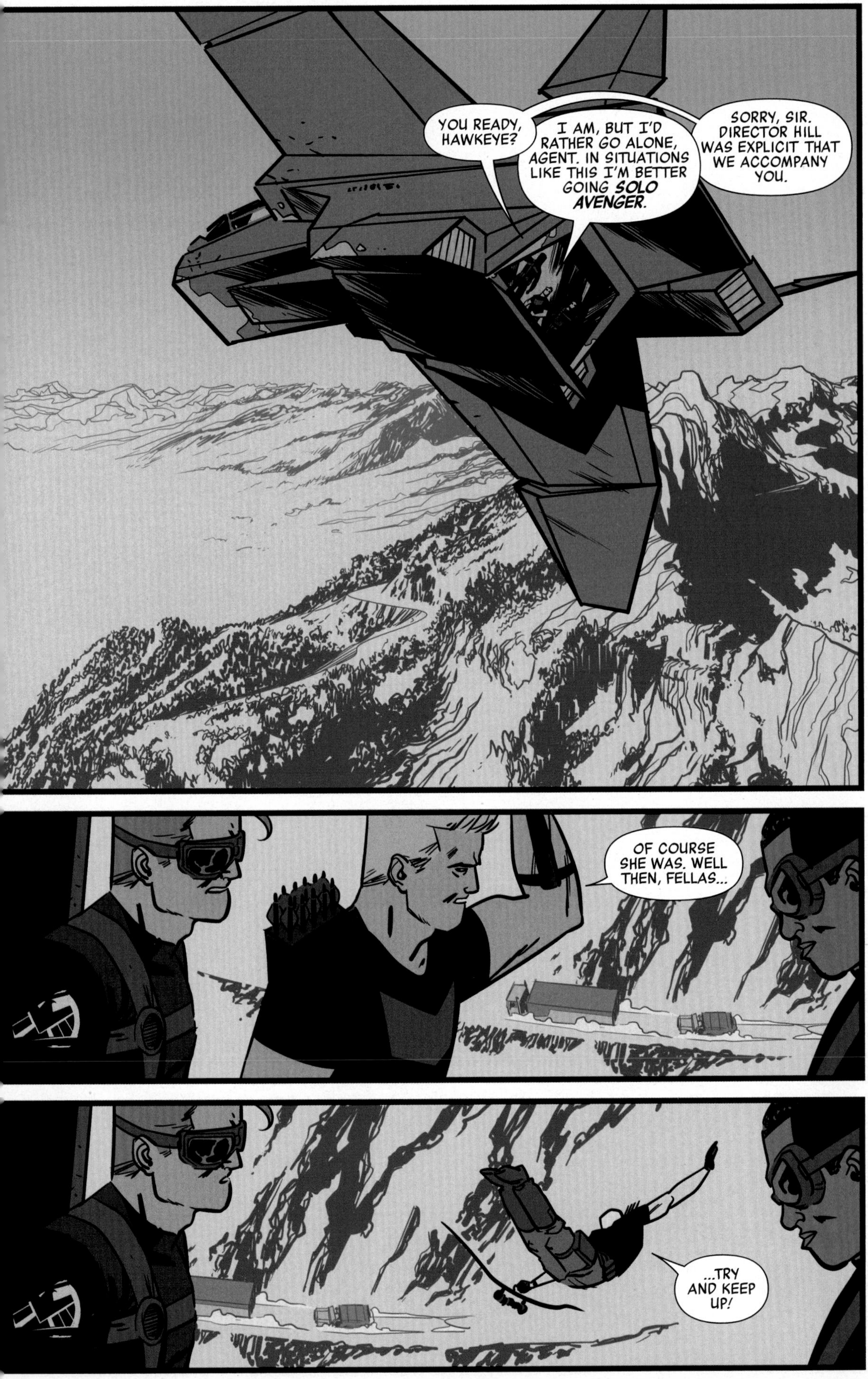
YOU READY, HAWKEYE?
I AM, BUT I'D RATHER GO ALONE, AGENT. IN SITUATIONS LIKE THIS I'M BETTER GOING SOLO AVENGER.
SORRY, SIR. DIRECTOR HILL WAS EXPLICIT THAT WE ACCOMPANY YOU.
OF COURSE SHE WAS. WELL THEN, FELLAS...
...TRY AND KEEP UP!

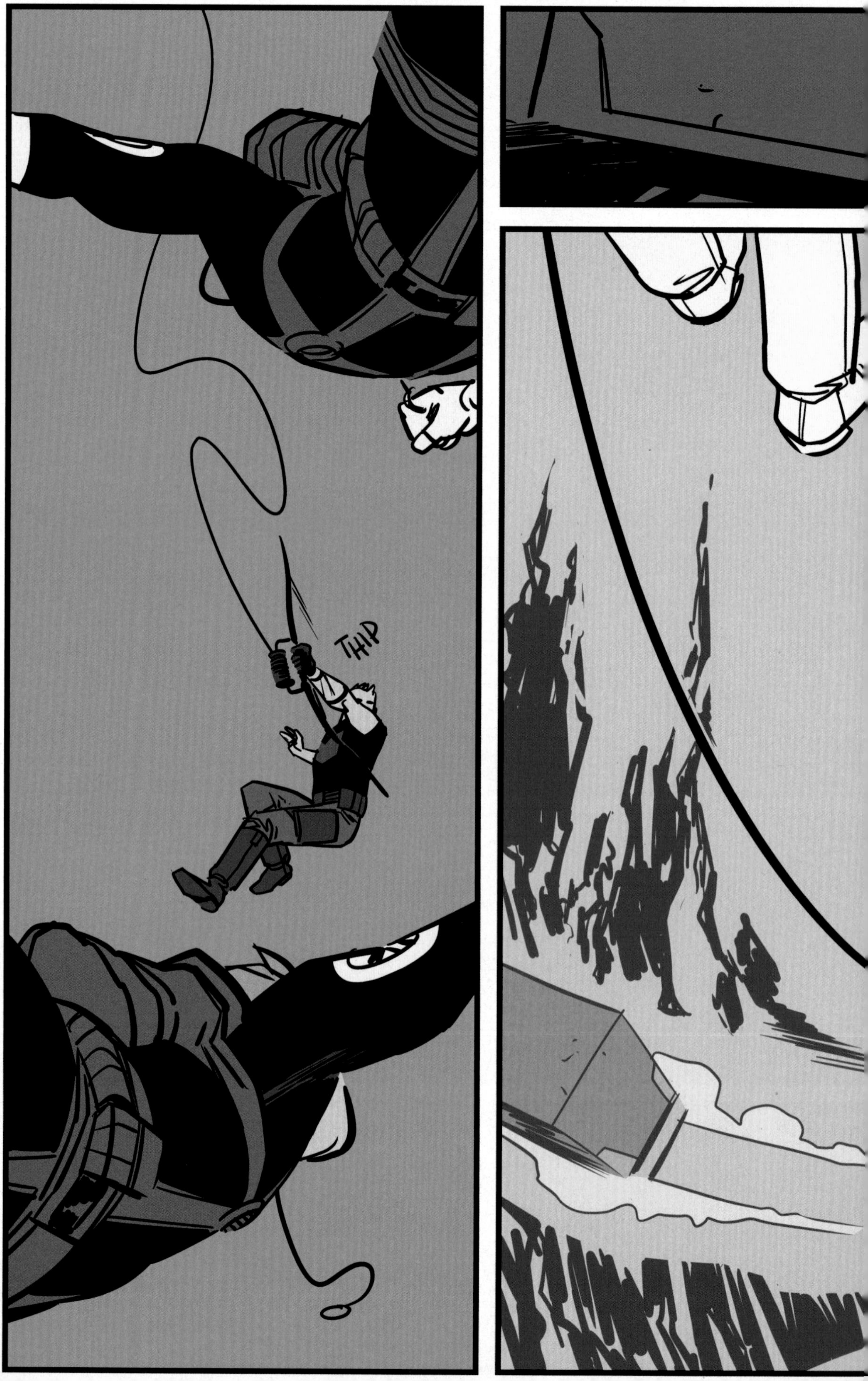
THIP

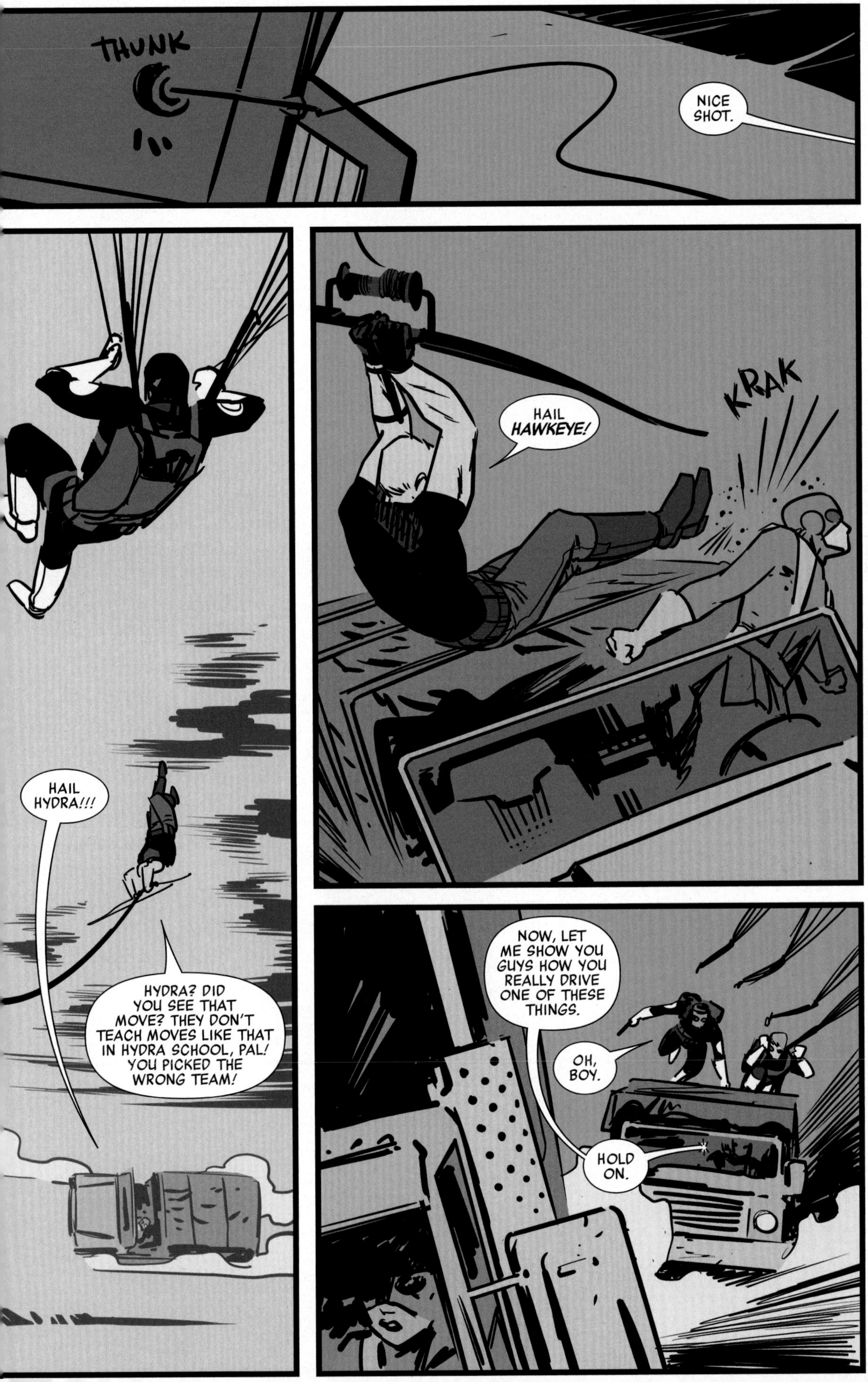
THUNK
NICE SHOT.
HAIL HYDRA!!!
HYDRA? DID YOU SEE THAT MOVE? THEY DON'T TEACH MOVES LIKE THAT IN HYDRA SCHOOL, PAL! YOU PICKED THE WRONG TEAM!
HAIL *HAWKEYE!*
KRAK
NOW, LET ME SHOW YOU GUYS HOW YOU REALLY DRIVE ONE OF THESE THINGS.
OH, BOY.
HOLD ON.

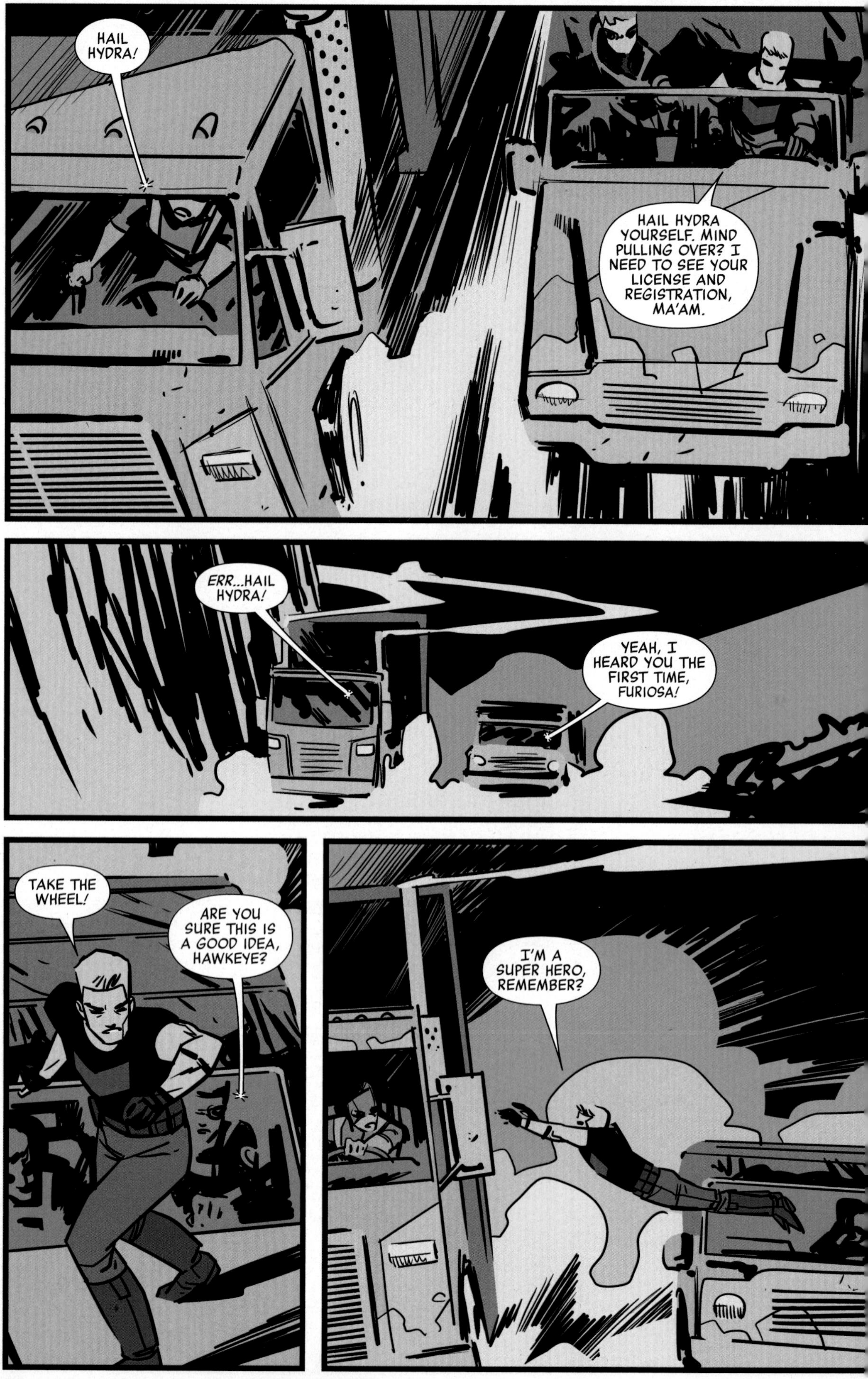
HAIL HYDRA!
HAIL HYDRA YOURSELF. MIND PULLING OVER? I NEED TO SEE YOUR LICENSE AND REGISTRATION, MA'AM.
ERR...HAIL HYDRA!
YEAH, I HEARD YOU THE FIRST TIME, FURIOSA!
TAKE THE WHEEL!
ARE YOU SURE THIS IS A GOOD IDEA, HAWKEYE?
I'M A SUPER HERO, REMEMBER?

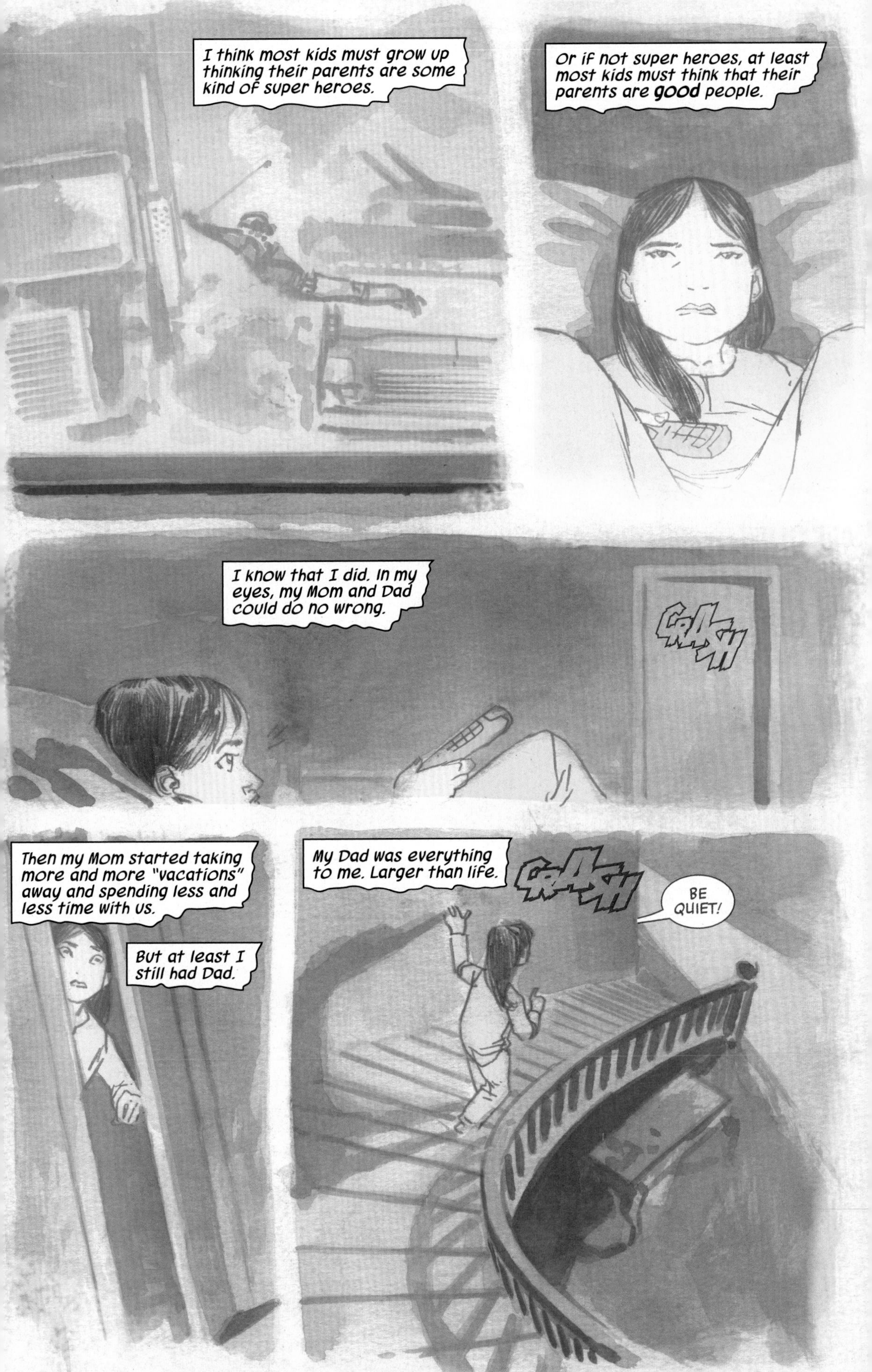
I think most kids must grow up thinking their parents are some kind of super heroes.
Or if not super heroes, at least most kids must think that their parents are **good** people.
I know that I did. In my eyes, my Mom and Dad could do no wrong.
CRASH
Then my Mom started taking more and more "vacations" away and spending less and less time with us.
But at least I still had Dad.
My Dad was everything to me. Larger than life.
CRASH
BE QUIET!

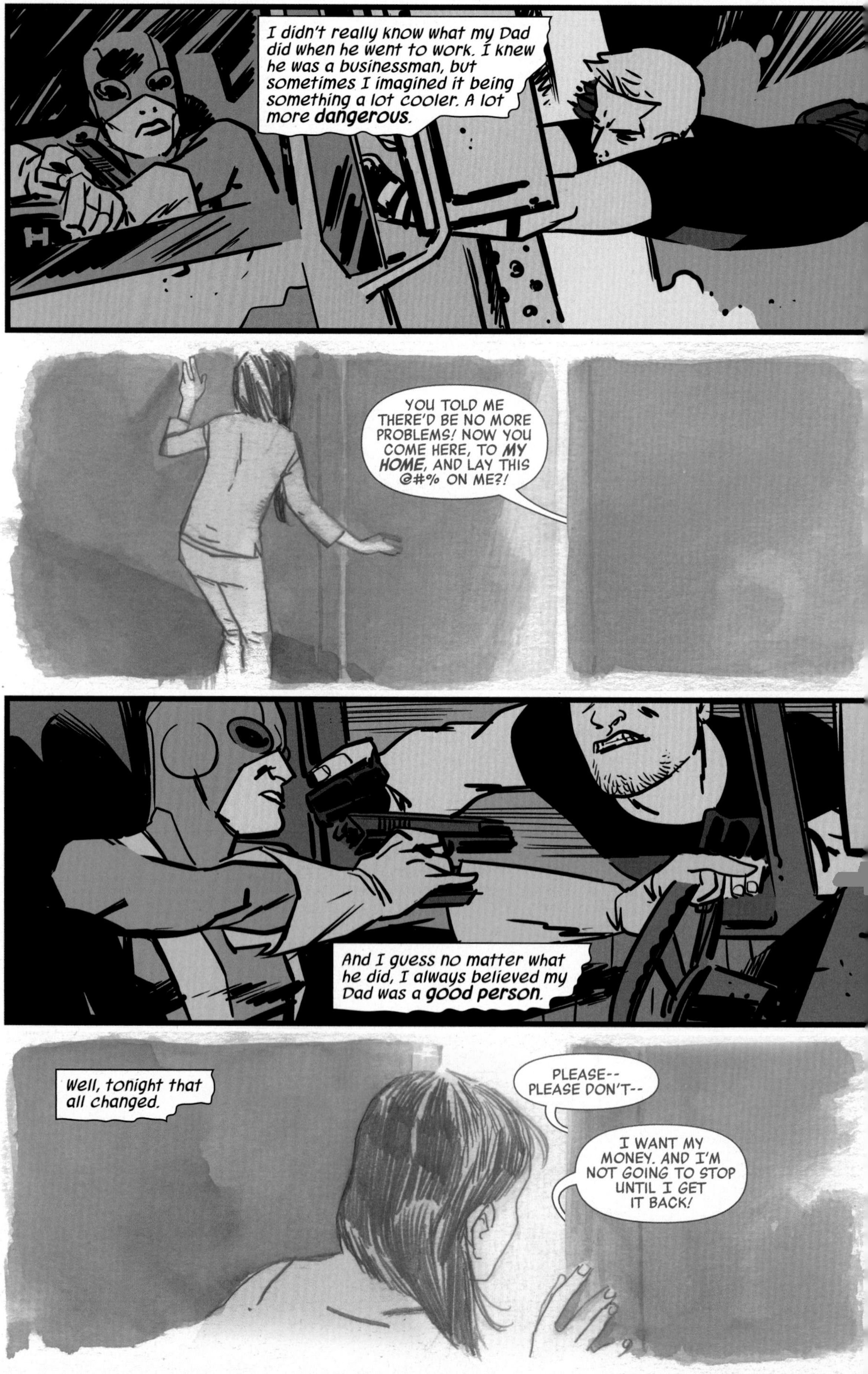
I didn't really know what my Dad did when he went to work. I knew he was a businessman, but sometimes I imagined it being something a lot cooler. A lot more **dangerous**.
YOU TOLD ME THERE'D BE NO MORE PROBLEMS! NOW YOU COME HERE, TO ***MY HOME***, AND LAY THIS @#% ON ME?!
And I guess no matter what he did, I always believed my Dad was a **good person**.
Well, tonight that all changed.
PLEASE-- PLEASE DON'T--
I WANT MY MONEY. AND I'M NOT GOING TO STOP UNTIL I GET IT BACK!

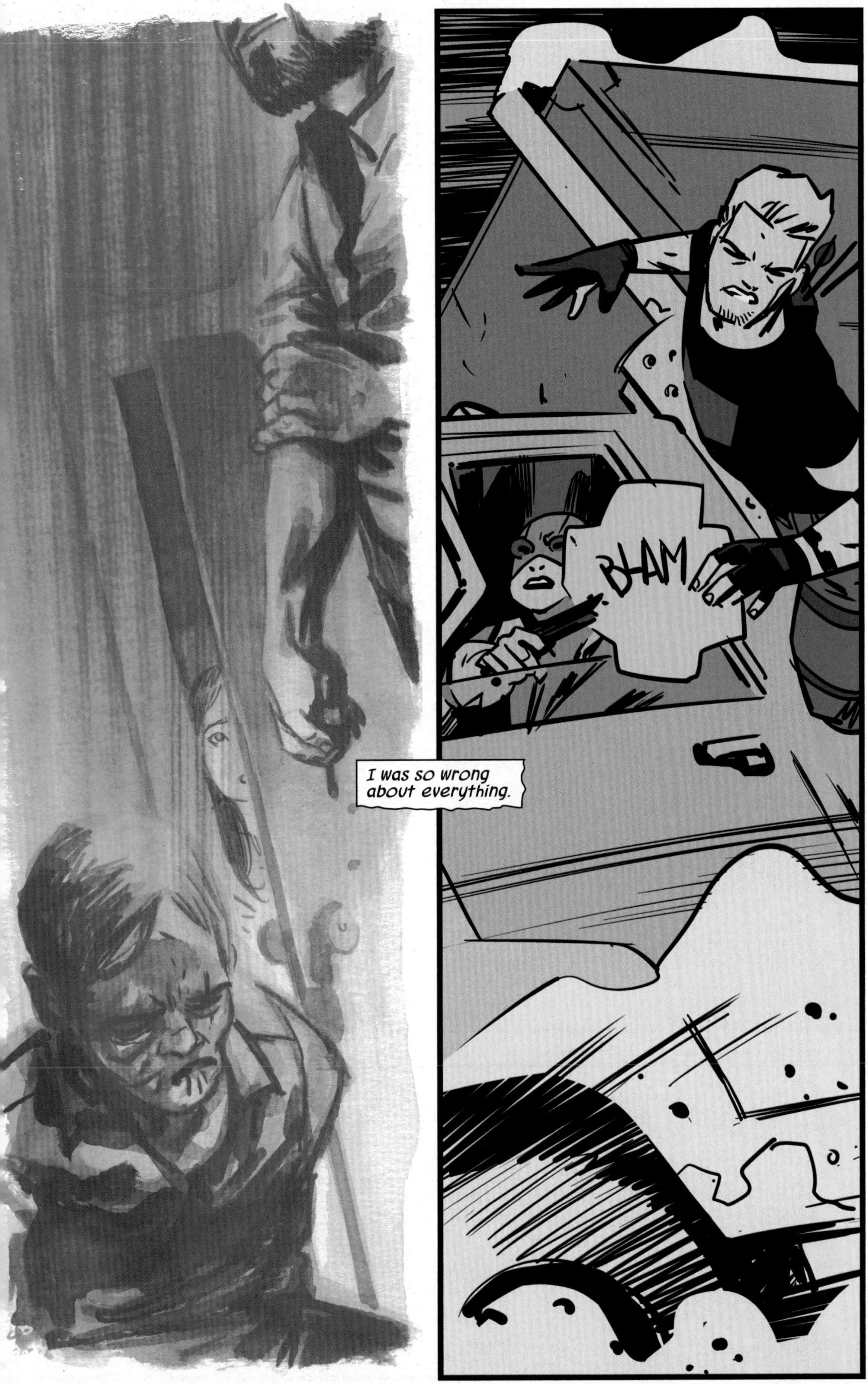

BLAM
I was so wrong about everything.

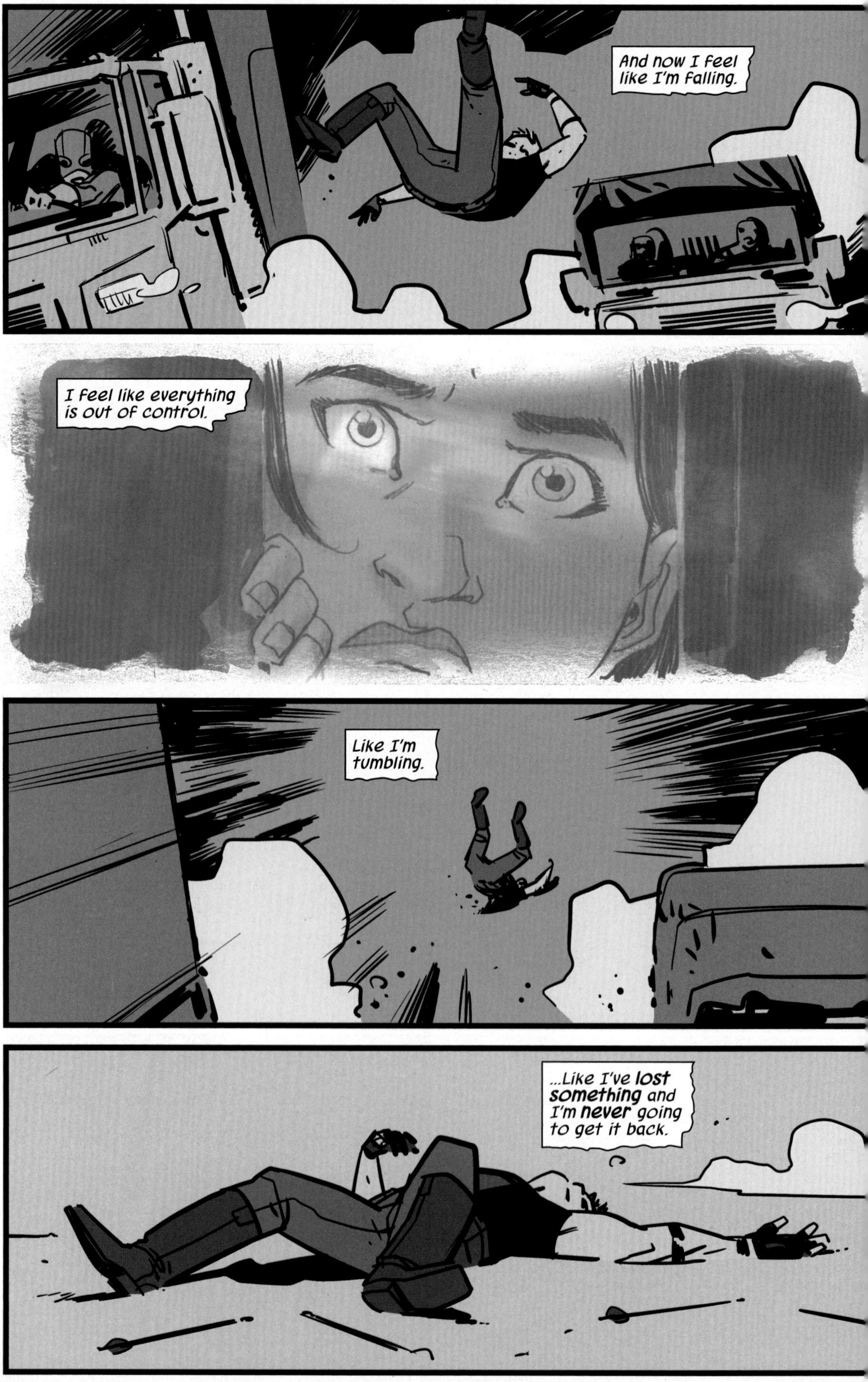
And now I feel like I'm falling.
I feel like everything is out of control.
Like I'm tumbling.
...Like I've **lost something** and I'm **never** going to get it back.

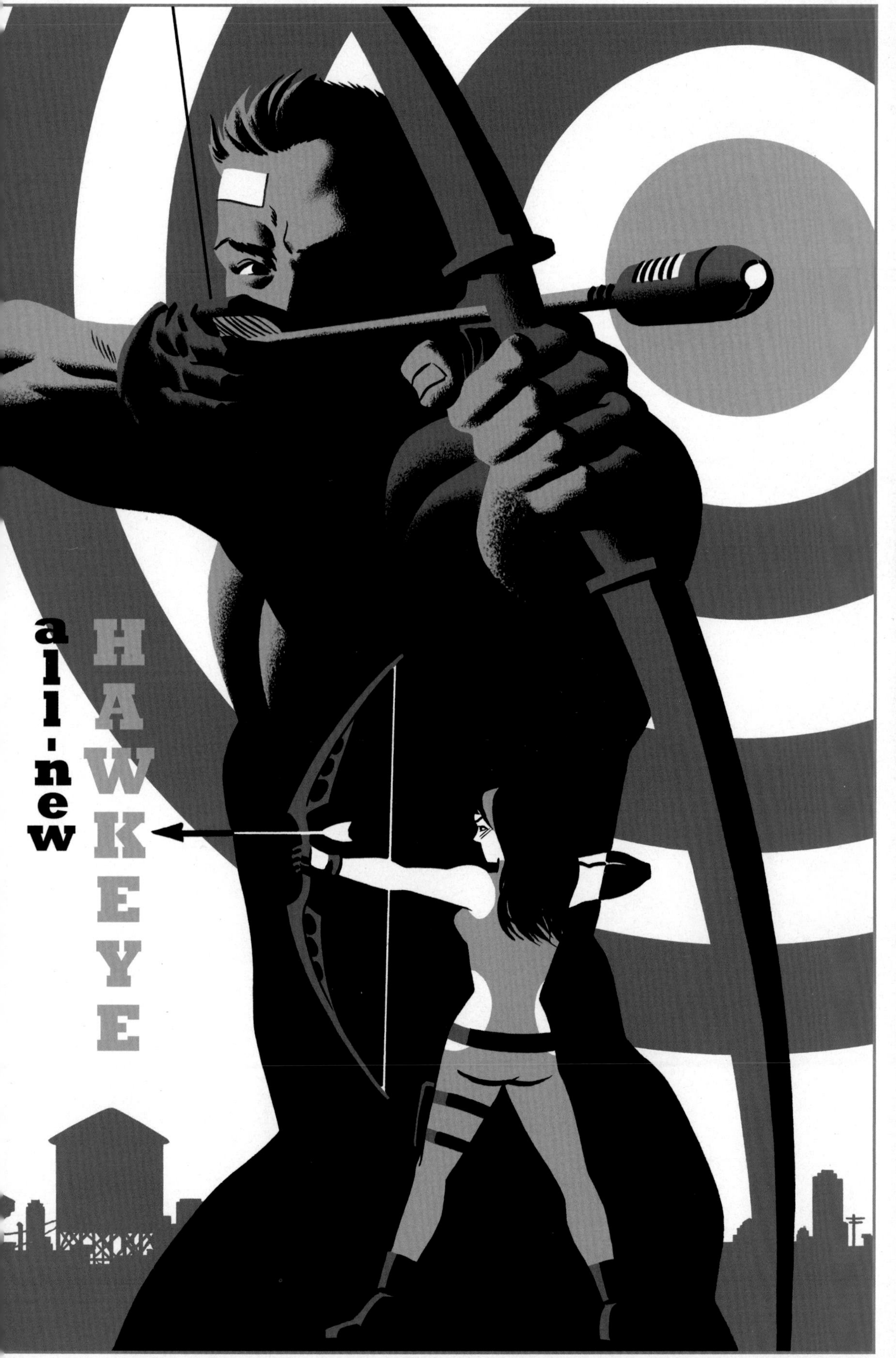
all-new
HAWKEYE

ALL-NEW HAWKEYE #4 VARIANT BY **MICHAEL CHO**

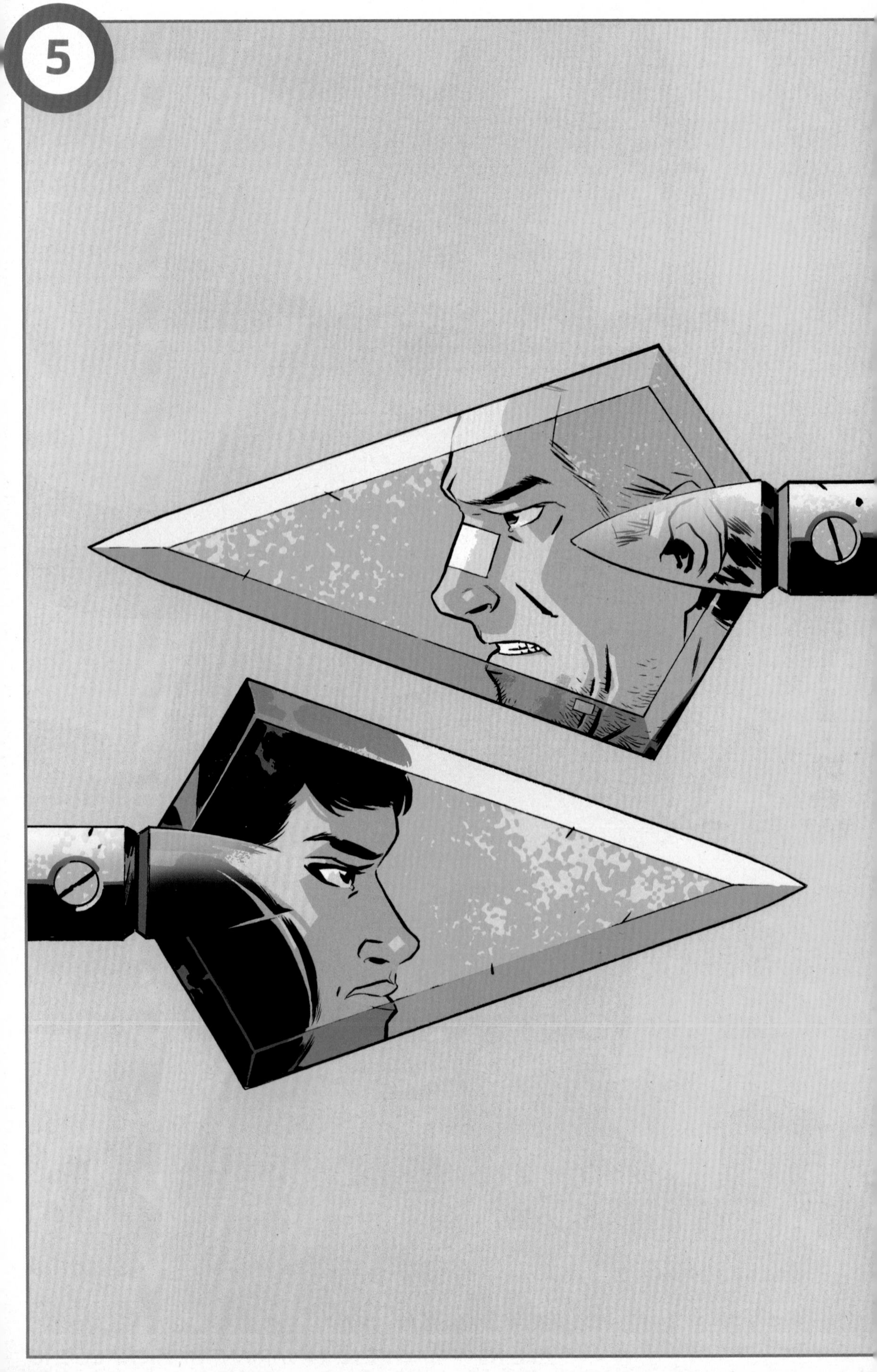
5

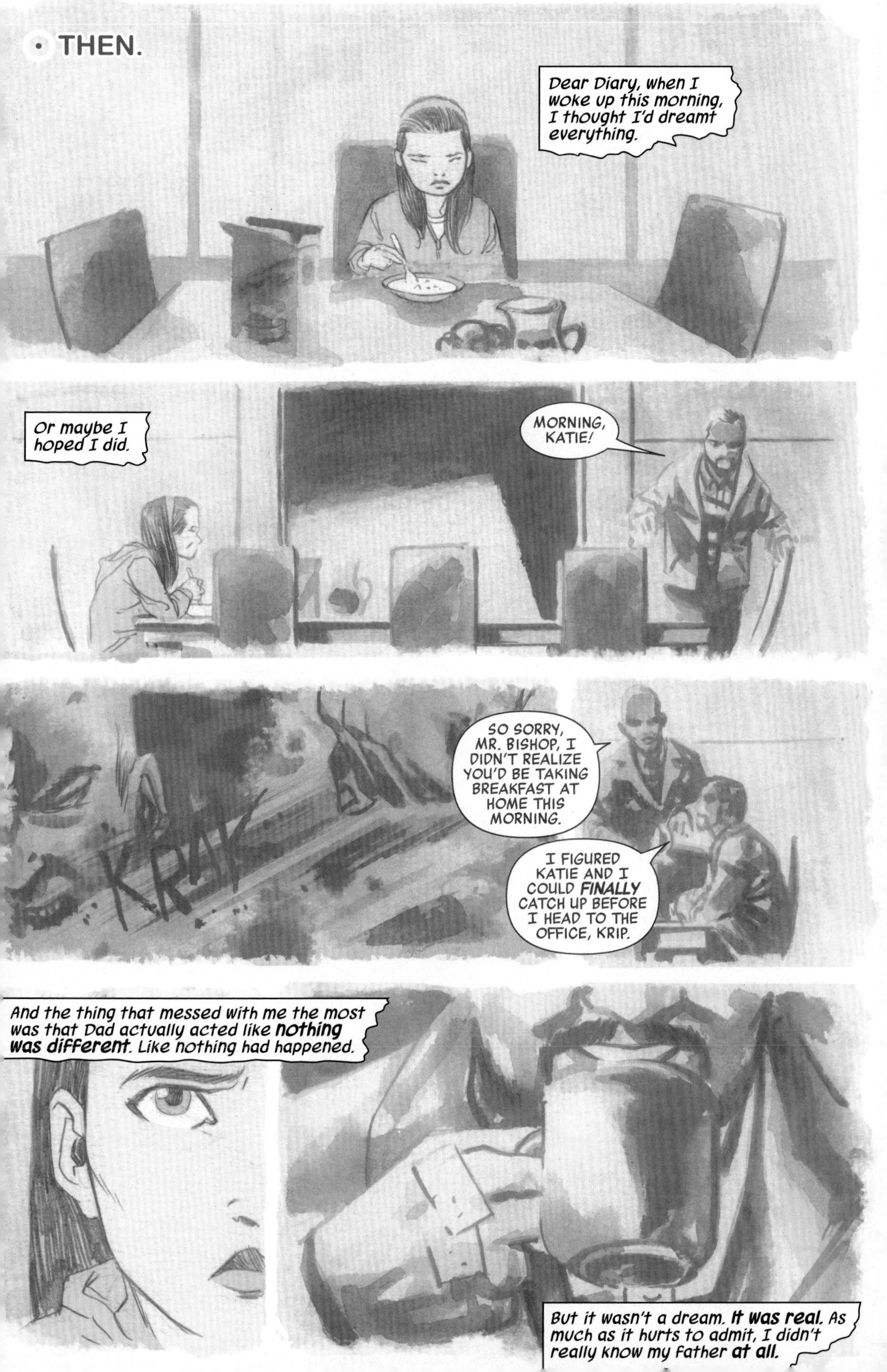
THEN.
Dear Diary, when I woke up this morning, I thought I'd dreamt everything.
Or maybe I hoped I did.
MORNING, KATIE!
KRAK
SO SORRY, MR. BISHOP, I DIDN'T REALIZE YOU'D BE TAKING BREAKFAST AT HOME THIS MORNING.
I FIGURED KATIE AND I COULD FINALLY CATCH UP BEFORE I HEAD TO THE OFFICE, KRIP.
And the thing that messed with me the most was that Dad actually acted like nothing was different. Like nothing had happened.
But it wasn't a dream. It was real. As much as it hurts to admit, I didn't really know my father at all.

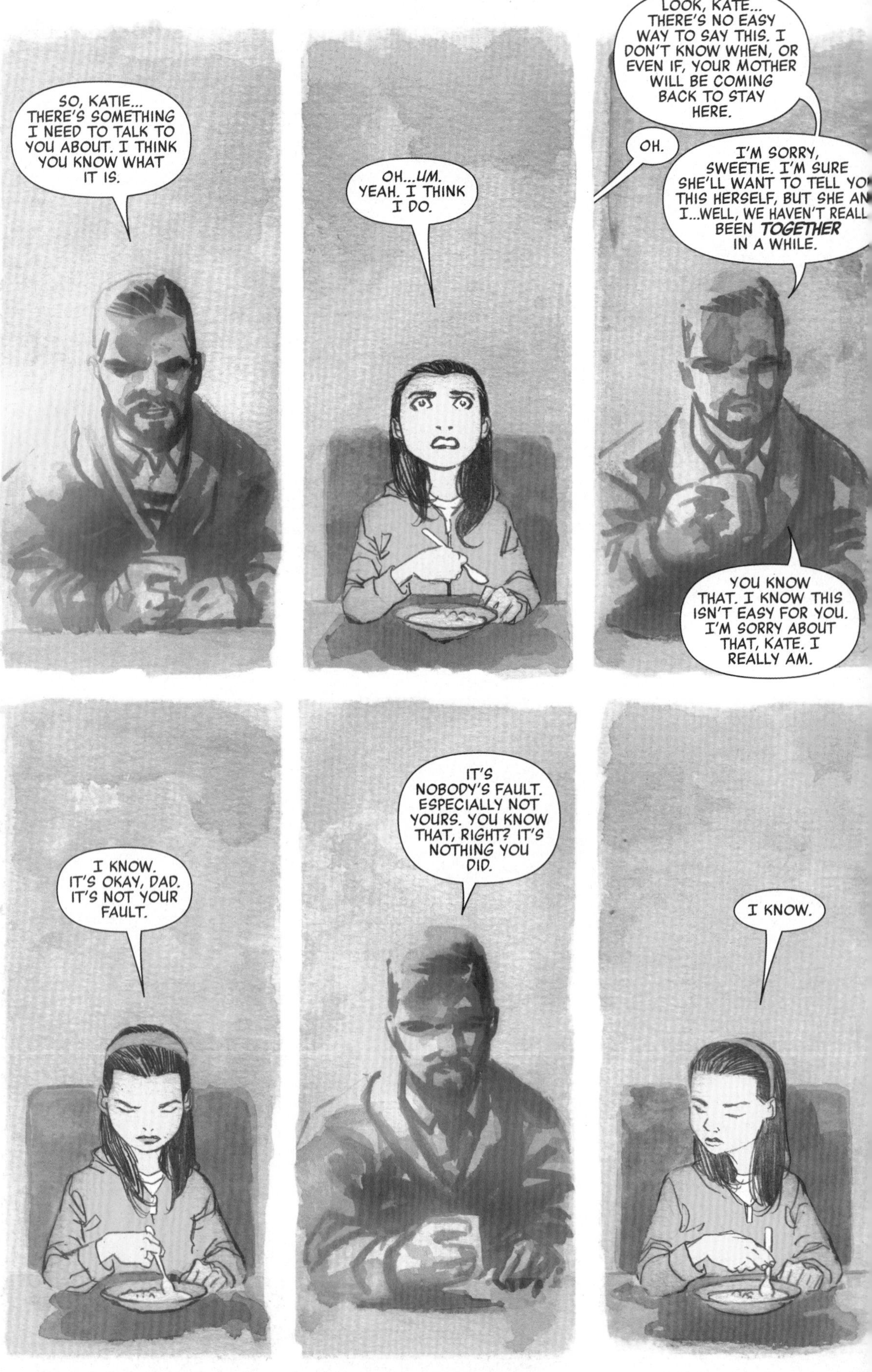
SO, KATIE... THERE'S SOMETHING I NEED TO TALK TO YOU ABOUT. I THINK YOU KNOW WHAT IT IS.
OH...UM. YEAH. I THINK I DO.
LOOK, KATE... THERE'S NO EASY WAY TO SAY THIS. I DON'T KNOW WHEN, OR EVEN IF, YOUR MOTHER WILL BE COMING BACK TO STAY HERE.
OH.
I'M SORRY, SWEETIE. I'M SURE SHE'LL WANT TO TELL YO THIS HERSELF, BUT SHE AN I...WELL, WE HAVEN'T REALL BEEN TOGETHER IN A WHILE.
YOU KNOW THAT. I KNOW THIS ISN'T EASY FOR YOU. I'M SORRY ABOUT THAT, KATE. I REALLY AM.
I KNOW. IT'S OKAY, DAD. IT'S NOT YOUR FAULT.
IT'S NOBODY'S FAULT. ESPECIALLY NOT YOURS. YOU KNOW THAT, RIGHT? IT'S NOTHING YOU DID.
I KNOW.

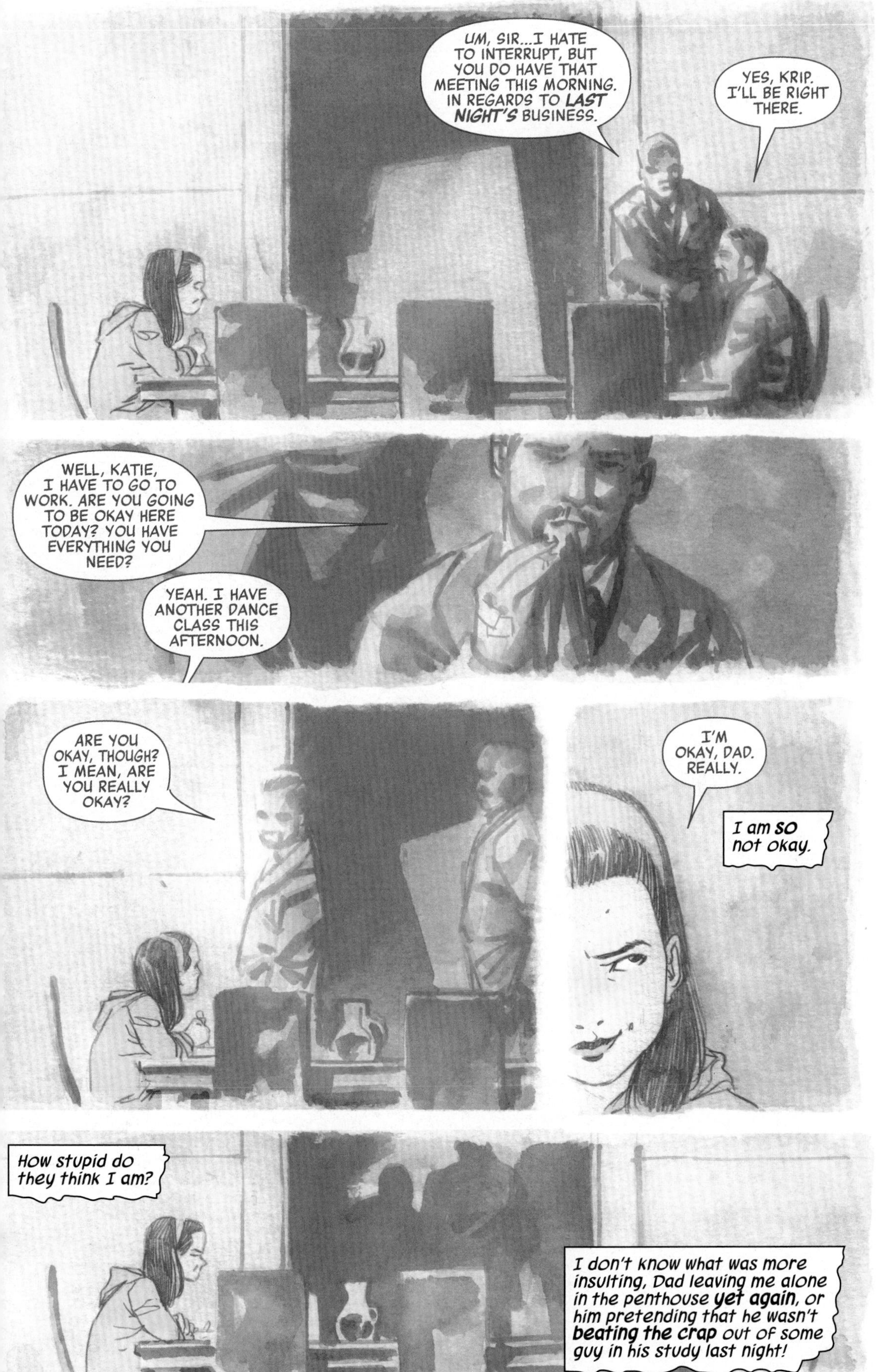
UM, SIR...I HATE TO INTERRUPT, BUT YOU DO HAVE THAT MEETING THIS MORNING. IN REGARDS TO LAST NIGHT'S BUSINESS.
YES, KRIP. I'LL BE RIGHT THERE.
WELL, KATIE, I HAVE TO GO TO WORK. ARE YOU GOING TO BE OKAY HERE TODAY? YOU HAVE EVERYTHING YOU NEED?
YEAH. I HAVE ANOTHER DANCE CLASS THIS AFTERNOON.
ARE YOU OKAY, THOUGH? I MEAN, ARE YOU REALLY OKAY?
I'M OKAY, DAD. REALLY.
I am SO not okay.
How stupid do they think I am?
I don't know what was more insulting, Dad leaving me alone in the penthouse yet again, or him pretending that he wasn't beating the crap out of some guy in his study last night!

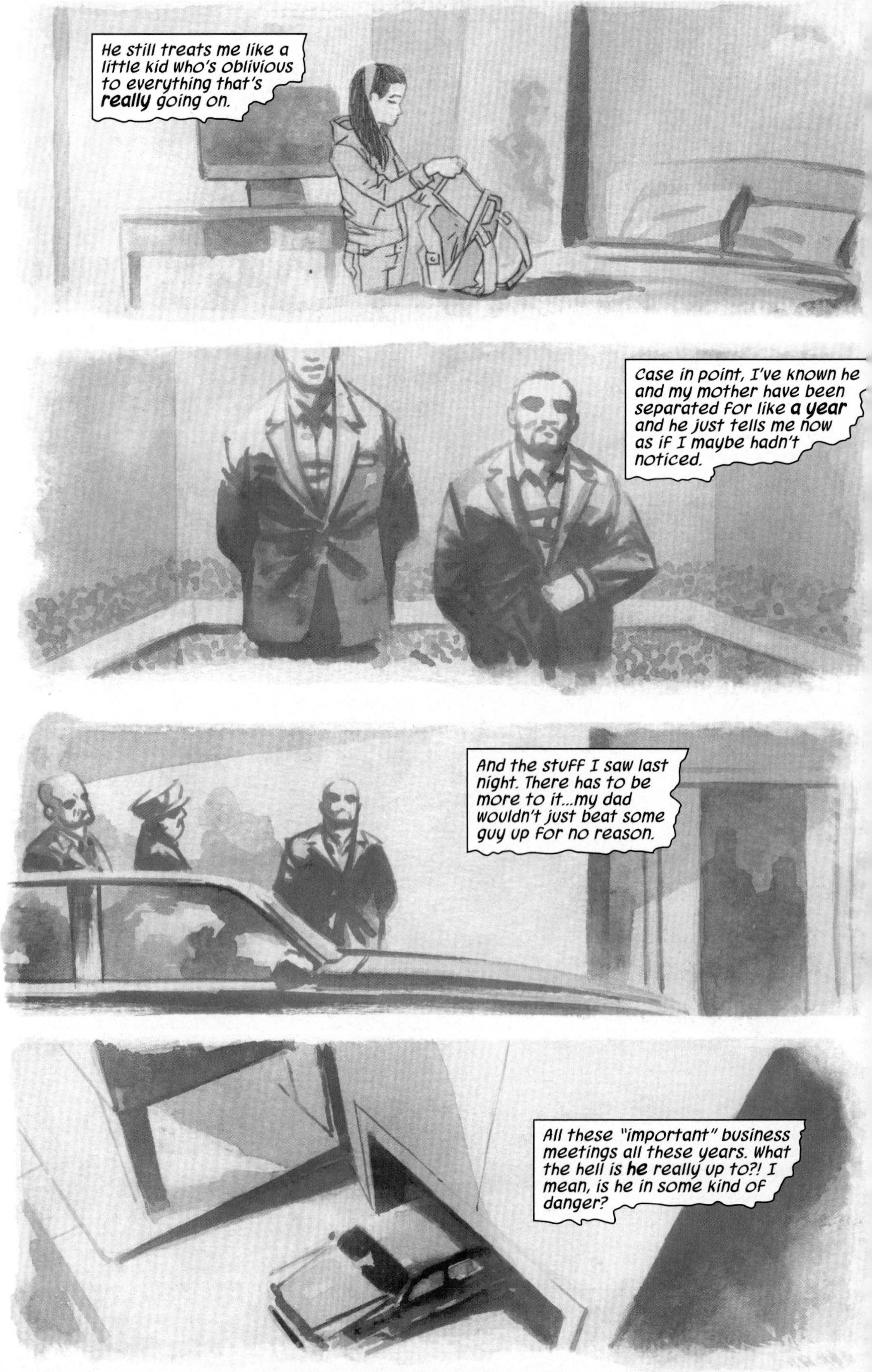
He still treats me like a little kid who's oblivious to everything that's **really** going on.
Case in point, I've known he and my mother have been separated for like **a year** and he just tells me now as if I maybe hadn't noticed.
And the stuff I saw last night. There has to be more to it...my dad wouldn't just beat some guy up for no reason.
All these "important" business meetings all these years. What the hell is **he** really up to?! I mean, is he in some kind of danger?

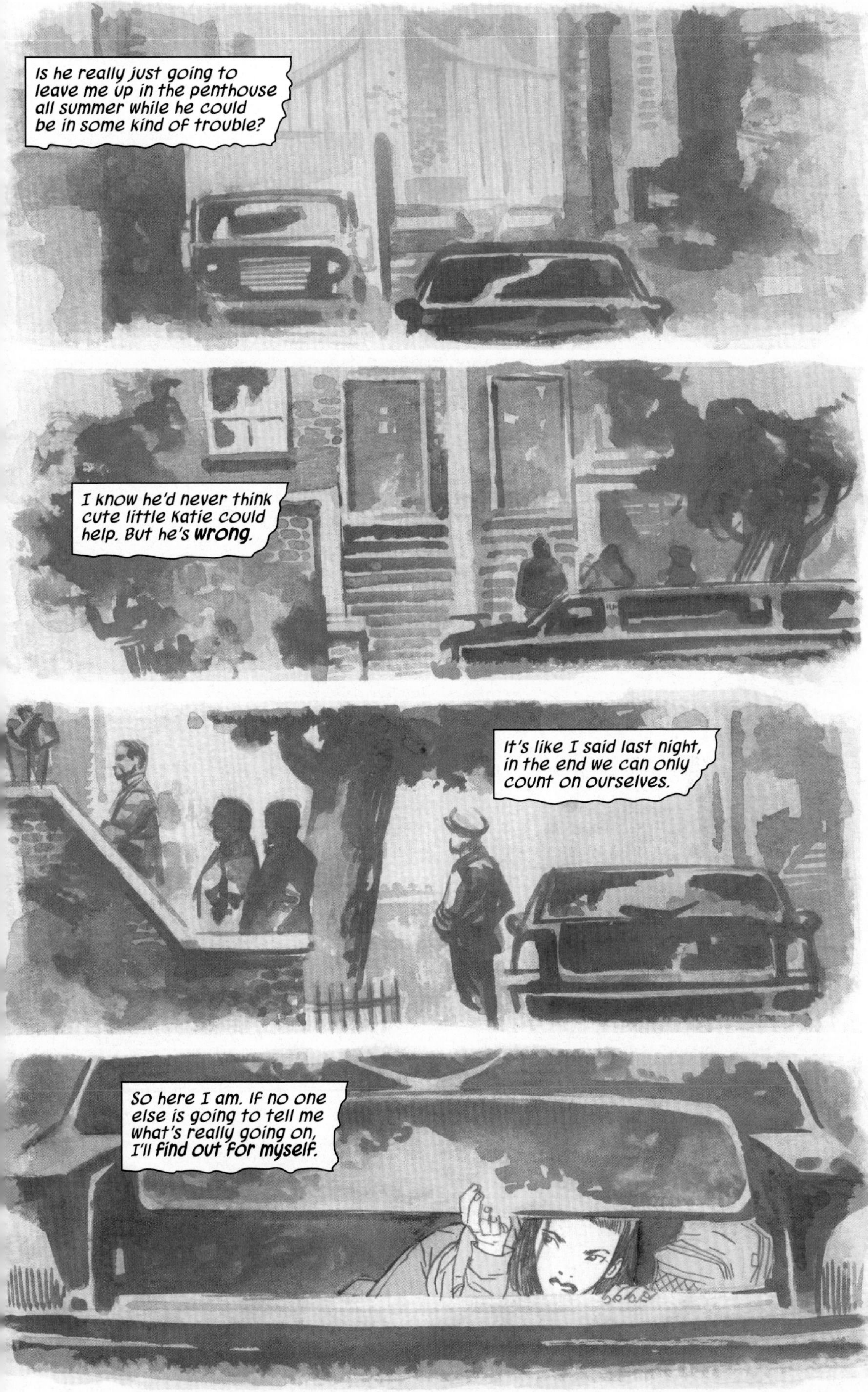
Is he really just going to leave me up in the penthouse all summer while he could be in some kind of trouble?
I know he'd never think cute little Katie could help. But he's wrong.
It's like I said last night, in the end we can only count on ourselves.
So here I am. If no one else is going to tell me what's really going on, I'll find out for myself.

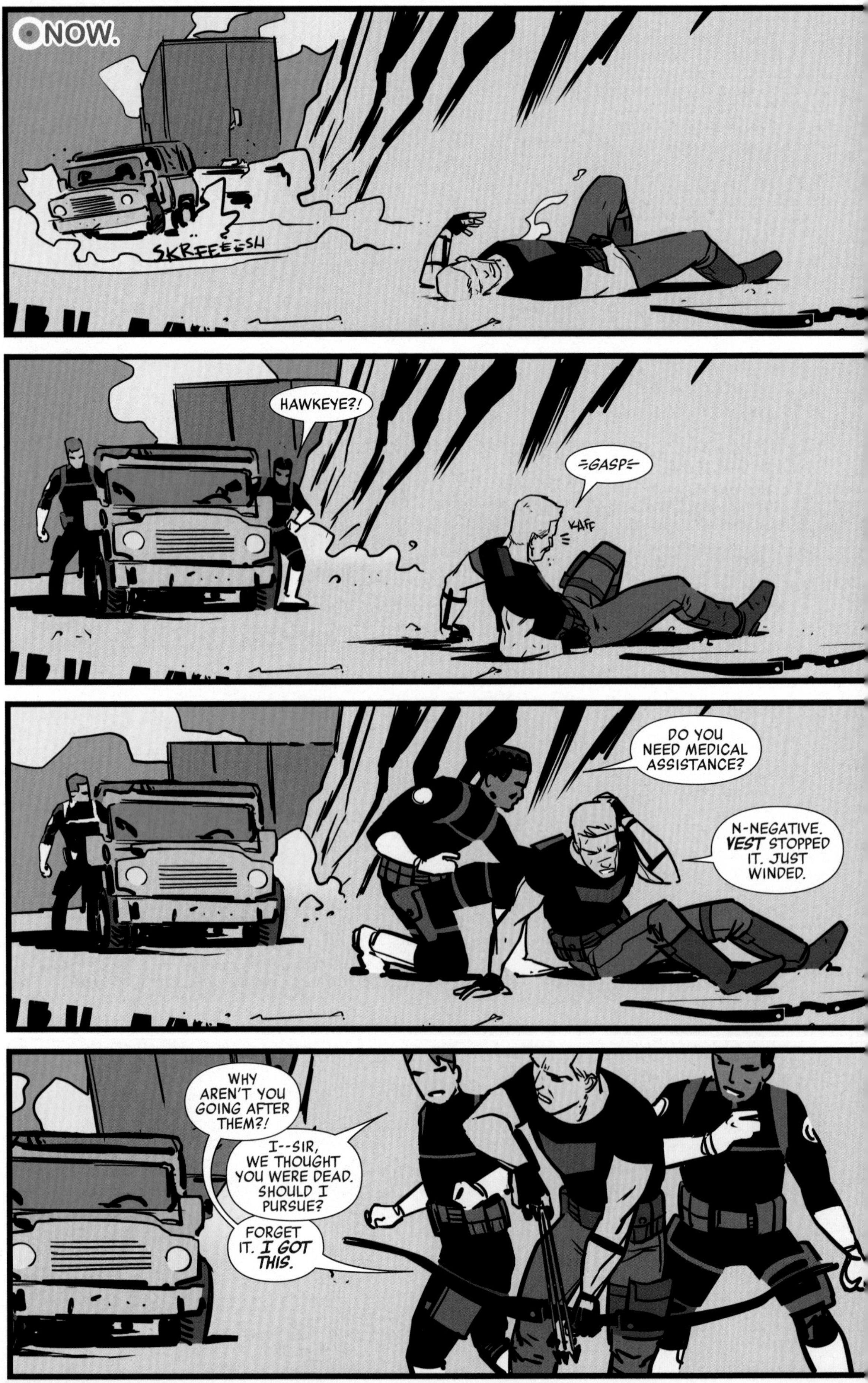
NOW.
SKREEEESH
HAWKEYE?!
=GASP=
KAFF
DO YOU NEED MEDICAL ASSISTANCE?
N-NEGATIVE. VEST STOPPED IT. JUST WINDED.
WHY AREN'T YOU GOING AFTER THEM?!
I--SIR, WE THOUGHT YOU WERE DEAD. SHOULD I PURSUE?
FORGET IT. I GOT THIS.

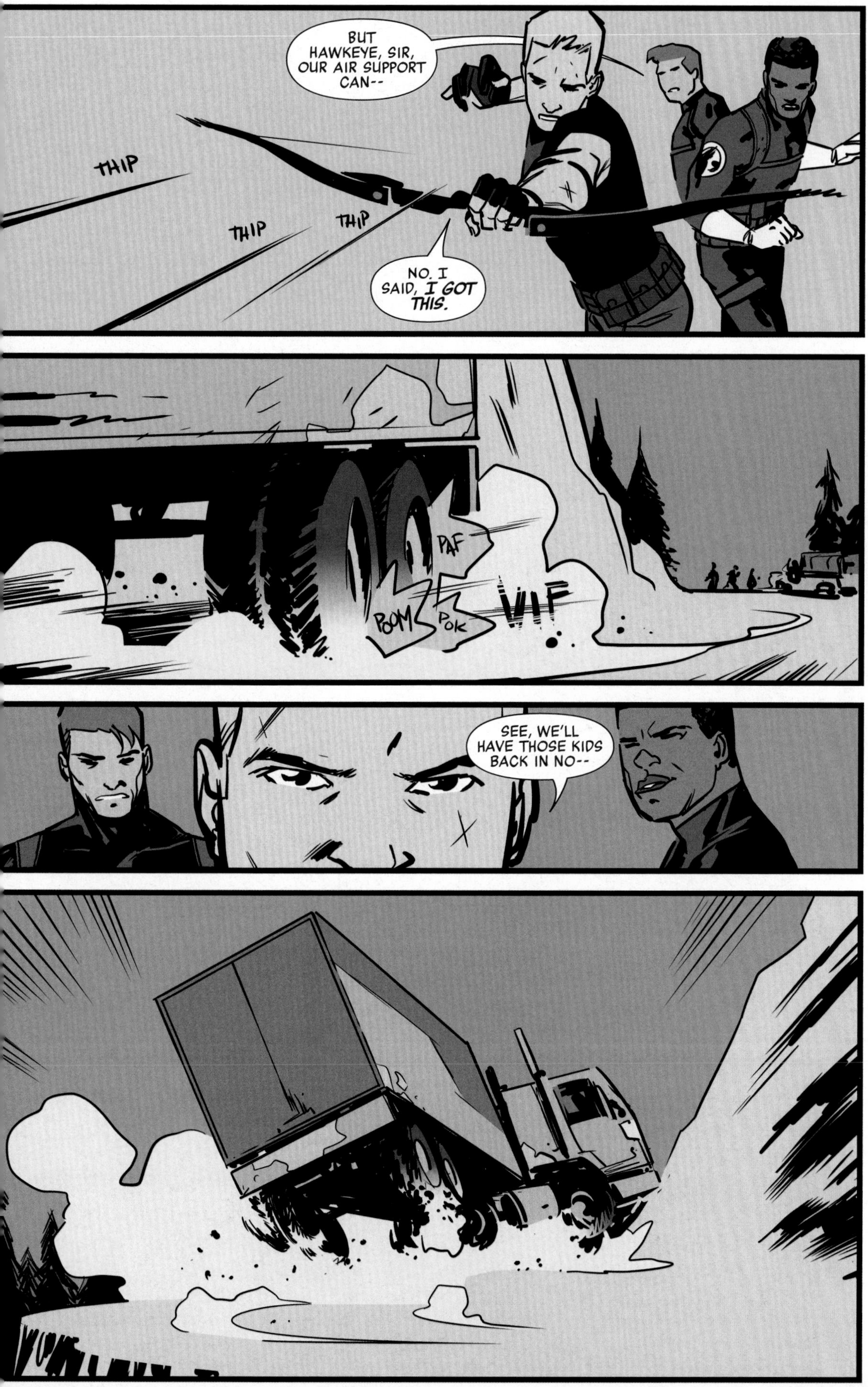
BUT HAWKEYE, SIR, OUR AIR SUPPORT CAN--
THIP
THIP
THIP
NO. I SAID, I GOT THIS.
PAF
POOM
POK
VIF
SEE, WE'LL HAVE THOSE KIDS BACK IN NO--

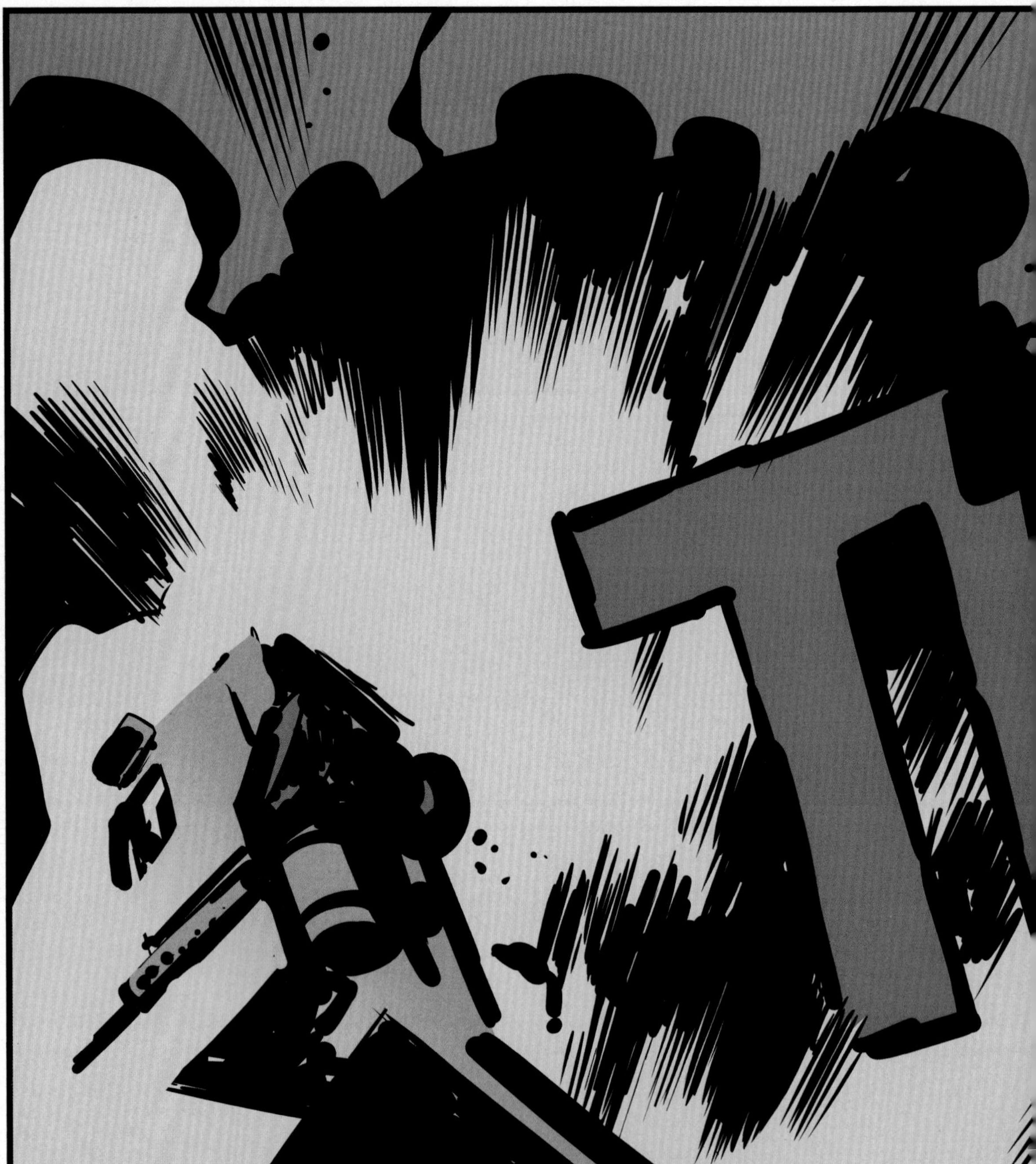

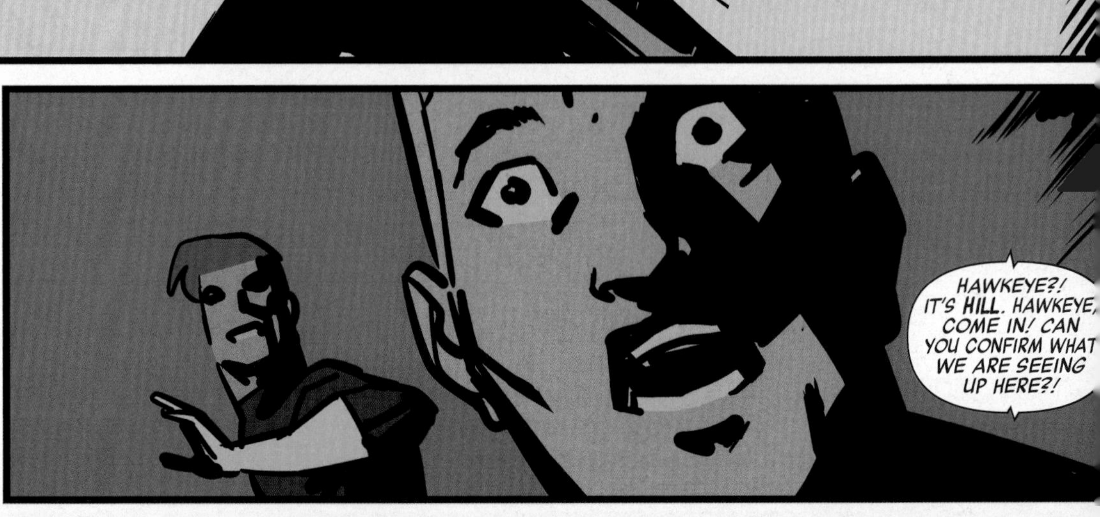
HAWKEYE?! IT'S HILL. HAWKEYE, COME IN! CAN YOU CONFIRM WHAT WE ARE SEEING UP HERE?!

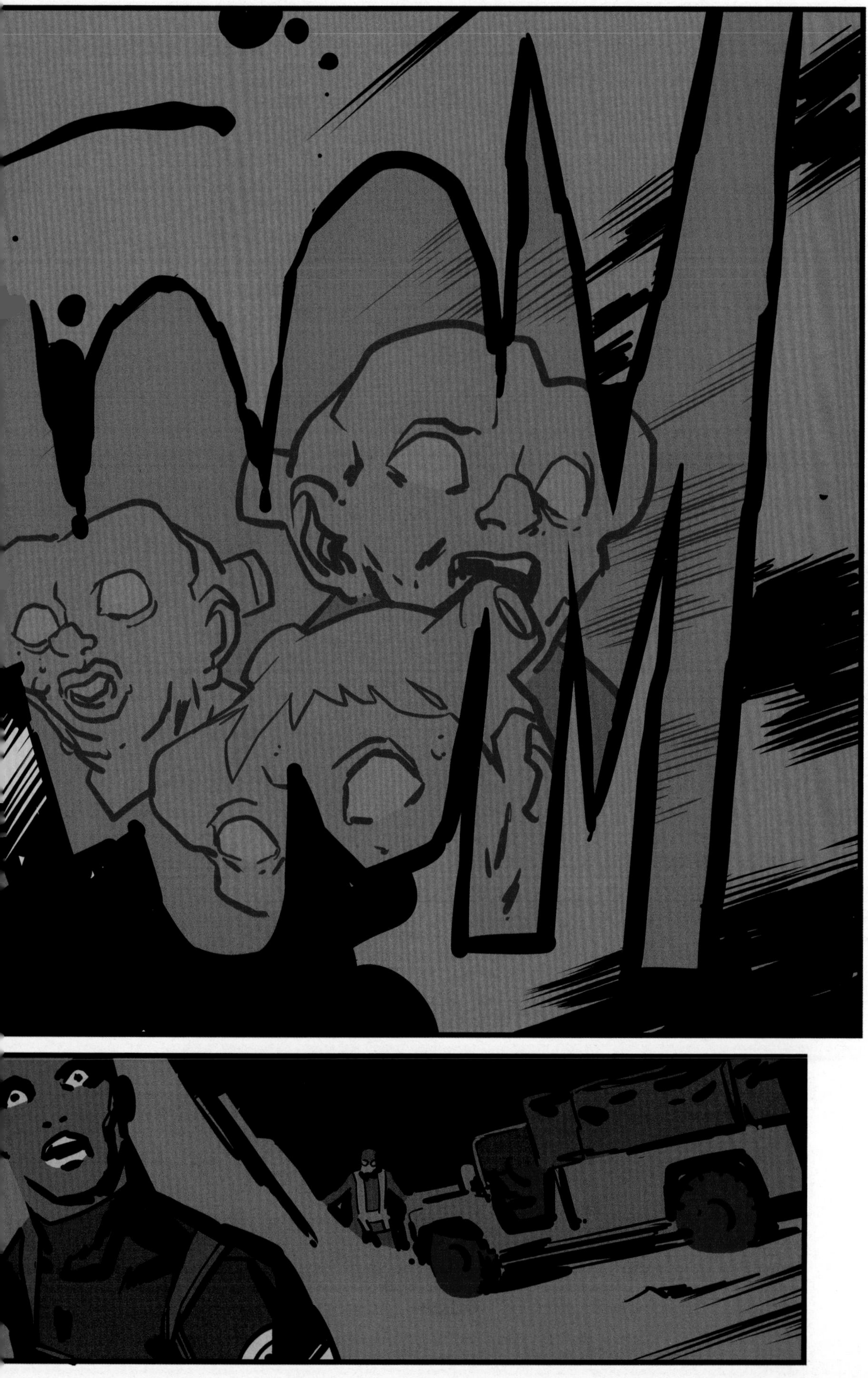

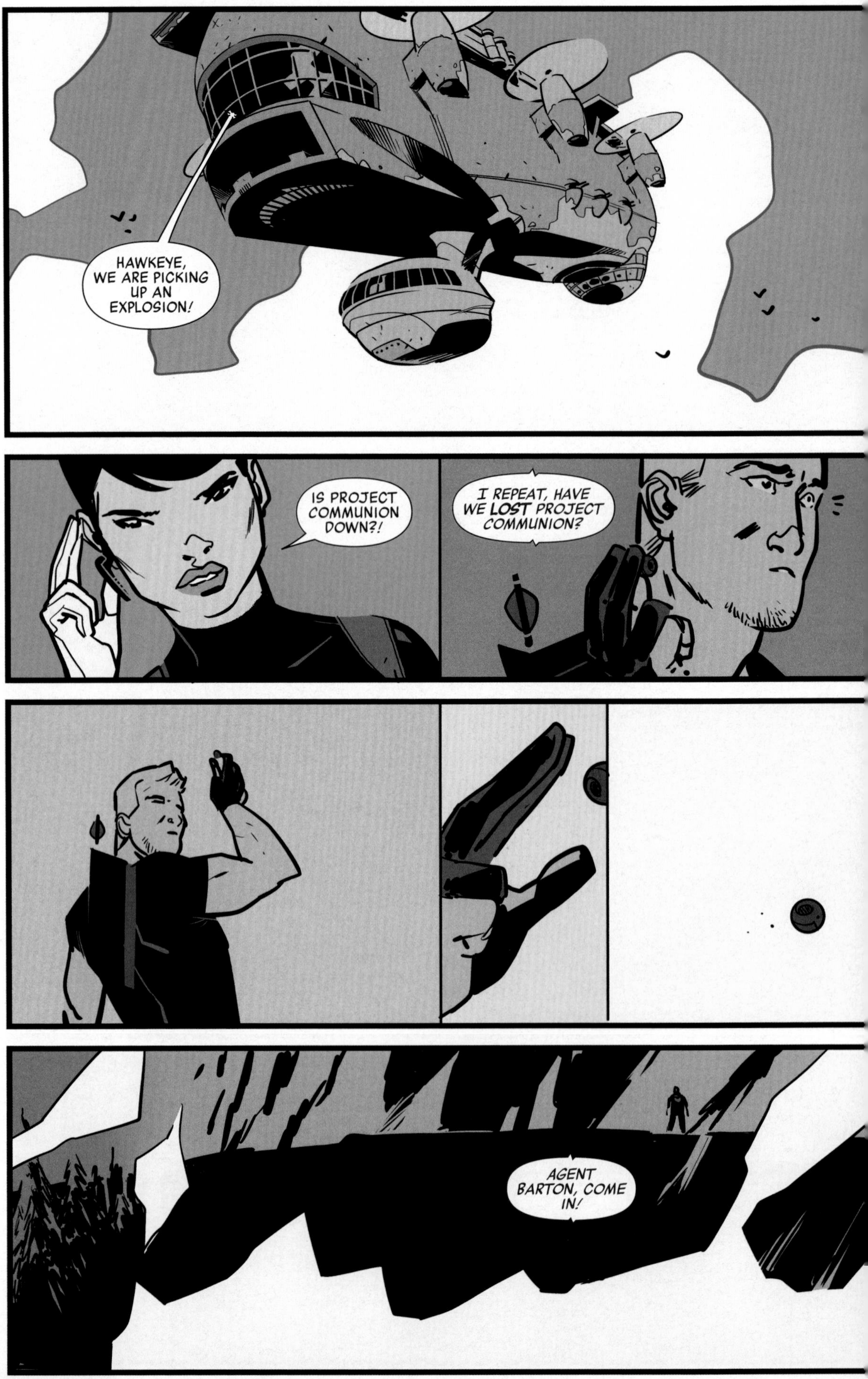
HAWKEYE, WE ARE PICKING UP AN EXPLOSION!
IS PROJECT COMMUNION DOWN?!
I REPEAT, HAVE WE LOST PROJECT COMMUNION?
AGENT BARTON, COME IN!

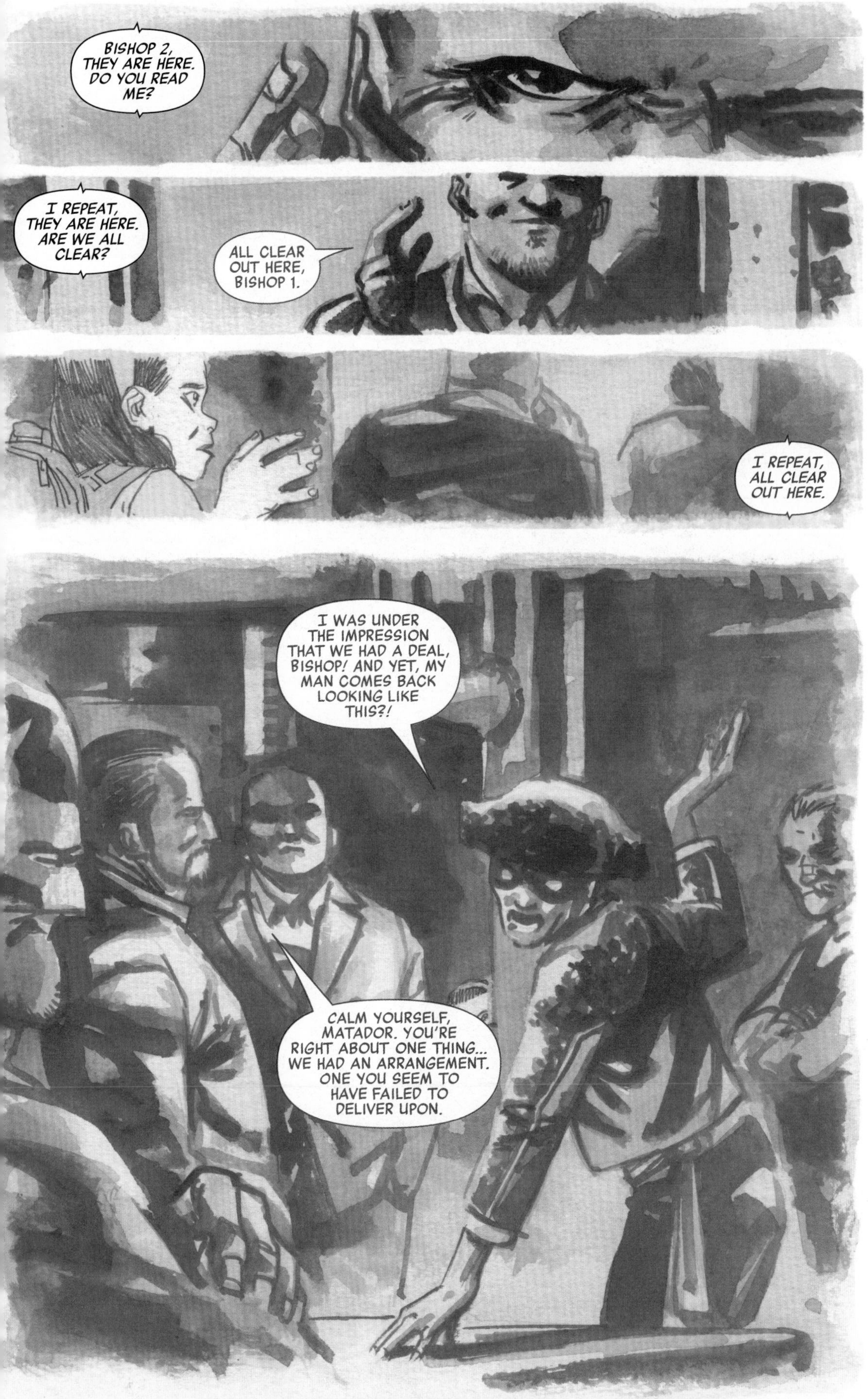
BISHOP 2, THEY ARE HERE. DO YOU READ ME?
I REPEAT, THEY ARE HERE. ARE WE ALL CLEAR?
ALL CLEAR OUT HERE, BISHOP 1.
I REPEAT, ALL CLEAR OUT HERE.
I WAS UNDER THE IMPRESSION THAT WE HAD A DEAL, BISHOP! AND YET, MY MAN COMES BACK LOOKING LIKE THIS?!
CALM YOURSELF, MATADOR. YOU'RE RIGHT ABOUT ONE THING... WE HAD AN ARRANGEMENT. ONE YOU SEEM TO HAVE FAILED TO DELIVER UPON.

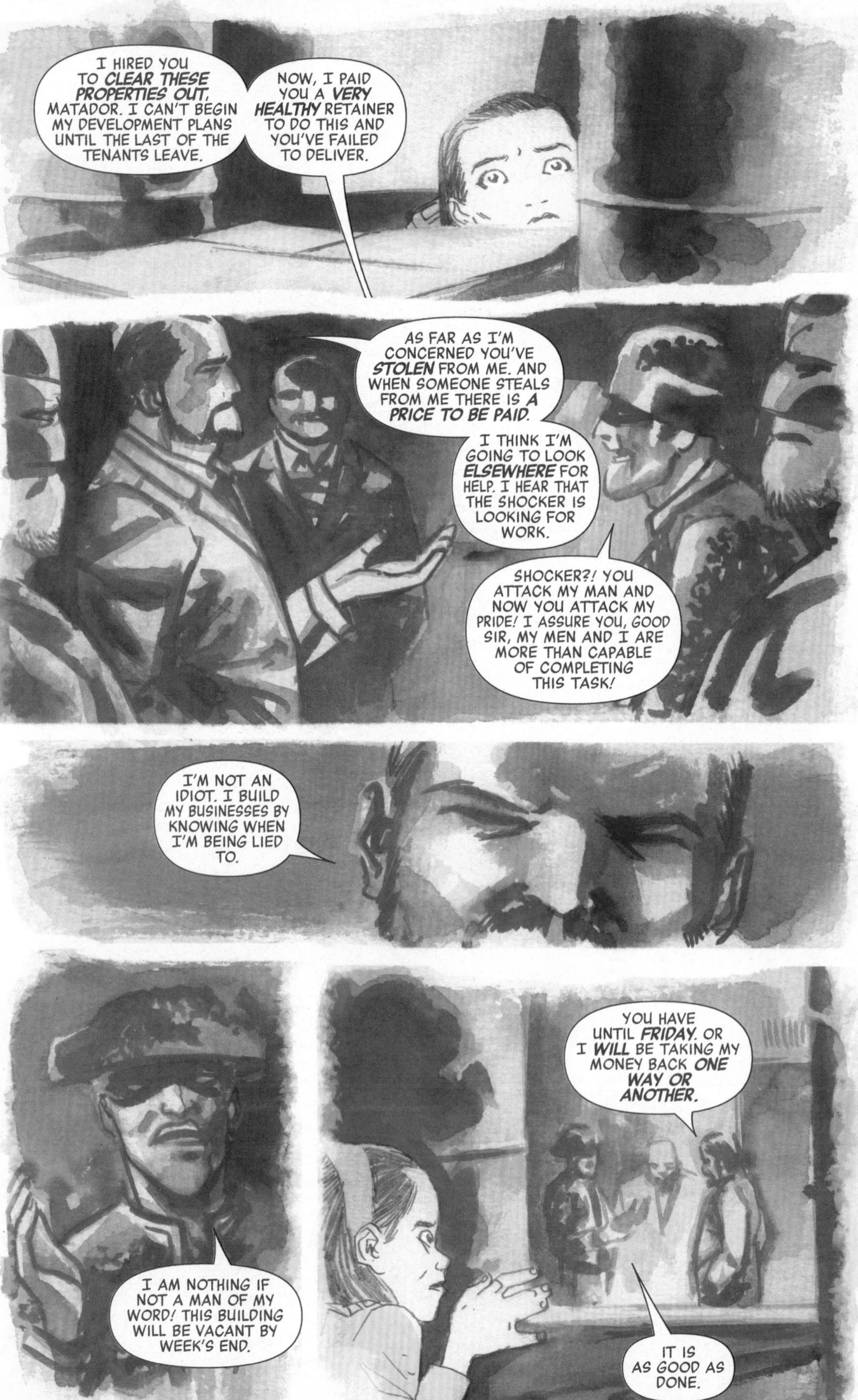
I HIRED YOU TO CLEAR THESE PROPERTIES OUT, MATADOR. I CAN'T BEGIN MY DEVELOPMENT PLANS UNTIL THE LAST OF THE TENANTS LEAVE.
NOW, I PAID YOU A VERY HEALTHY RETAINER TO DO THIS AND YOU'VE FAILED TO DELIVER.
AS FAR AS I'M CONCERNED YOU'VE STOLEN FROM ME. AND WHEN SOMEONE STEALS FROM ME THERE IS A PRICE TO BE PAID.
I THINK I'M GOING TO LOOK ELSEWHERE FOR HELP. I HEAR THAT THE SHOCKER IS LOOKING FOR WORK.
SHOCKER?! YOU ATTACK MY MAN AND NOW YOU ATTACK MY PRIDE! I ASSURE YOU, GOOD SIR, MY MEN AND I ARE MORE THAN CAPABLE OF COMPLETING THIS TASK!
I'M NOT AN IDIOT. I BUILD MY BUSINESSES BY KNOWING WHEN I'M BEING LIED TO.
I AM NOTHING IF NOT A MAN OF MY WORD! THIS BUILDING WILL BE VACANT BY WEEK'S END.
YOU HAVE UNTIL FRIDAY. OR I WILL BE TAKING MY MONEY BACK ONE WAY OR ANOTHER.
IT IS AS GOOD AS DONE.

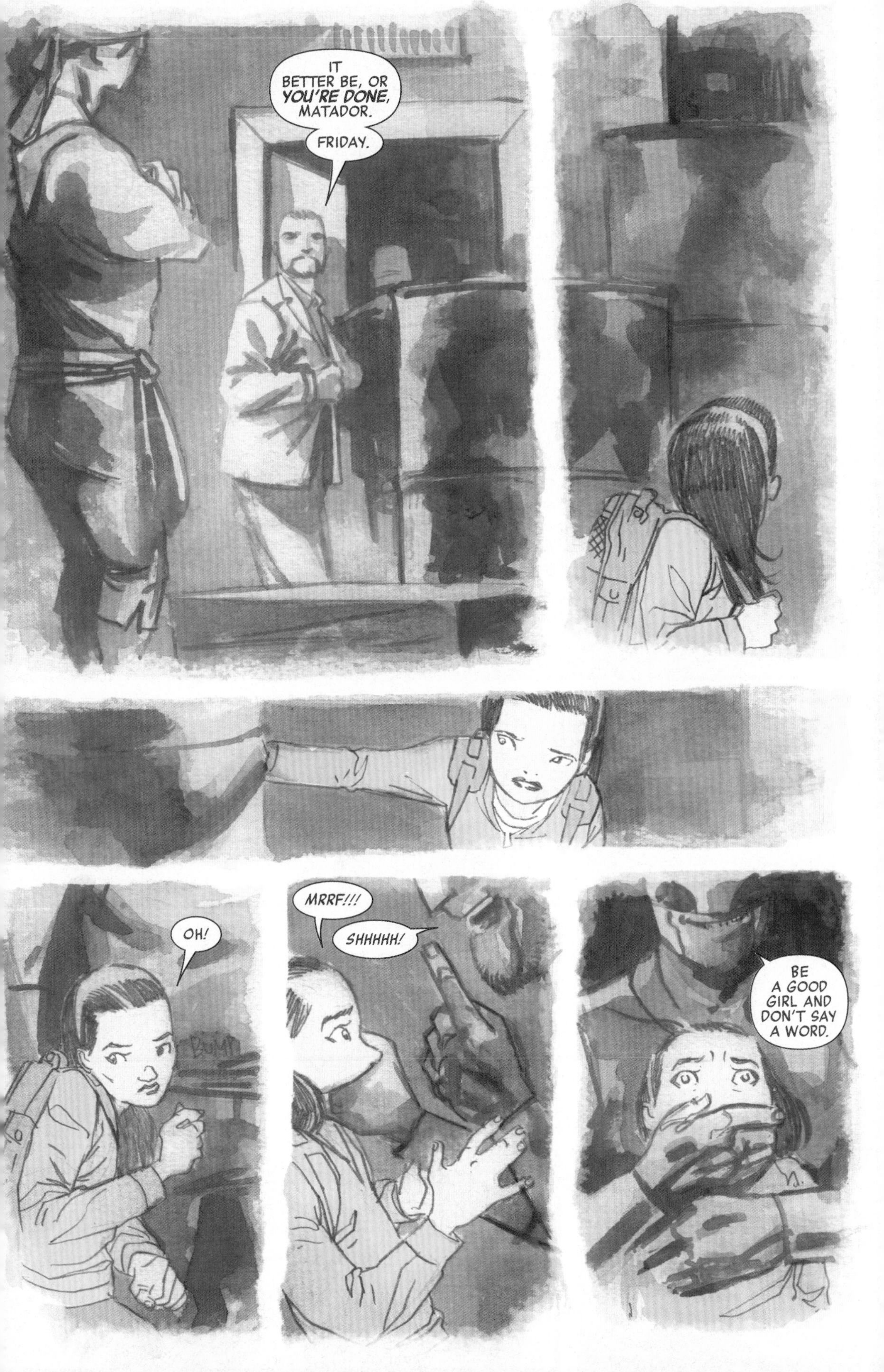
IT BETTER BE, OR YOU'RE DONE, MATADOR.
FRIDAY.
OH!
BUMP
MRRF!!!
SHHHHH!
BE A GOOD GIRL AND DON'T SAY A WORD.

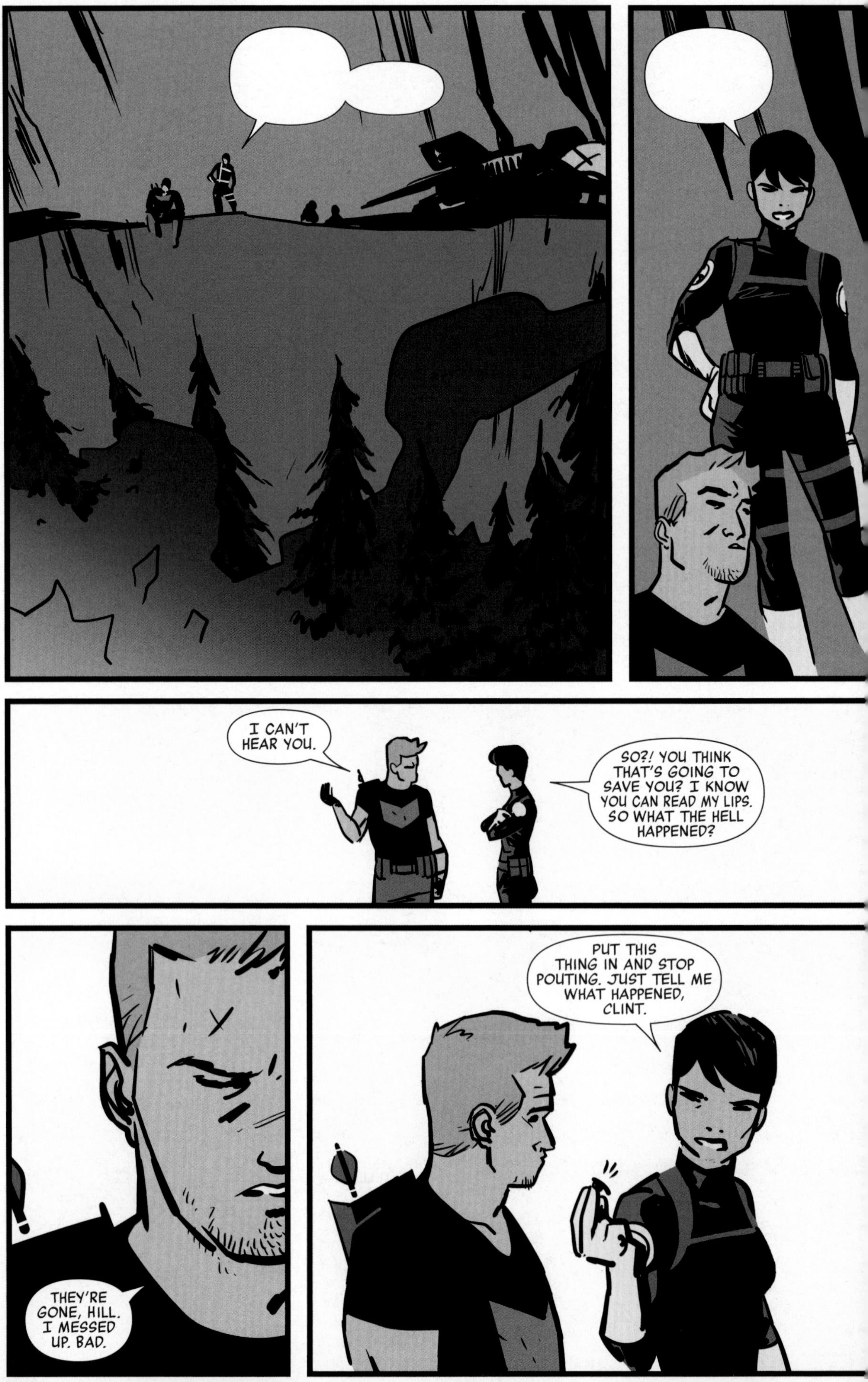
I CAN'T HEAR YOU.
SO?! YOU THINK THAT'S GOING TO SAVE YOU? I KNOW YOU CAN READ MY LIPS. SO WHAT THE HELL HAPPENED?
THEY'RE GONE, HILL. I MESSED UP. BAD.
PUT THIS THING IN AND STOP POUTING. JUST TELL ME WHAT HAPPENED, CLINT.

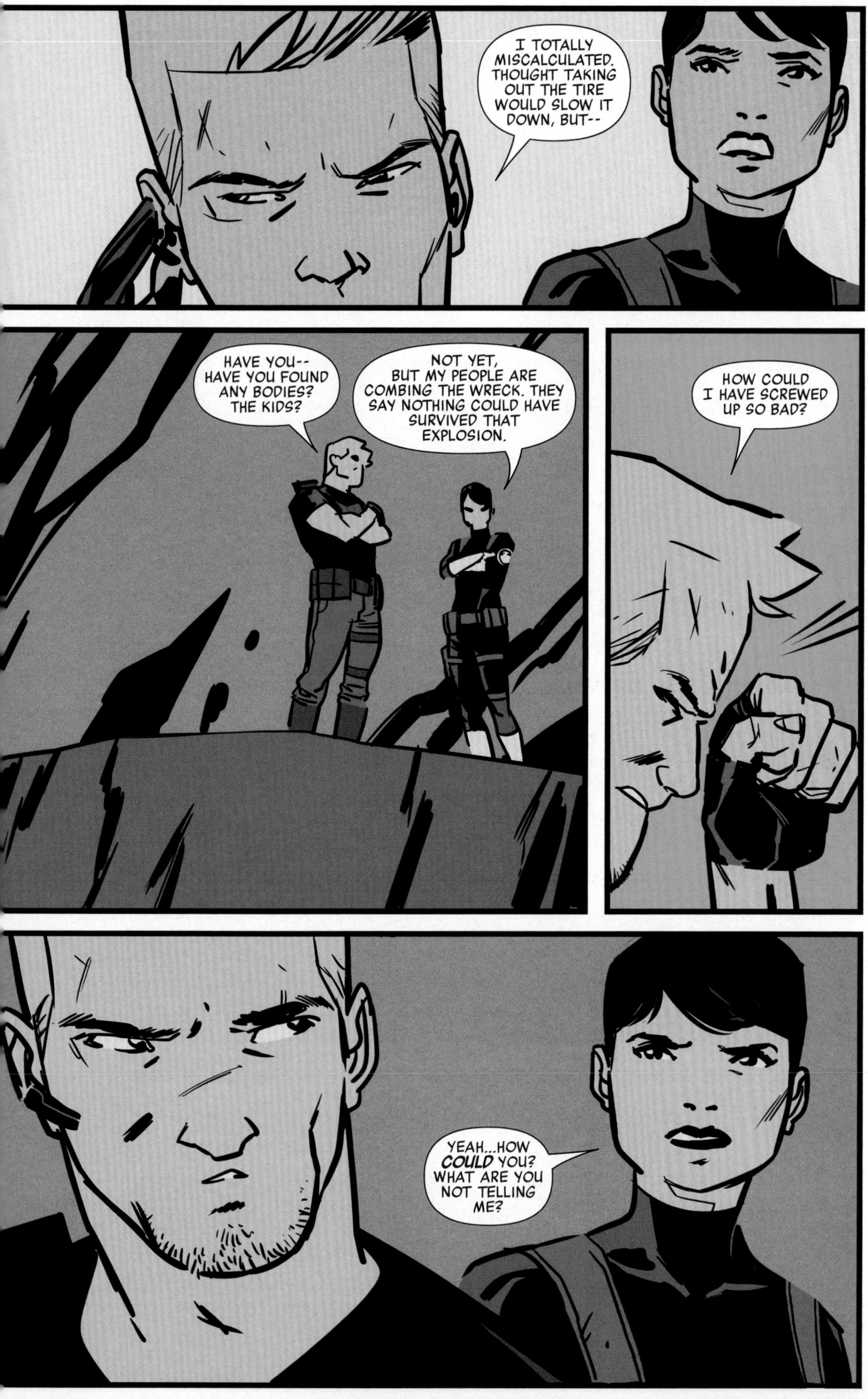
I TOTALLY MISCALCULATED. THOUGHT TAKING OUT THE TIRE WOULD SLOW IT DOWN, BUT--
HAVE YOU-- HAVE YOU FOUND ANY BODIES? THE KIDS?
NOT YET, BUT MY PEOPLE ARE COMBING THE WRECK. THEY SAY NOTHING COULD HAVE SURVIVED THAT EXPLOSION.
HOW COULD I HAVE SCREWED UP SO BAD?
YEAH...HOW *COULD* YOU? WHAT ARE YOU NOT TELLING ME?

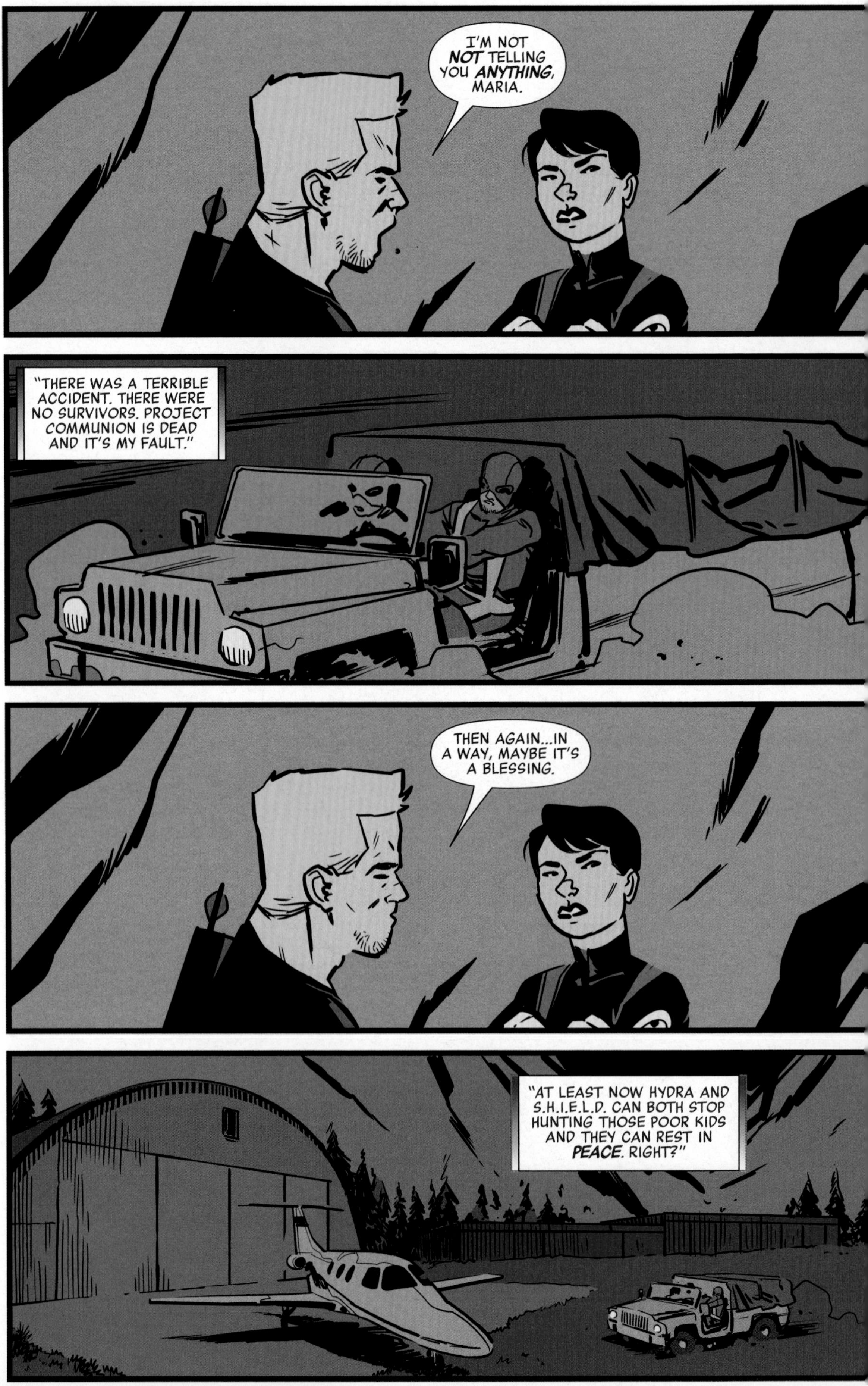

I'M NOT NOT TELLING YOU ANYTHING, MARIA.
"THERE WAS A TERRIBLE ACCIDENT. THERE WERE NO SURVIVORS. PROJECT COMMUNION IS DEAD AND IT'S MY FAULT."
THEN AGAIN...IN A WAY, MAYBE IT'S A BLESSING.
"AT LEAST NOW HYDRA AND S.H.I.E.L.D. CAN BOTH STOP HUNTING THOSE POOR KIDS AND THEY CAN REST IN PEACE. RIGHT?"

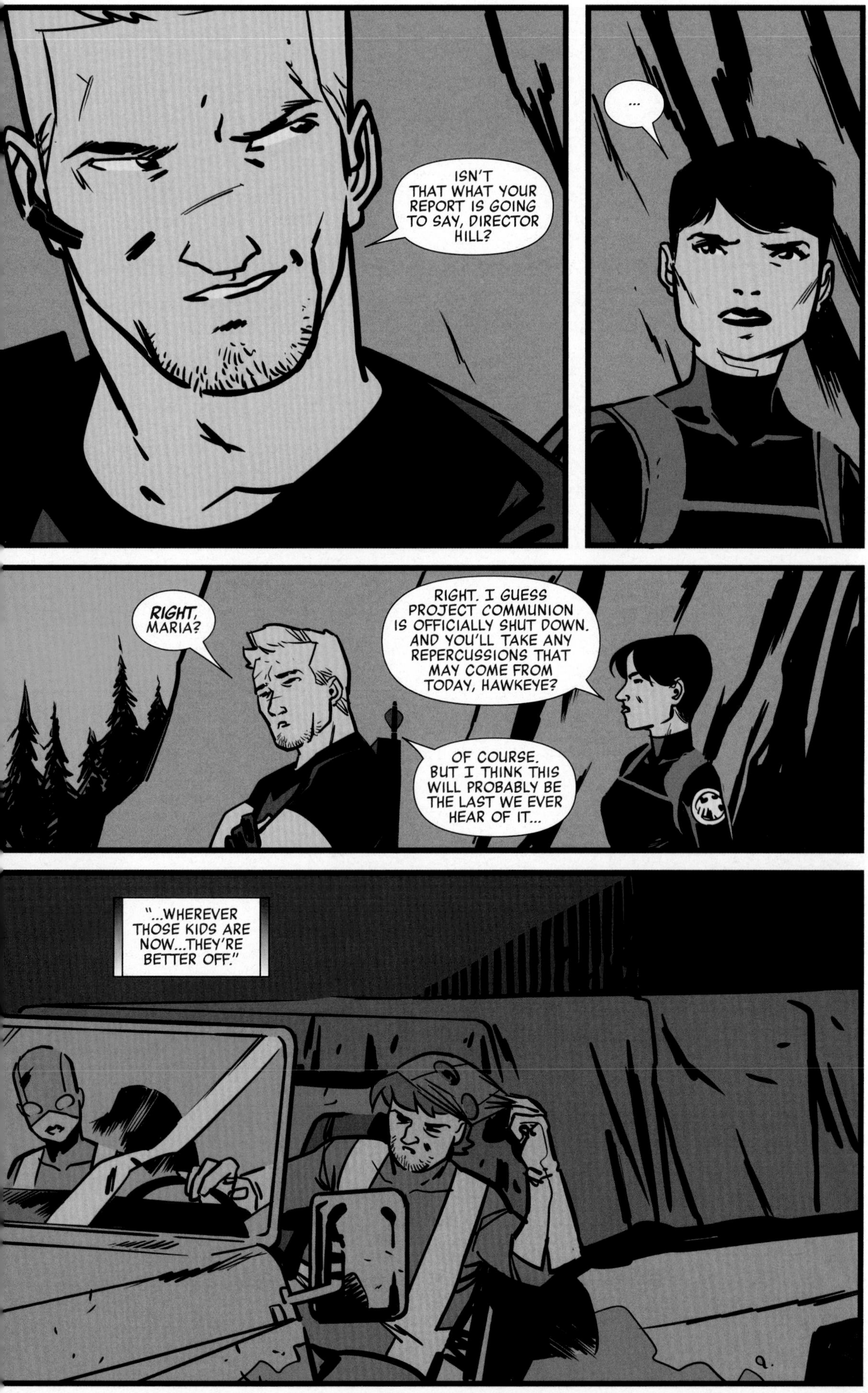
ISN'T THAT WHAT YOUR REPORT IS GOING TO SAY, DIRECTOR HILL?
...
RIGHT, MARIA?
RIGHT. I GUESS PROJECT COMMUNION IS OFFICIALLY SHUT DOWN. AND YOU'LL TAKE ANY REPERCUSSIONS THAT MAY COME FROM TODAY, HAWKEYE?
OF COURSE. BUT I THINK THIS WILL PROBABLY BE THE LAST WE EVER HEAR OF IT...
"...WHEREVER THOSE KIDS ARE NOW...THEY'RE BETTER OFF."

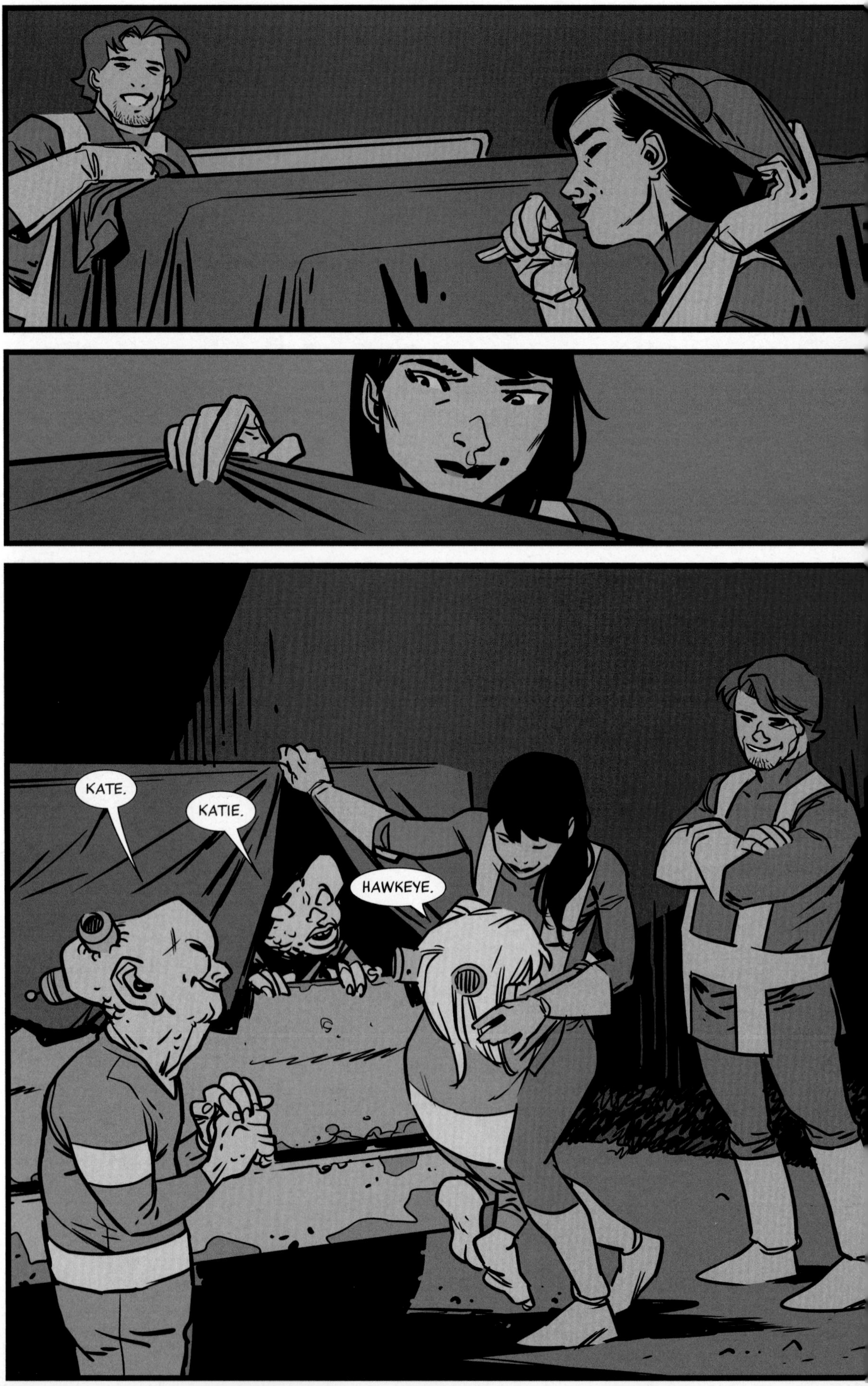
KATE.
KATIE.
HAWKEYE.

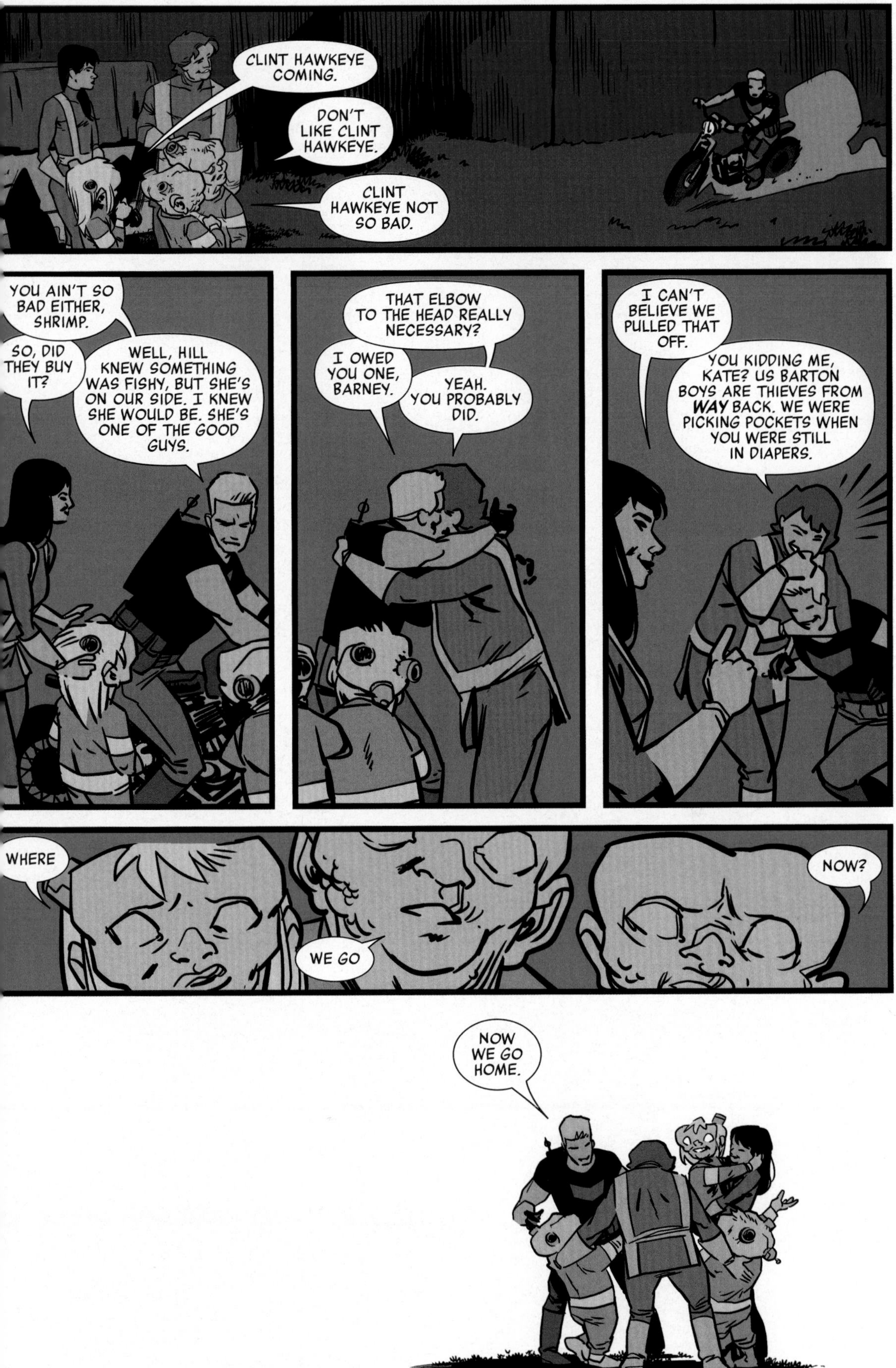
CLINT HAWKEYE COMING.
DON'T LIKE CLINT HAWKEYE.
CLINT HAWKEYE NOT SO BAD.
YOU AIN'T SO BAD EITHER, SHRIMP.
SO, DID THEY BUY IT?
WELL, HILL KNEW SOMETHING WAS FISHY, BUT SHE'S ON OUR SIDE. I KNEW SHE WOULD BE. SHE'S ONE OF THE GOOD GUYS.
THAT ELBOW TO THE HEAD REALLY NECESSARY?
I OWED YOU ONE, BARNEY.
YEAH. YOU PROBABLY DID.
I CAN'T BELIEVE WE PULLED THAT OFF.
YOU KIDDING ME, KATE? US BARTON BOYS ARE THIEVES FROM WAY BACK. WE WERE PICKING POCKETS WHEN YOU WERE STILL IN DIAPERS.
WHERE
WE GO
NOW?
NOW WE GO HOME.

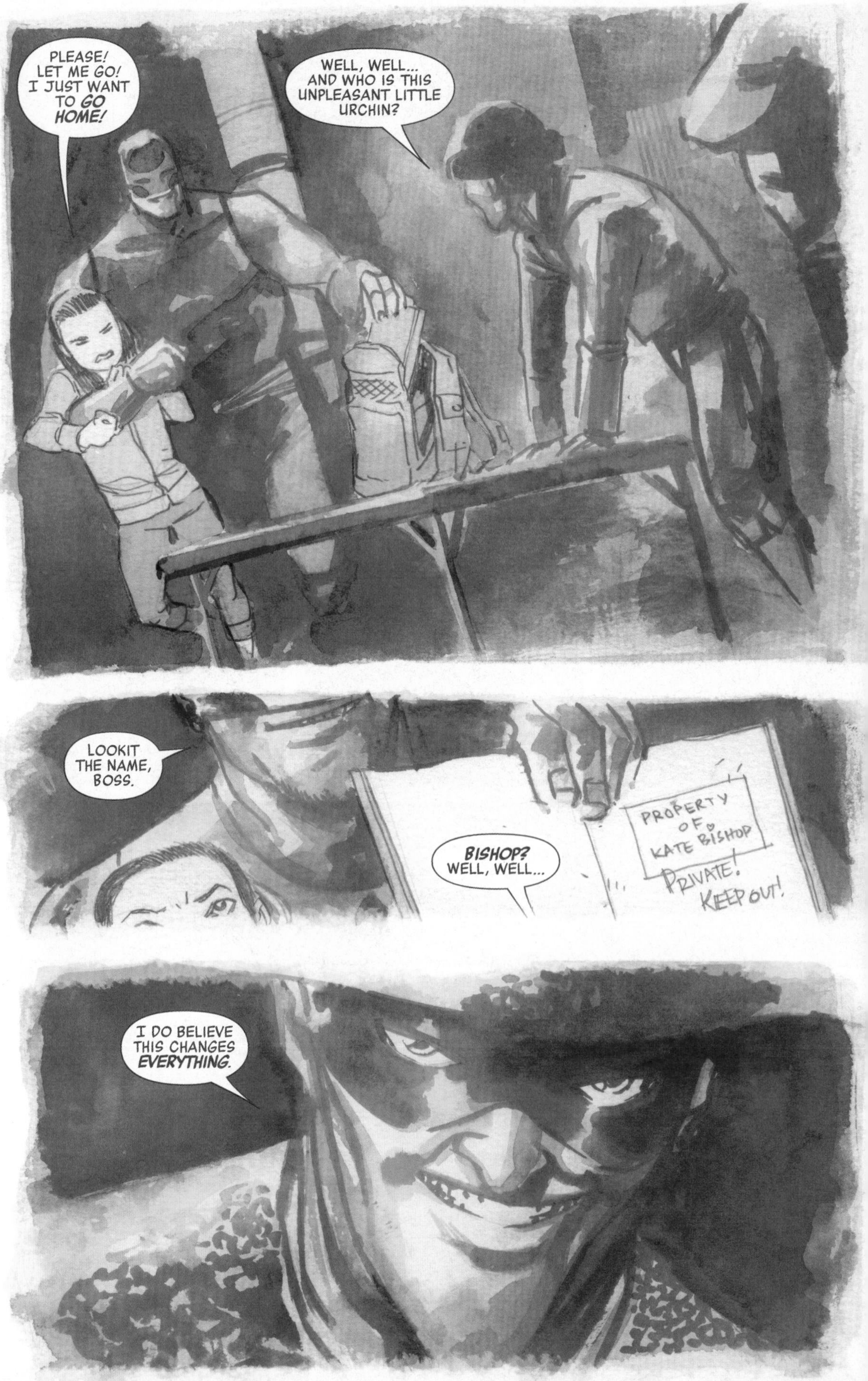
PLEASE! LET ME GO! I JUST WANT TO *GO HOME!*
WELL, WELL... AND WHO IS THIS UNPLEASANT LITTLE URCHIN?
LOOKIT THE NAME, BOSS.
PROPERTY OF KATE BISHOP
PRIVATE! KEEP OUT!
BISHOP? WELL, WELL...
I DO BELIEVE THIS CHANGES *EVERYTHING.*

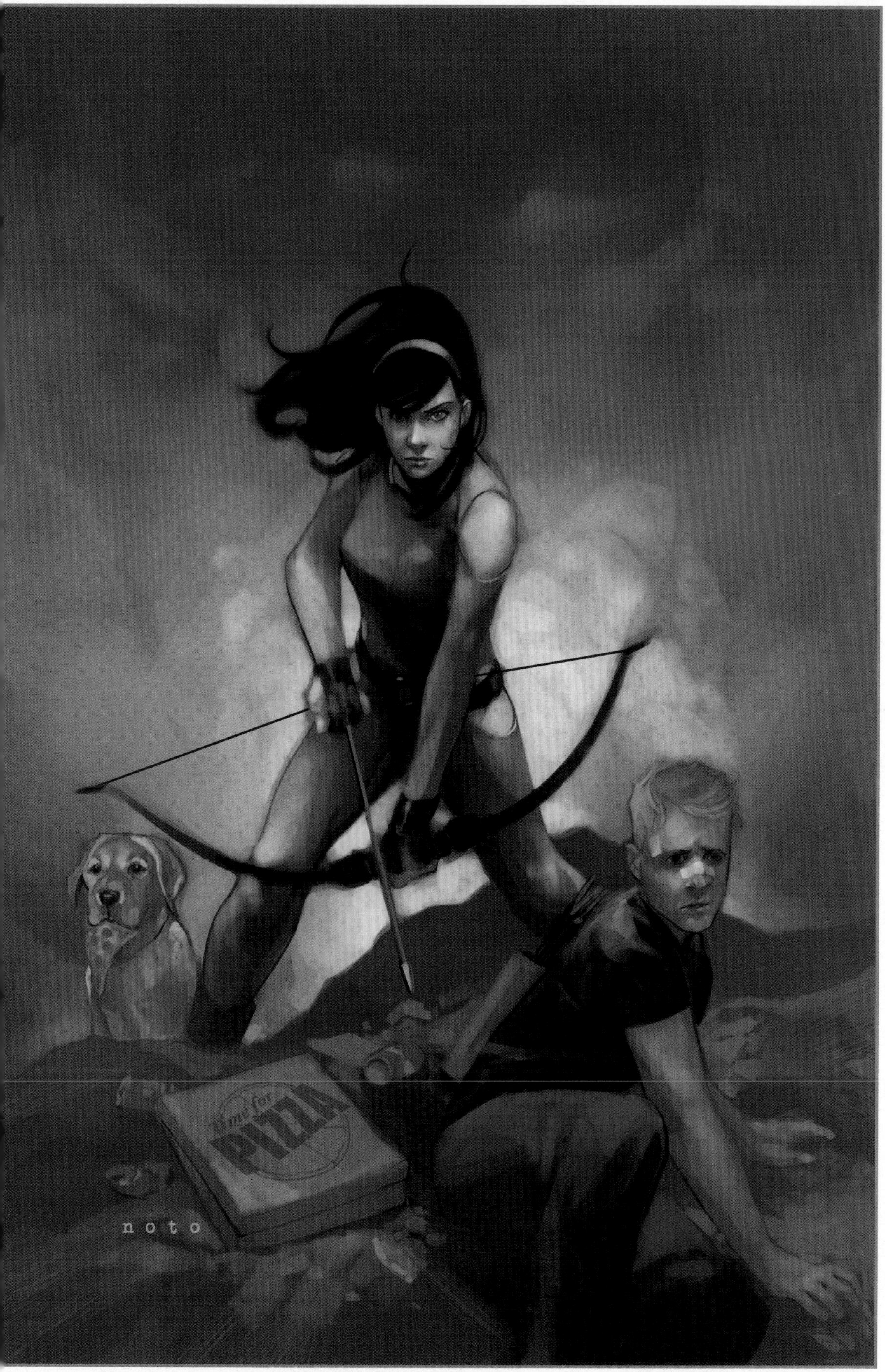
Time for PIZZA
noto

ALL-NEW HAWKEYE #5 WOMEN OF POWER VARIANT BY **PHIL NOTO**

6

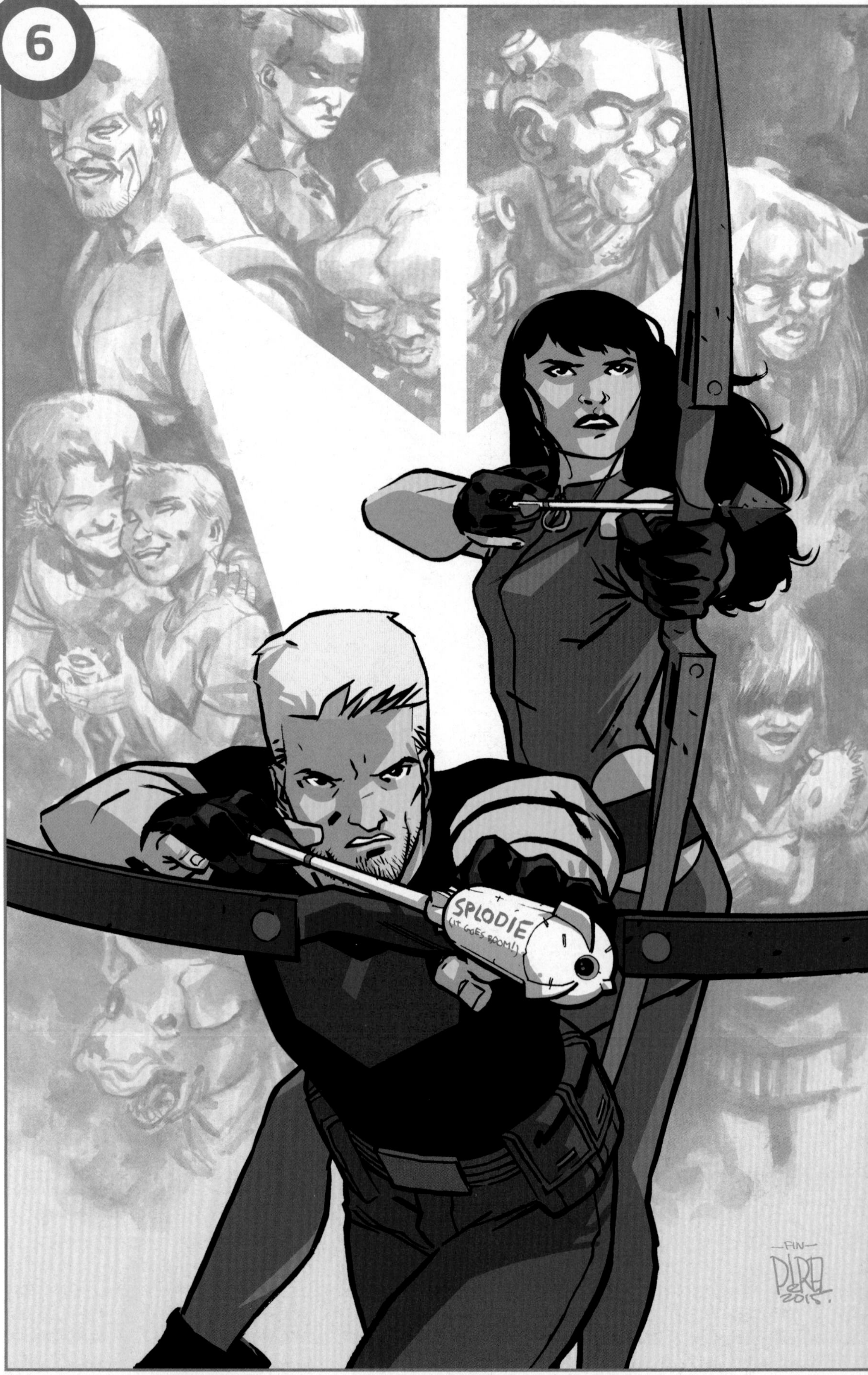
SPLODIE
(IT GOES BOOM!)
-FIN-

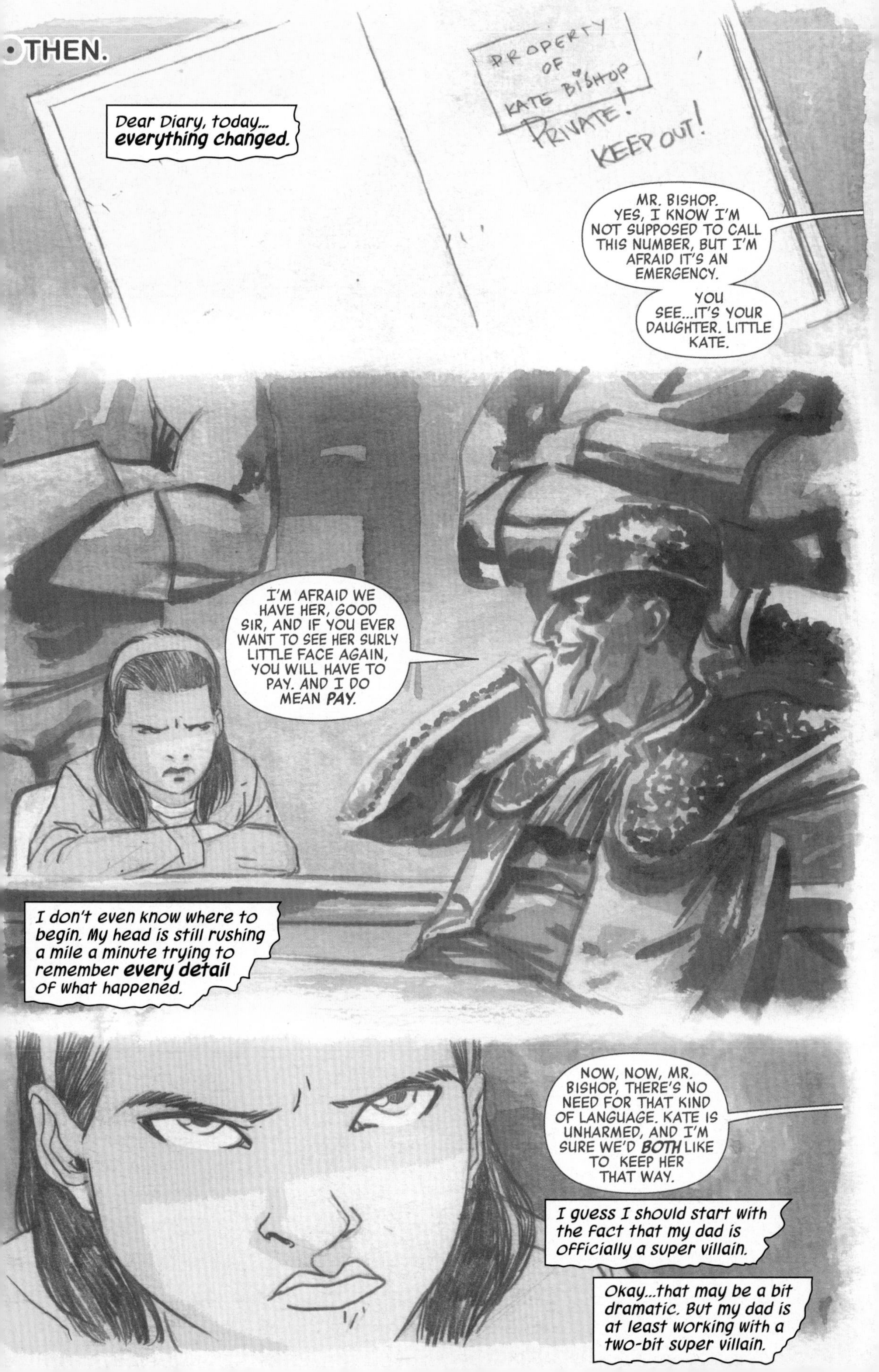
THEN.
PROPERTY OF KATE BISHOP
PRIVATE! KEEP OUT!
Dear Diary, today... everything changed.
MR. BISHOP. YES, I KNOW I'M NOT SUPPOSED TO CALL THIS NUMBER, BUT I'M AFRAID IT'S AN EMERGENCY.
YOU SEE...IT'S YOUR DAUGHTER. LITTLE KATE.
I'M AFRAID WE HAVE HER, GOOD SIR, AND IF YOU EVER WANT TO SEE HER SURLY LITTLE FACE AGAIN, YOU WILL HAVE TO PAY. AND I DO MEAN PAY.
I don't even know where to begin. My head is still rushing a mile a minute trying to remember every detail of what happened.
NOW, NOW, MR. BISHOP, THERE'S NO NEED FOR THAT KIND OF LANGUAGE. KATE IS UNHARMED, AND I'M SURE WE'D BOTH LIKE TO KEEP HER THAT WAY.
I guess I should start with the fact that my dad is officially a super villain.
Okay...that may be a bit dramatic. But my dad is at least working with a two-bit super villain.

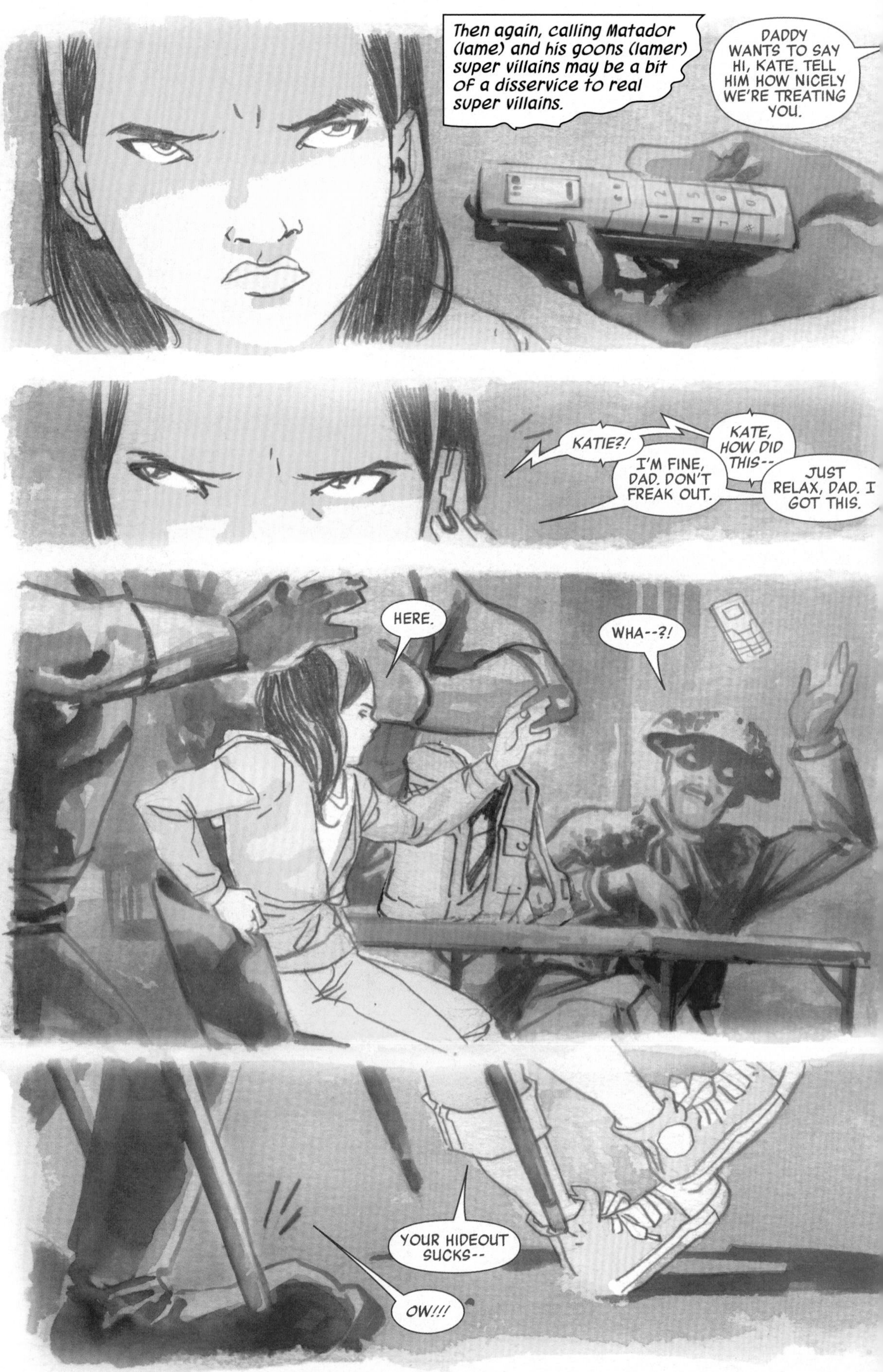

Then again, calling Matador (lame) and his goons (lamer) super villains may be a bit of a disservice to real super villains.
DADDY WANTS TO SAY HI, KATE. TELL HIM HOW NICELY WE'RE TREATING YOU.
KATIE?!
KATE, HOW DID THIS--
I'M FINE, DAD. DON'T FREAK OUT.
JUST RELAX, DAD. I GOT THIS.
HERE.
WHA--?!
YOUR HIDEOUT SUCKS--
OW!!!

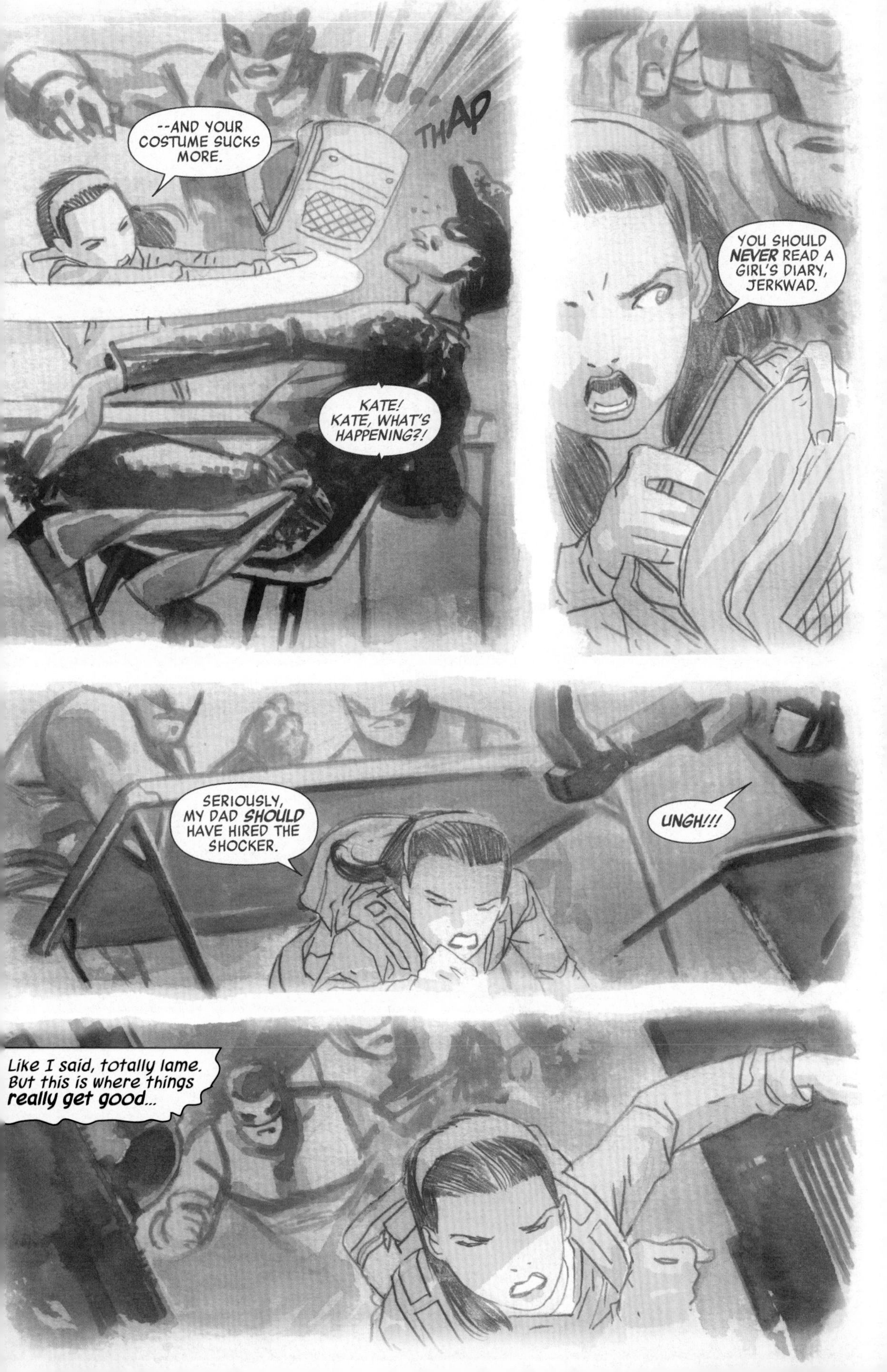
--AND YOUR COSTUME SUCKS MORE.
THAP
KATE! KATE, WHAT'S HAPPENING?!
YOU SHOULD NEVER READ A GIRL'S DIARY, JERKWAD.
SERIOUSLY, MY DAD SHOULD HAVE HIRED THE SHOCKER.
UNGH!!!
Like I said, totally lame. But this is where things really get good...

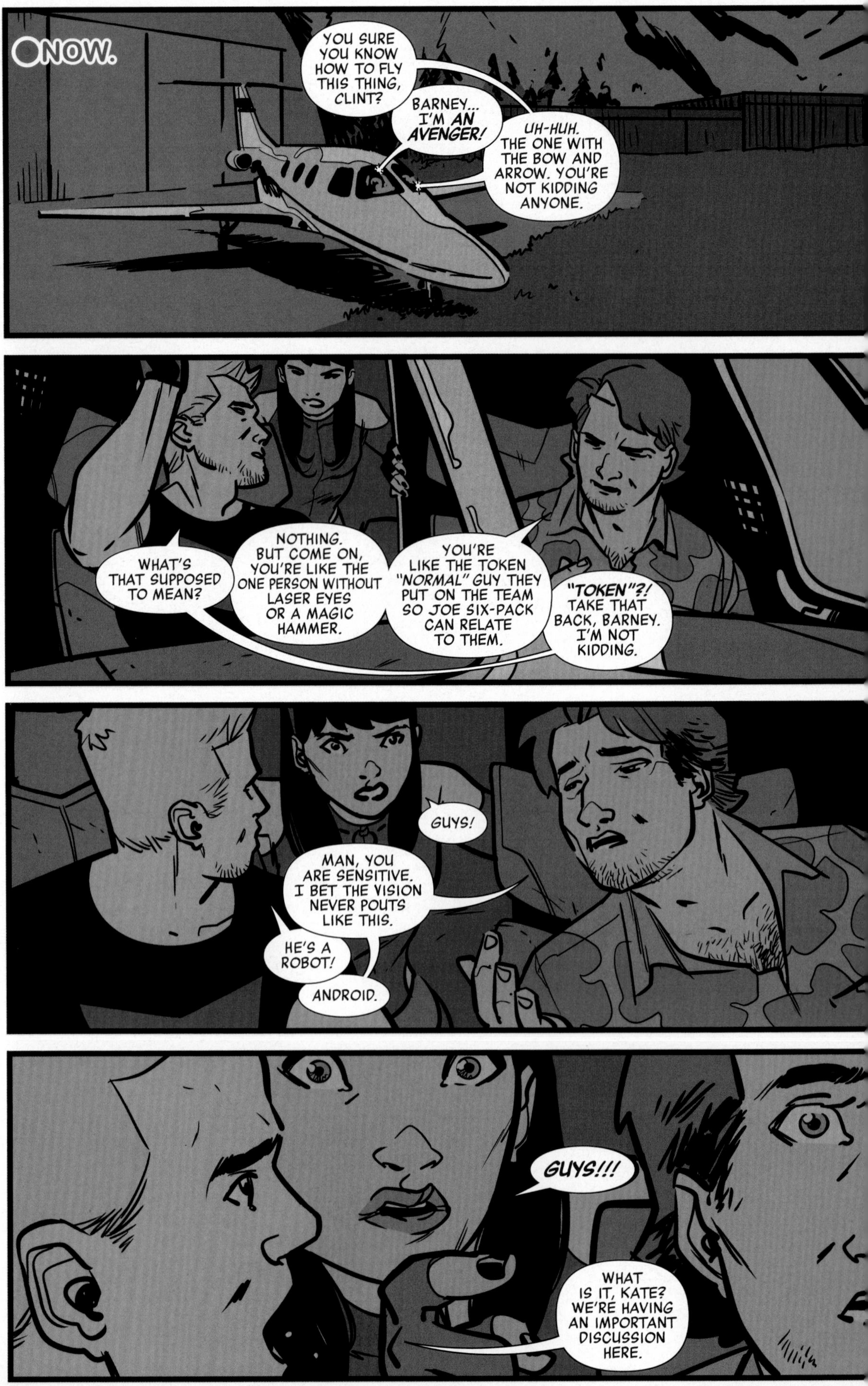
NOW.
YOU SURE YOU KNOW HOW TO FLY THIS THING, CLINT?
BARNEY... I'M AN AVENGER!
UH-HUH. THE ONE WITH THE BOW AND ARROW. YOU'RE NOT KIDDING ANYONE.
WHAT'S THAT SUPPOSED TO MEAN?
NOTHING. BUT COME ON, YOU'RE LIKE THE ONE PERSON WITHOUT LASER EYES OR A MAGIC HAMMER.
YOU'RE LIKE THE TOKEN "NORMAL" GUY THEY PUT ON THE TEAM SO JOE SIX-PACK CAN RELATE TO THEM.
"TOKEN"?! TAKE THAT BACK, BARNEY. I'M NOT KIDDING.
GUYS!
MAN, YOU ARE SENSITIVE. I BET THE VISION NEVER POUTS LIKE THIS.
HE'S A ROBOT!
ANDROID.
GUYS!!!
WHAT IS IT, KATE? WE'RE HAVING AN IMPORTANT DISCUSSION HERE.

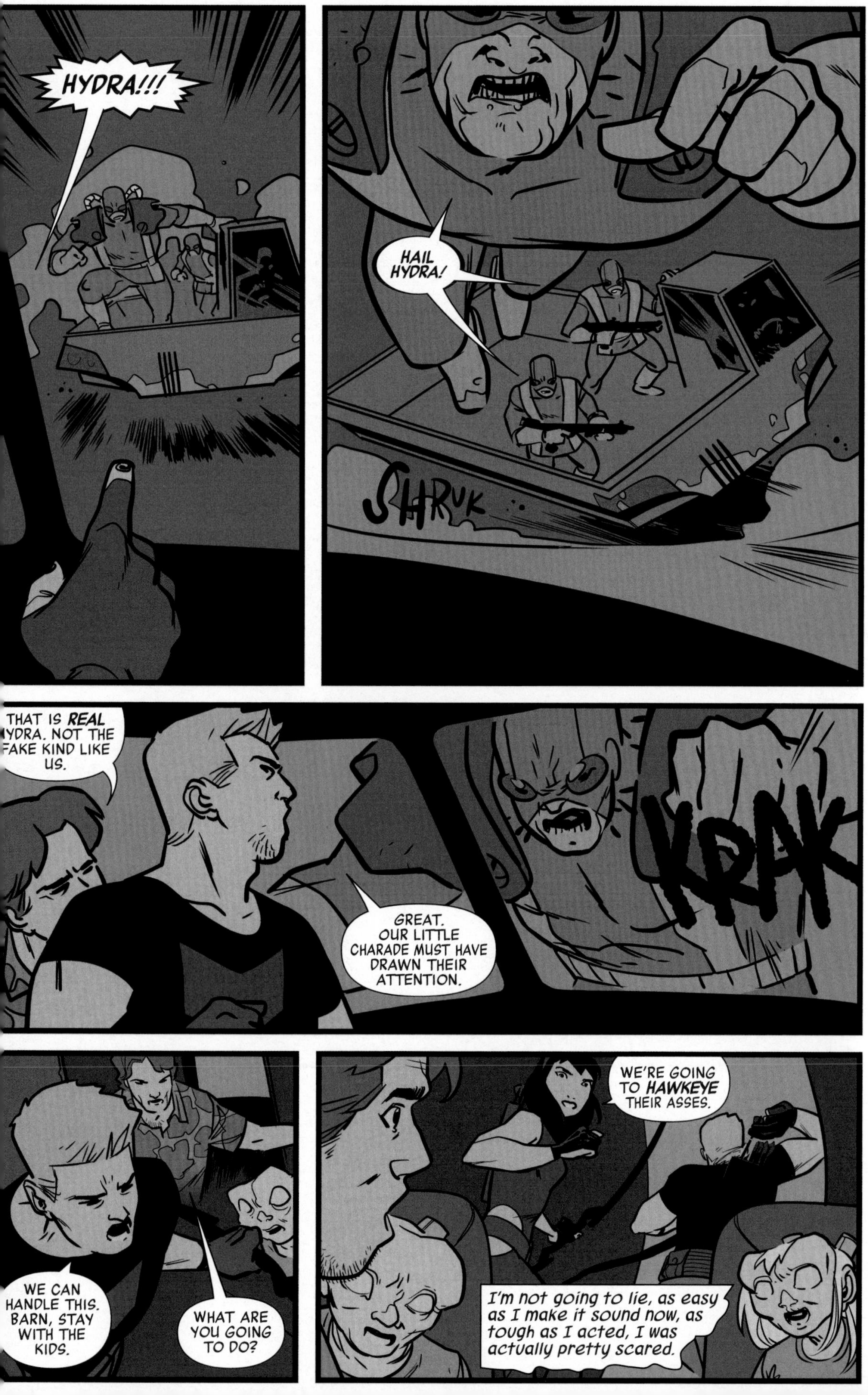
HYDRA!!!
HAIL HYDRA!
SHRUK
THAT IS REAL HYDRA. NOT THE FAKE KIND LIKE US.
GREAT. OUR LITTLE CHARADE MUST HAVE DRAWN THEIR ATTENTION.
KRAK
WE CAN HANDLE THIS. BARN, STAY WITH THE KIDS.
WHAT ARE YOU GOING TO DO?
WE'RE GOING TO HAWKEYE THEIR ASSES.
I'm not going to lie, as easy as I make it sound now, as tough as I acted, I was actually pretty scared.

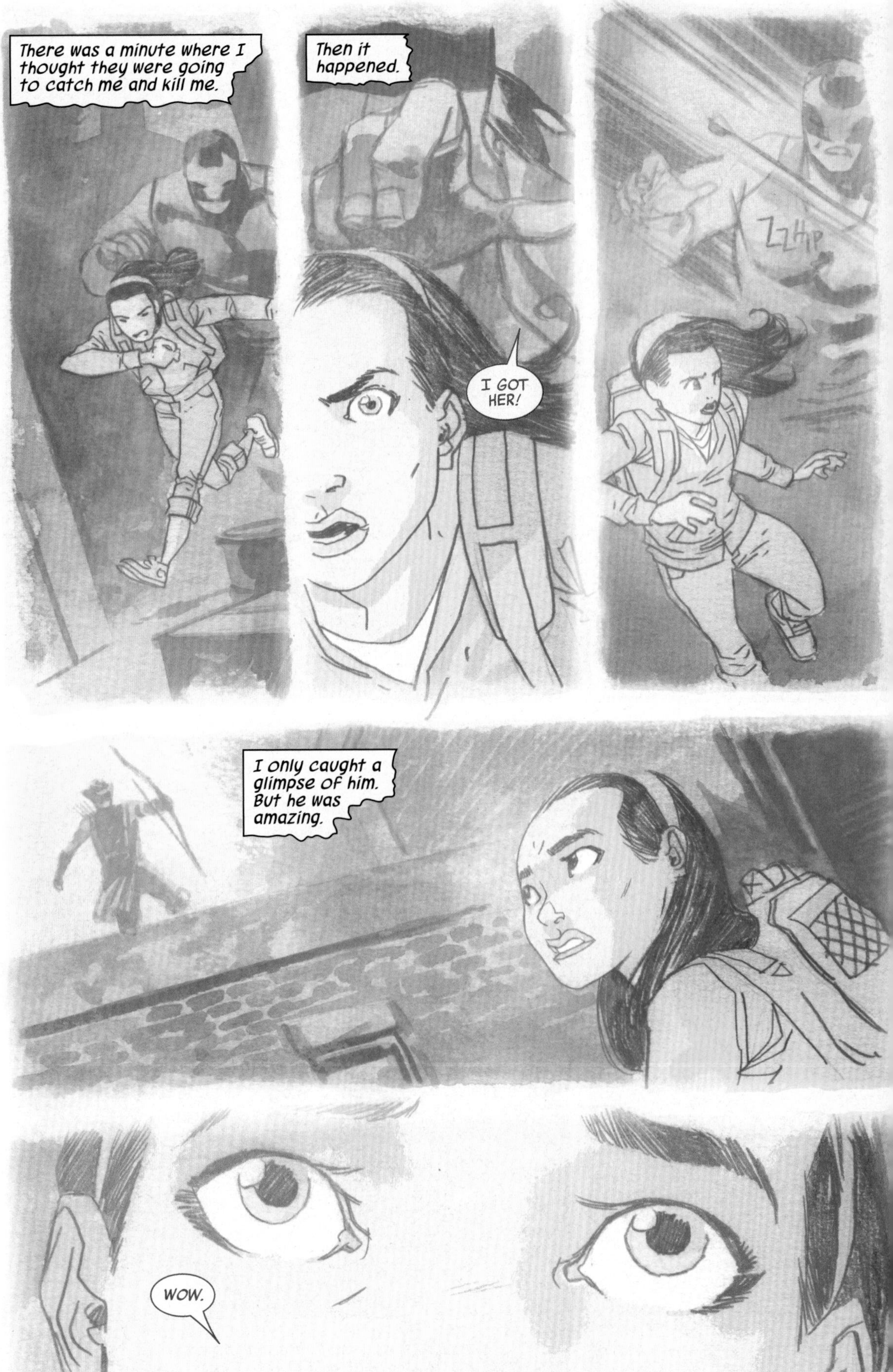
There was a minute where I thought they were going to catch me and kill me.
Then it happened.
I GOT HER!
ZZHIP
I only caught a glimpse of him. But he was amazing.
WOW.

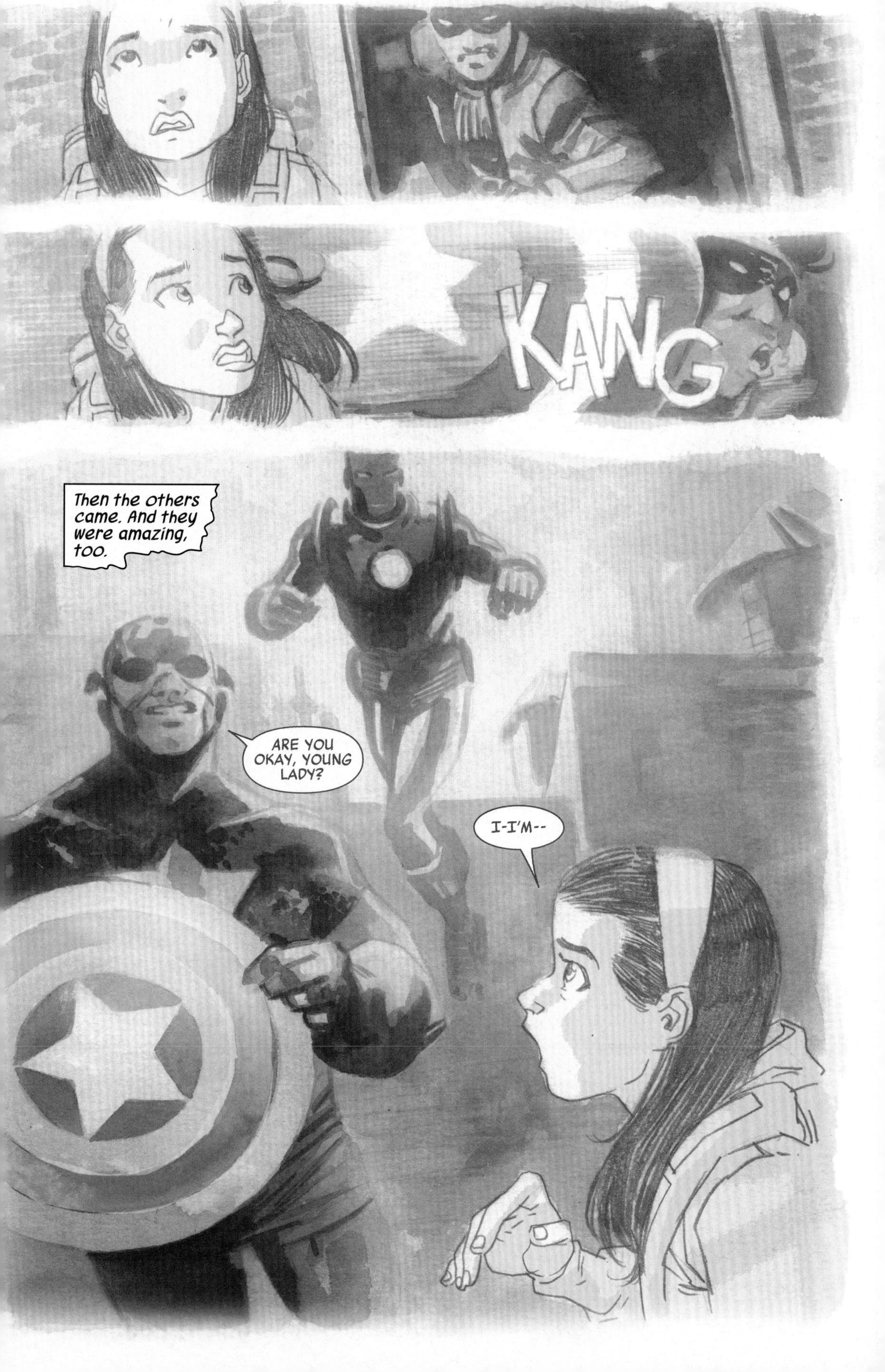
KANG
Then the others came. And they were amazing, too.
ARE YOU OKAY, YOUNG LADY?
I-I'M--

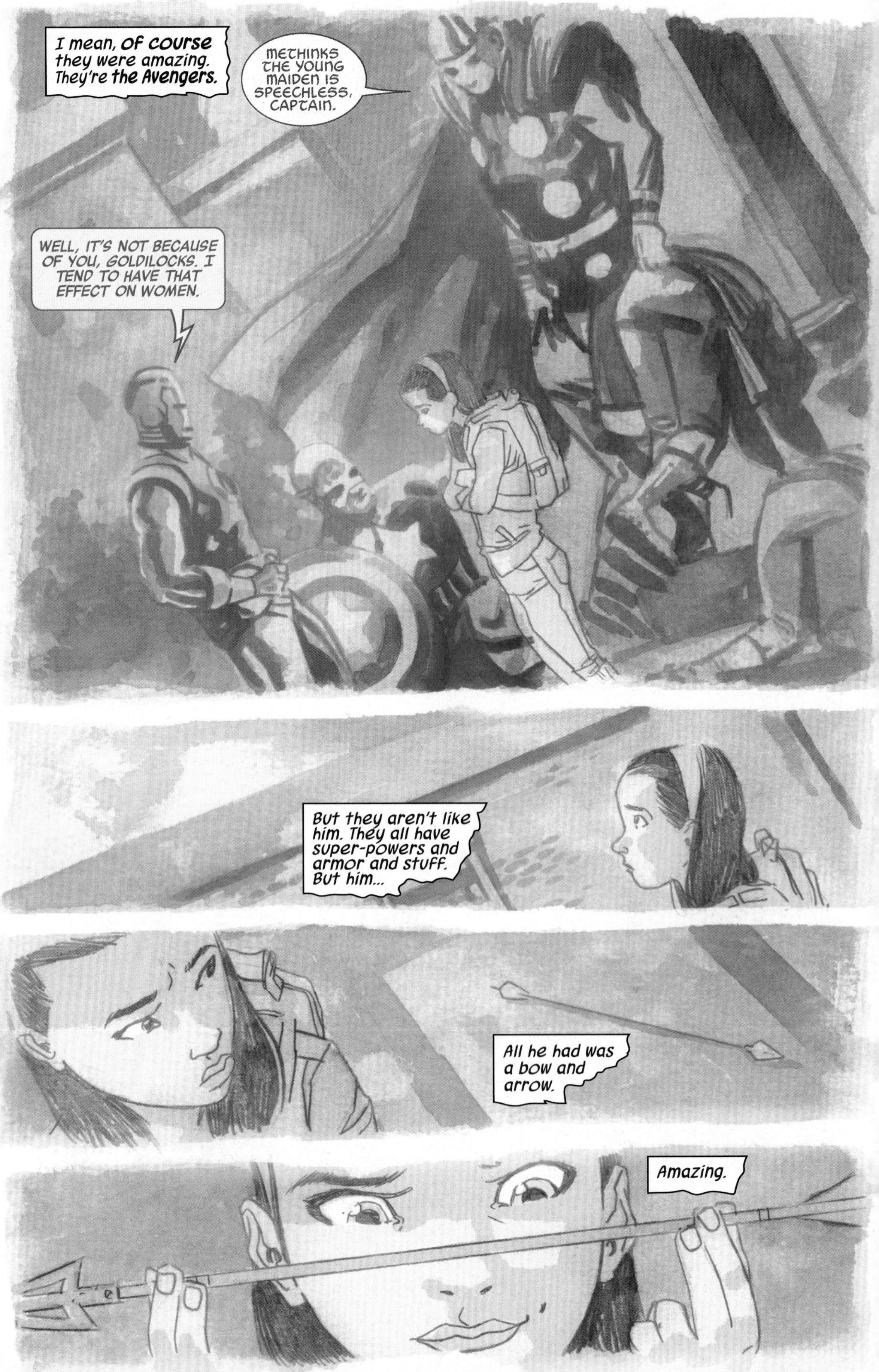
I mean, OF COURSE they were amazing. They're the Avengers.
METHINKS THE YOUNG MAIDEN IS SPEECHLESS, CAPTAIN.
WELL, IT'S NOT BECAUSE OF YOU, GOLDILOCKS. I TEND TO HAVE THAT EFFECT ON WOMEN.
But they aren't like him. They all have super-powers and armor and stuff. But him...
All he had was a bow and arrow.
Amazing.

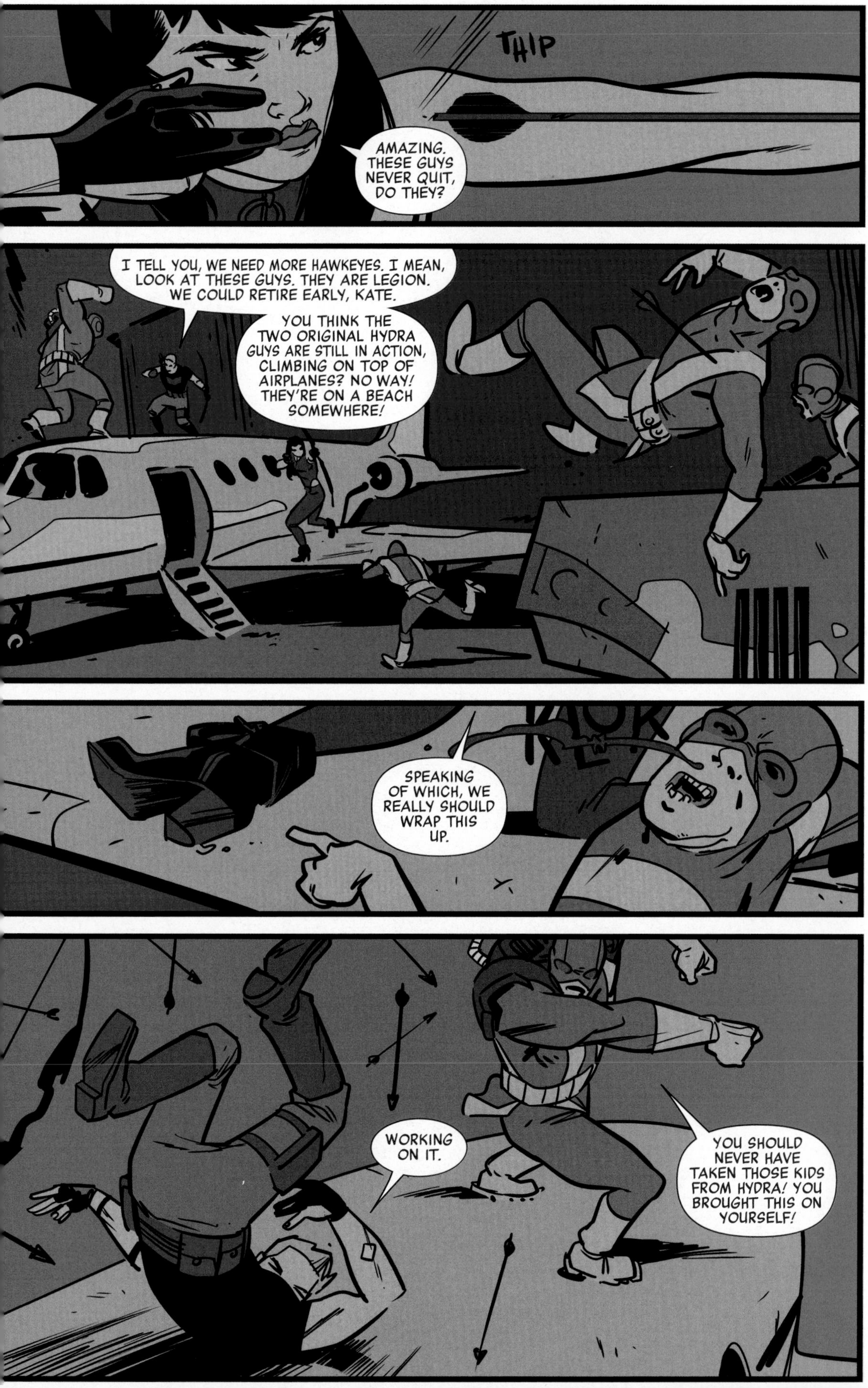
THIP
AMAZING. THESE GUYS NEVER QUIT, DO THEY?
I TELL YOU, WE NEED MORE HAWKEYES. I MEAN, LOOK AT THESE GUYS. THEY ARE LEGION. WE COULD RETIRE EARLY, KATE.
YOU THINK THE TWO ORIGINAL HYDRA GUYS ARE STILL IN ACTION, CLIMBING ON TOP OF AIRPLANES? NO WAY! THEY'RE ON A BEACH SOMEWHERE!
SPEAKING OF WHICH, WE REALLY SHOULD WRAP THIS UP.
WORKING ON IT.
YOU SHOULD NEVER HAVE TAKEN THOSE KIDS FROM HYDRA! YOU BROUGHT THIS ON YOURSELF!

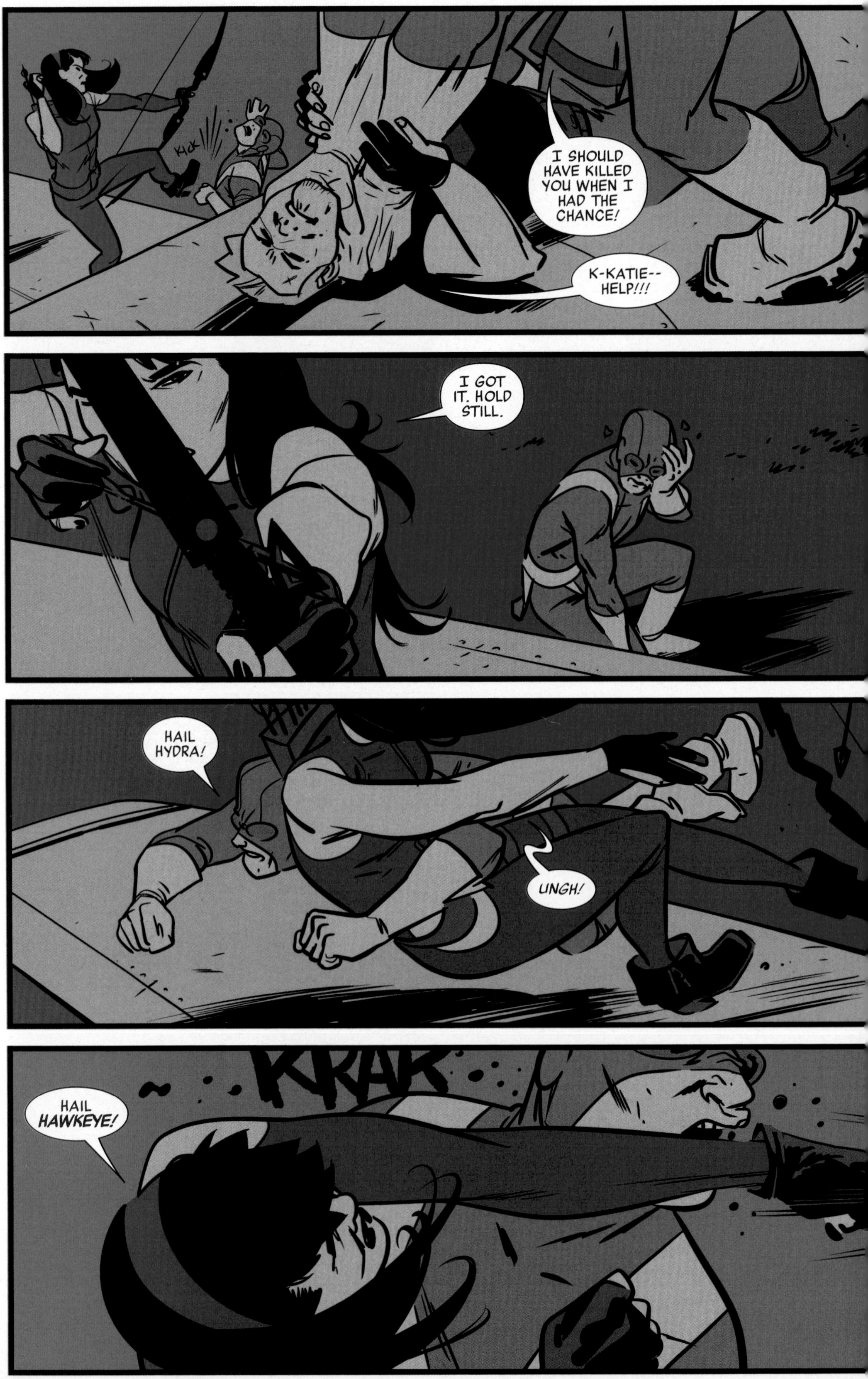
KICK
I SHOULD HAVE KILLED YOU WHEN I HAD THE CHANCE!
K-KATIE-- HELP!!!
I GOT IT. HOLD STILL.
HAIL HYDRA!
UNGH!
KRAK
HAIL HAWKEYE!

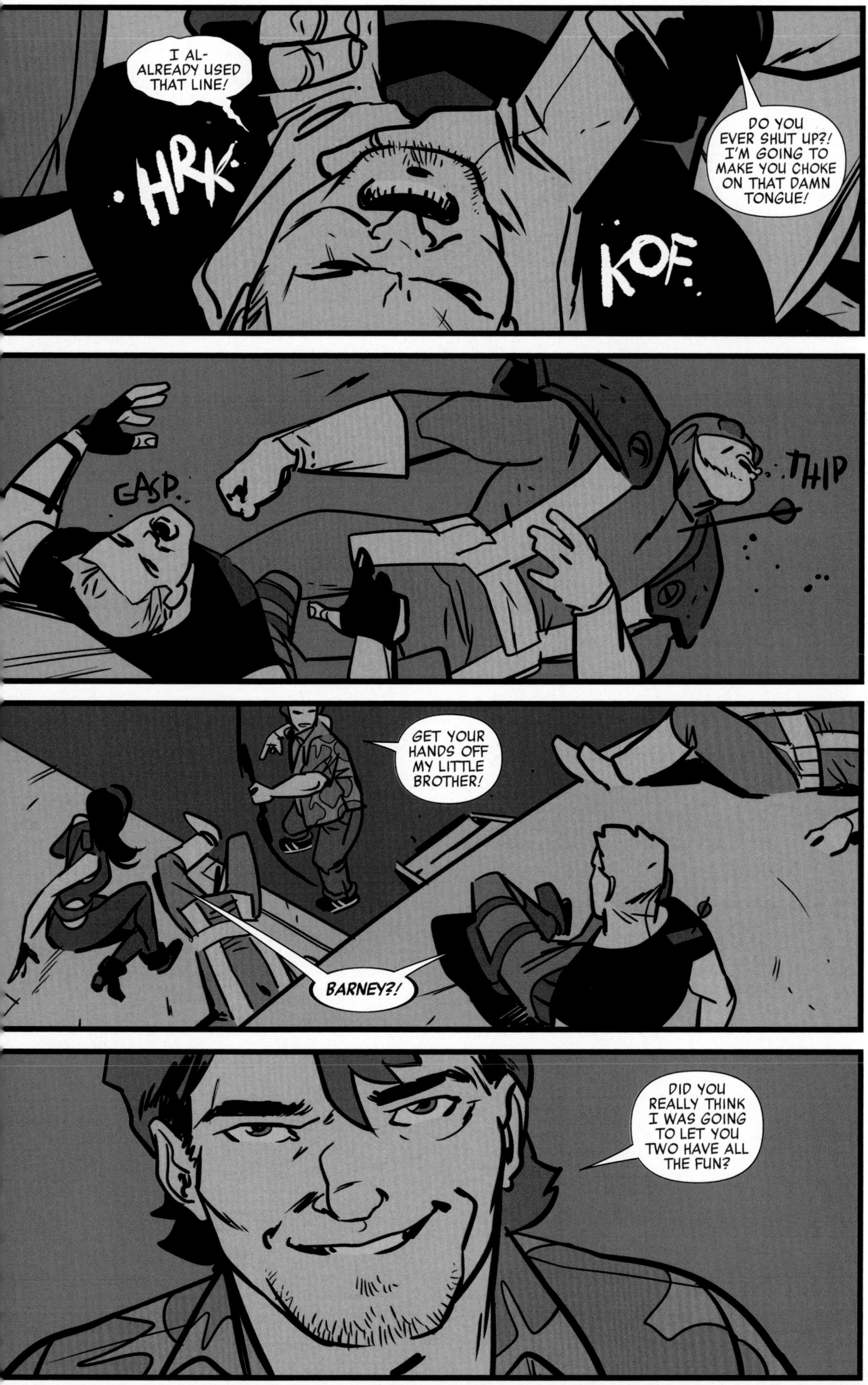
I AL-
ALREADY USED
THAT LINE!
HRK
DO YOU
EVER SHUT UP?!
I'M GOING TO
MAKE YOU CHOKE
ON THAT DAMN
TONGUE!
KOF
GASP
THIP
GET YOUR
HANDS OFF
MY LITTLE
BROTHER!
BARNEY?!
DID YOU
REALLY THINK
I WAS GOING
TO LET YOU
TWO HAVE ALL
THE FUN?

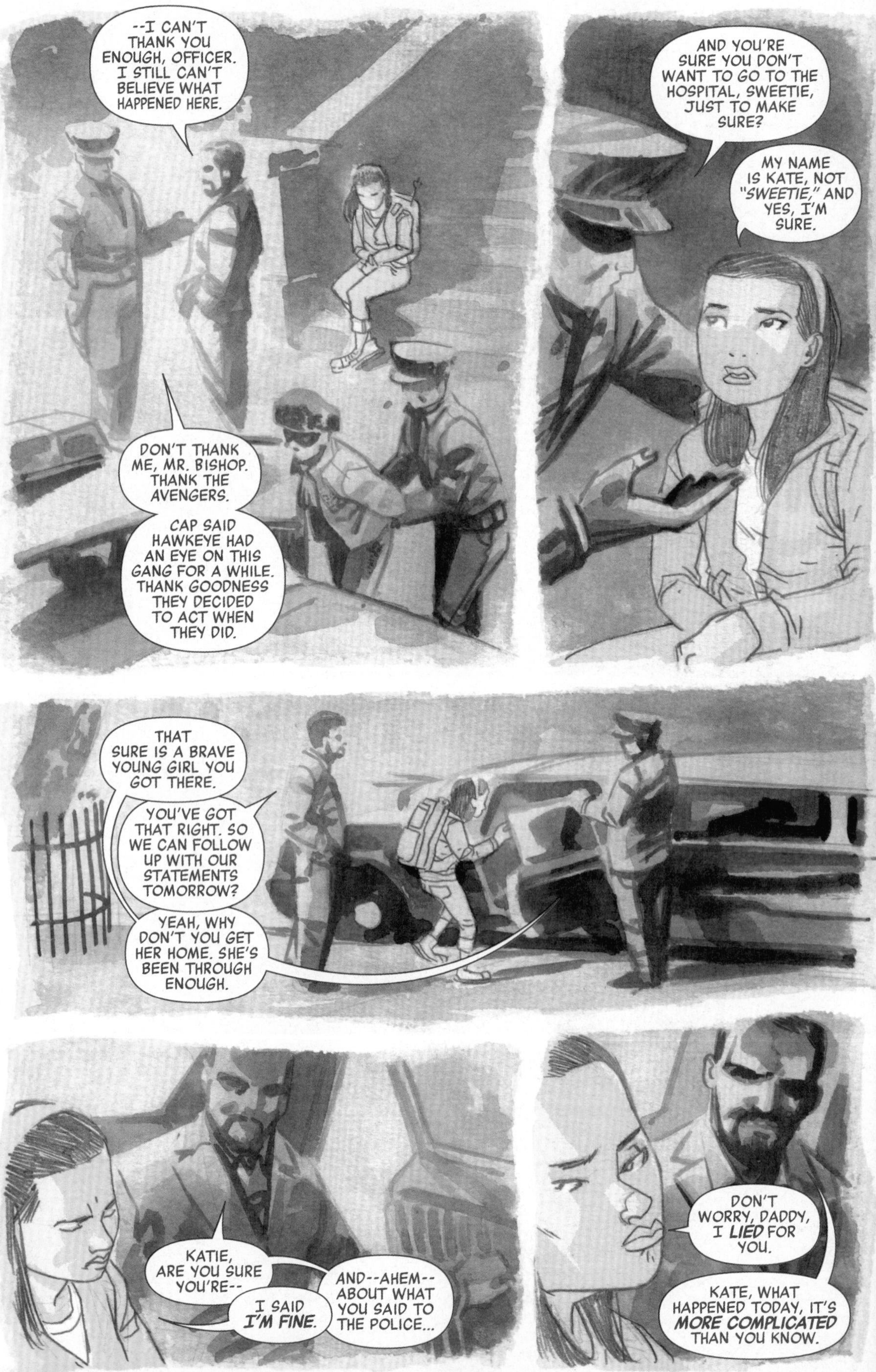
--I CAN'T THANK YOU ENOUGH, OFFICER. I STILL CAN'T BELIEVE WHAT HAPPENED HERE.
DON'T THANK ME, MR. BISHOP. THANK THE AVENGERS.
CAP SAID HAWKEYE HAD AN EYE ON THIS GANG FOR A WHILE. THANK GOODNESS THEY DECIDED TO ACT WHEN THEY DID.
AND YOU'RE SURE YOU DON'T WANT TO GO TO THE HOSPITAL, SWEETIE, JUST TO MAKE SURE?
MY NAME IS KATE, NOT "SWEETIE," AND YES, I'M SURE.
THAT SURE IS A BRAVE YOUNG GIRL YOU GOT THERE.
YOU'VE GOT THAT RIGHT. SO WE CAN FOLLOW UP WITH OUR STATEMENTS TOMORROW?
YEAH, WHY DON'T YOU GET HER HOME. SHE'S BEEN THROUGH ENOUGH.
KATIE, ARE YOU SURE YOU'RE--
I SAID *I'M FINE*.
AND--AHEM--ABOUT WHAT YOU SAID TO THE POLICE...
DON'T WORRY, DADDY, I *LIED* FOR YOU.
KATE, WHAT HAPPENED TODAY, IT'S *MORE COMPLICATED* THAN YOU KNOW.

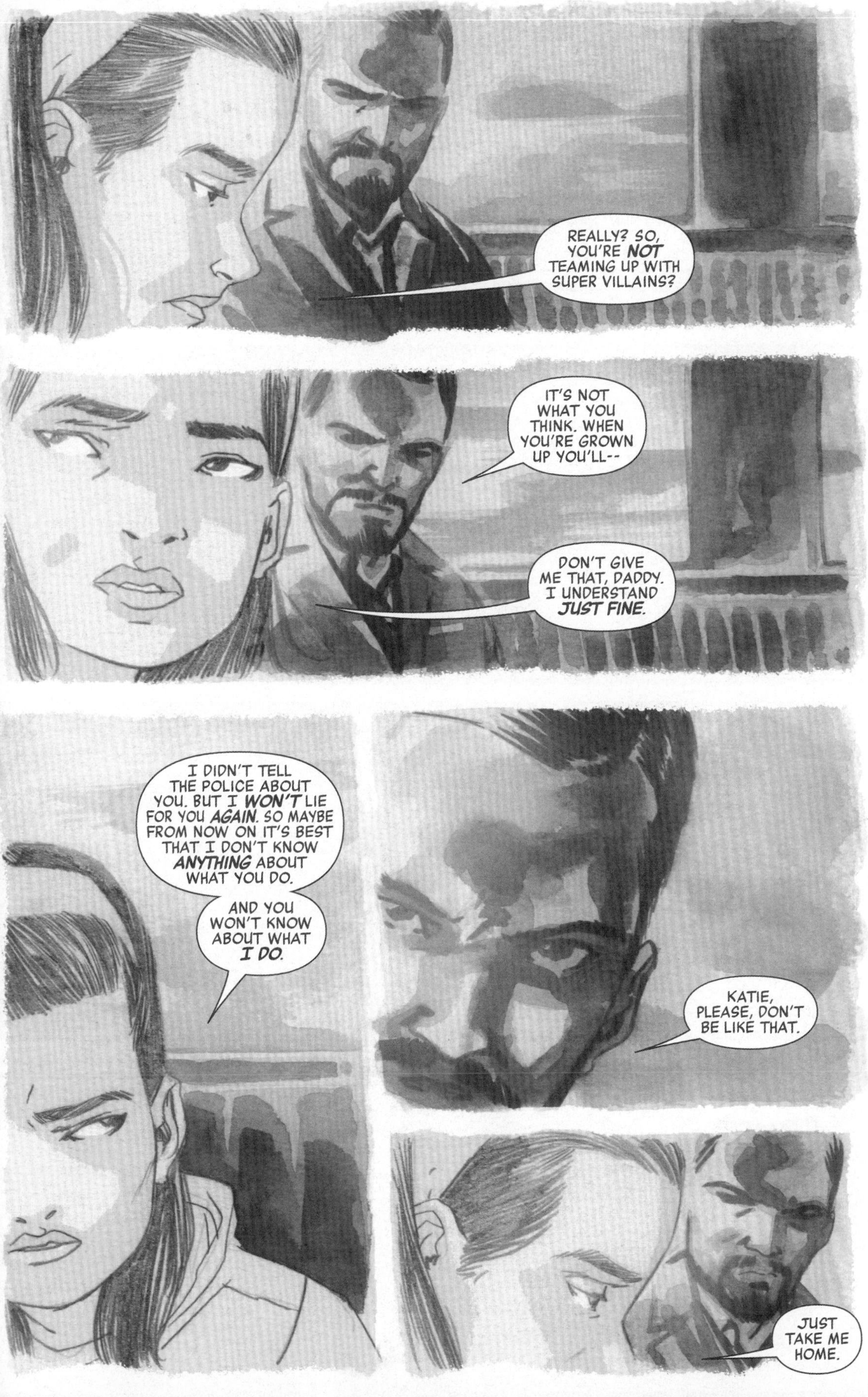
REALLY? SO, YOU'RE **NOT** TEAMING UP WITH SUPER VILLAINS?
IT'S NOT WHAT YOU THINK. WHEN YOU'RE GROWN UP YOU'LL--
DON'T GIVE ME THAT, DADDY. I UNDERSTAND **JUST FINE**.
I DIDN'T TELL THE POLICE ABOUT YOU. BUT I **WON'T** LIE FOR YOU **AGAIN**. SO MAYBE FROM NOW ON IT'S BEST THAT I DON'T KNOW **ANYTHING** ABOUT WHAT YOU DO.
AND YOU WON'T KNOW ABOUT WHAT **I DO**.
KATIE, PLEASE, DON'T BE LIKE THAT.
JUST TAKE ME HOME.

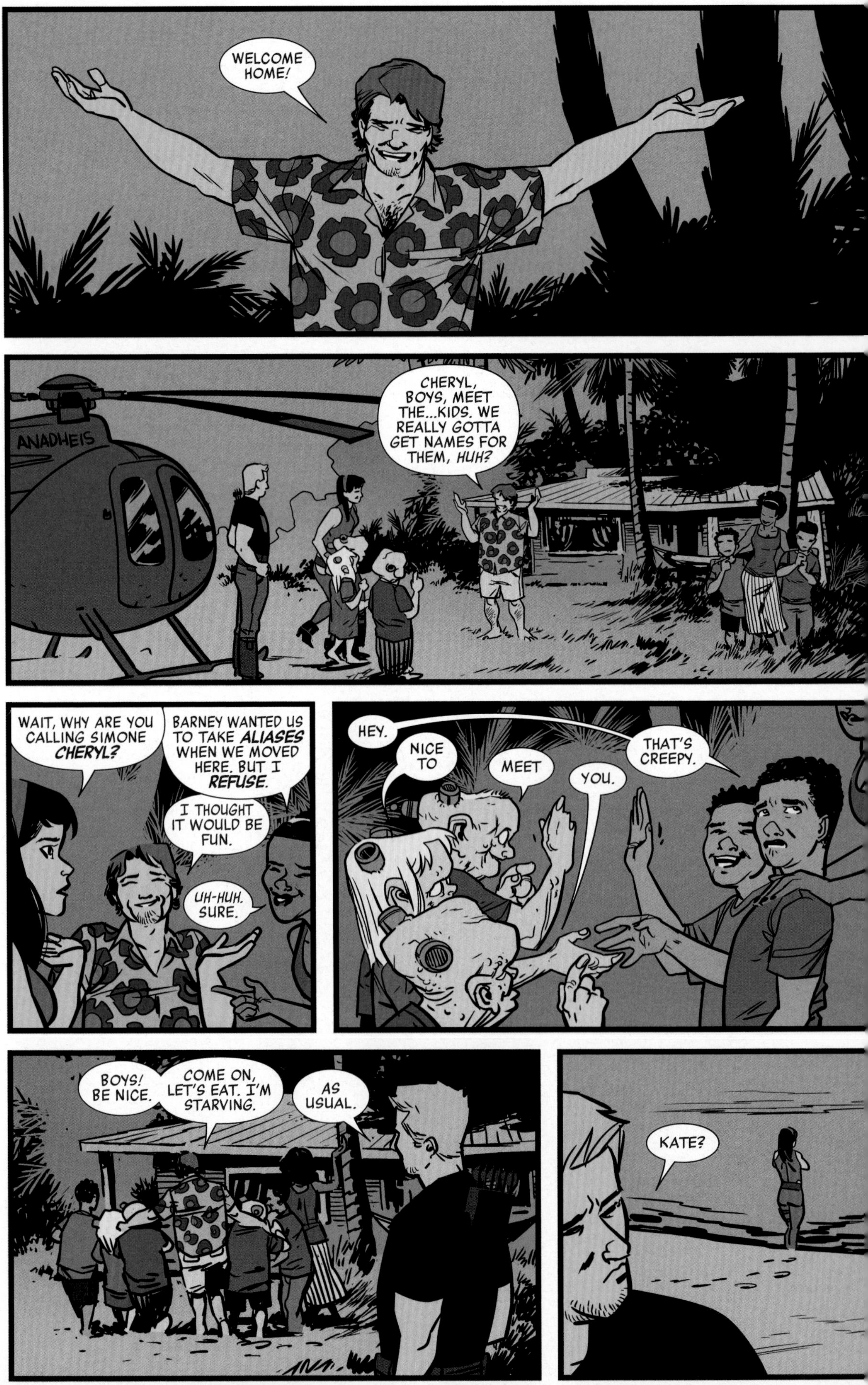
WELCOME HOME!
ANADHEIS
CHERYL, BOYS, MEET THE...KIDS. WE REALLY GOTTA GET NAMES FOR THEM, HUH?
WAIT, WHY ARE YOU CALLING SIMONE CHERYL?
BARNEY WANTED US TO TAKE ALIASES WHEN WE MOVED HERE. BUT I REFUSE.
I THOUGHT IT WOULD BE FUN.
UH-HUH. SURE.
HEY.
NICE TO
MEET
YOU.
THAT'S CREEPY.
BOYS! BE NICE.
COME ON, LET'S EAT. I'M STARVING.
AS USUAL.
KATE?

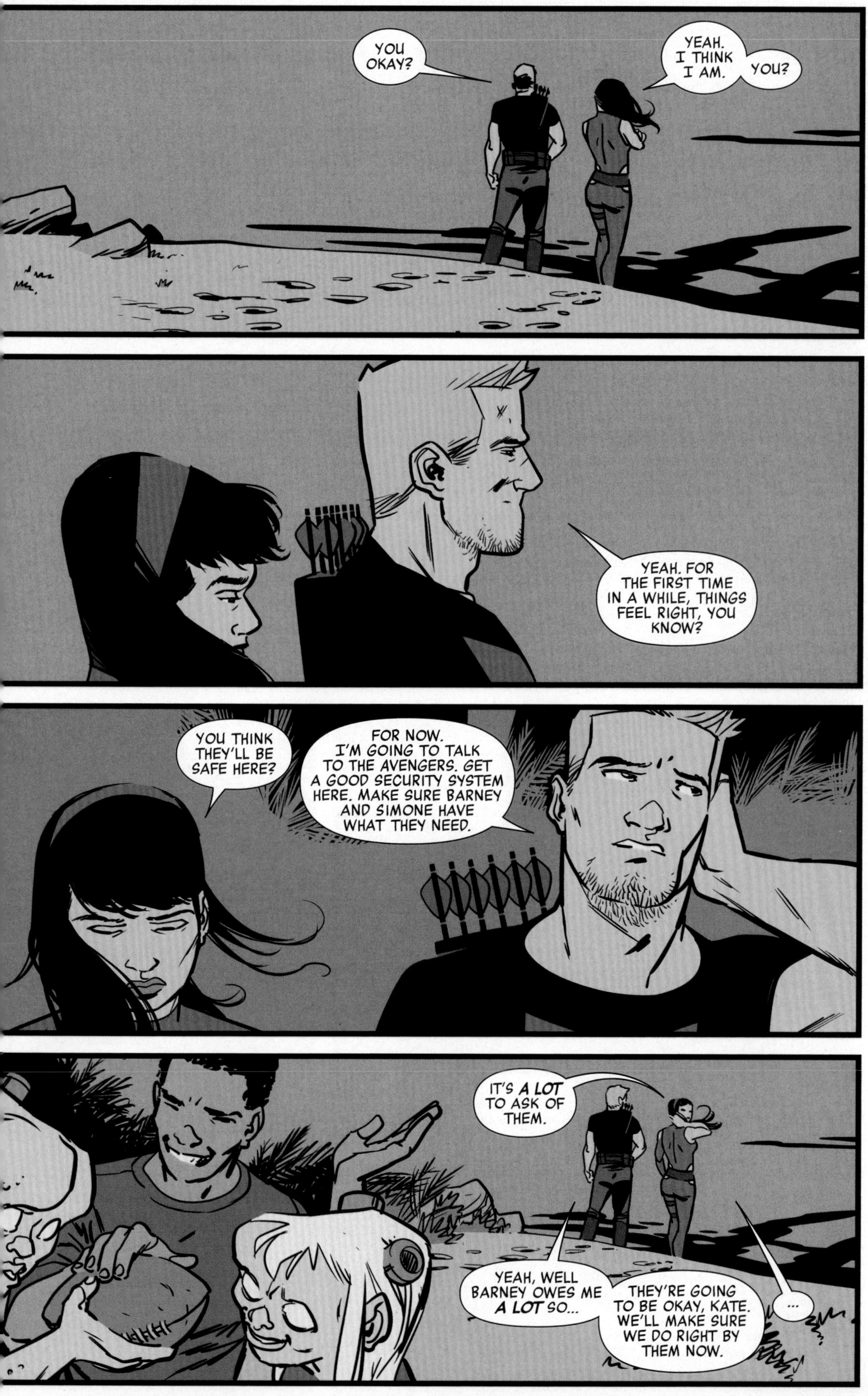
YOU OKAY?
YEAH. I THINK I AM.
YOU?
YEAH. FOR THE FIRST TIME IN A WHILE, THINGS FEEL RIGHT, YOU KNOW?
YOU THINK THEY'LL BE SAFE HERE?
FOR NOW. I'M GOING TO TALK TO THE AVENGERS. GET A GOOD SECURITY SYSTEM HERE. MAKE SURE BARNEY AND SIMONE HAVE WHAT THEY NEED.
IT'S A LOT TO ASK OF THEM.
YEAH, WELL BARNEY OWES ME A LOT SO...
THEY'RE GOING TO BE OKAY, KATE. WE'LL MAKE SURE WE DO RIGHT BY THEM NOW.
...

YES, CLINT. US. WHAT DO **WE** DO NOW?

WELL, WE'RE BACK IN ACTION, RIGHT?

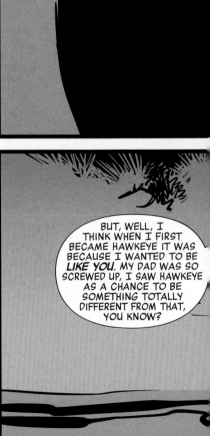

BUT, WELL, I THINK WHEN I FIRST BECAME HAWKEYE IT WAS BECAUSE I WANTED TO BE *LIKE YOU.* MY DAD WAS SO SCREWED UP, I SAW HAWKEYE AS A CHANCE TO BE SOMETHING TOTALLY DIFFERENT FROM THAT, YOU KNOW?

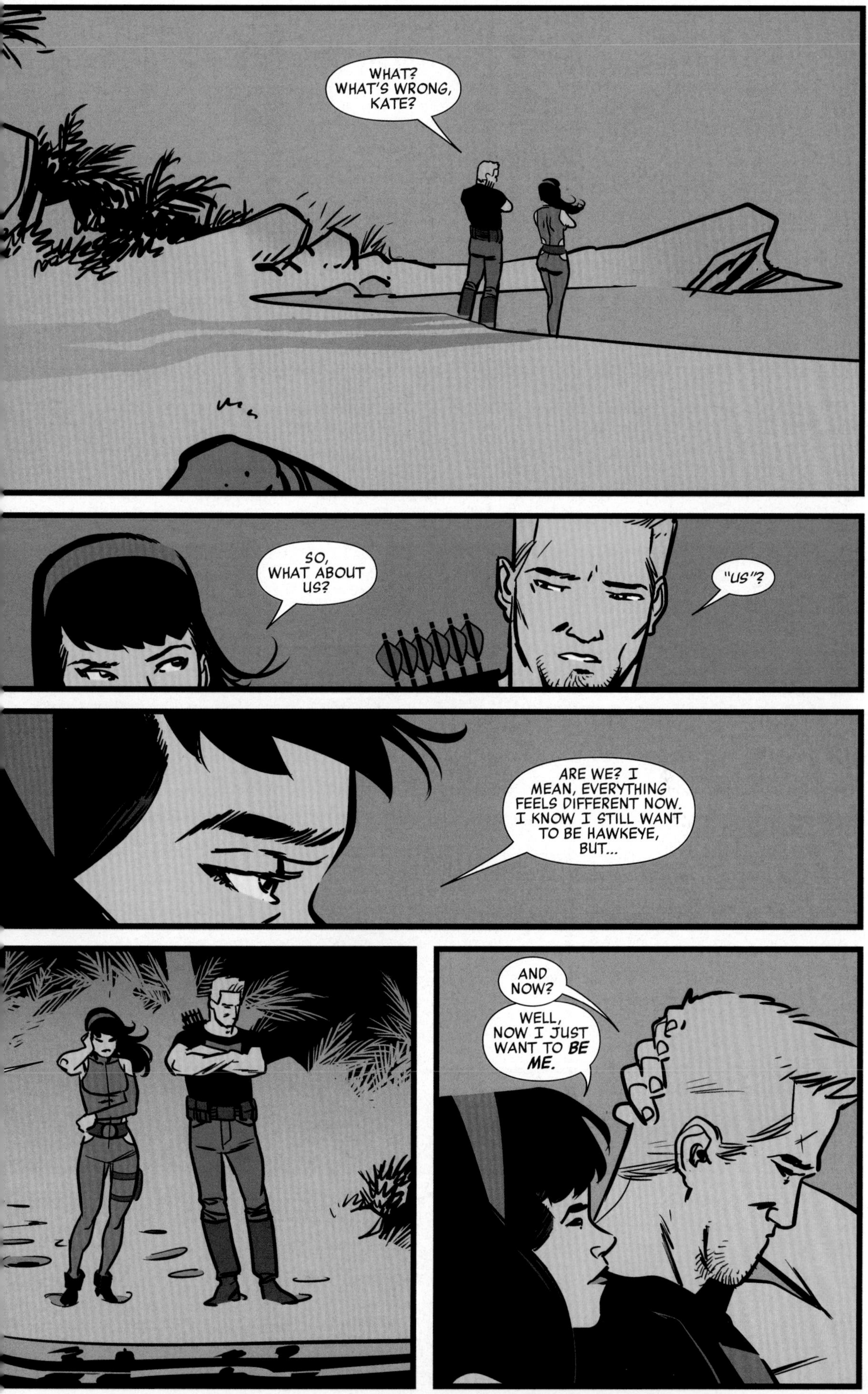
WHAT? WHAT'S WRONG, KATE?
SO, WHAT ABOUT US?
"US"?
ARE WE? I MEAN, EVERYTHING FEELS DIFFERENT NOW. I KNOW I STILL WANT TO BE HAWKEYE, BUT...
AND NOW?
WELL, NOW I JUST WANT TO *BE ME.*

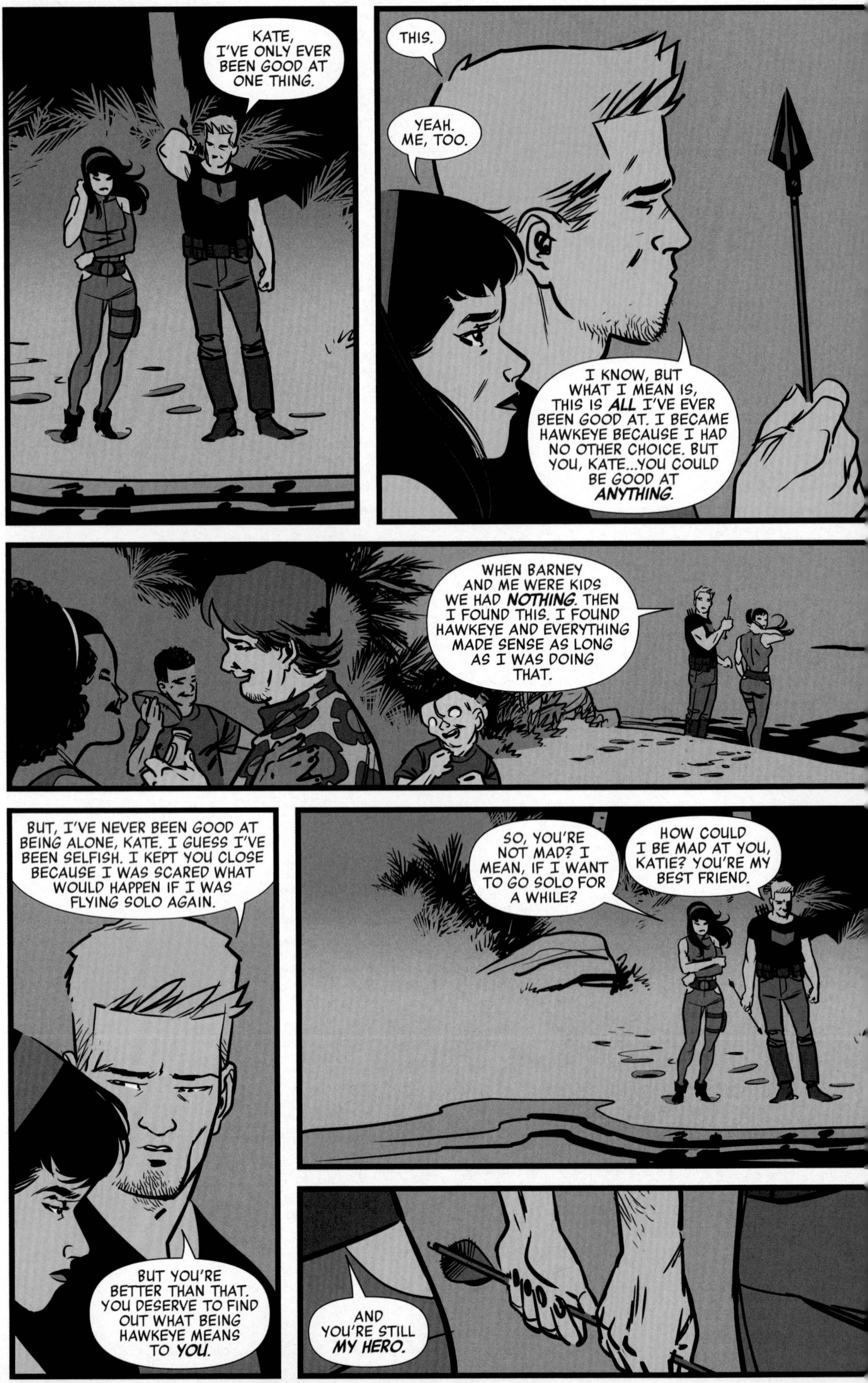
KATE, I'VE ONLY EVER BEEN GOOD AT ONE THING.
THIS.
YEAH. ME, TOO.
I KNOW, BUT WHAT I MEAN IS, THIS IS ALL I'VE EVER BEEN GOOD AT. I BECAME HAWKEYE BECAUSE I HAD NO OTHER CHOICE. BUT YOU, KATE...YOU COULD BE GOOD AT ANYTHING.
WHEN BARNEY AND ME WERE KIDS WE HAD NOTHING. THEN I FOUND THIS. I FOUND HAWKEYE AND EVERYTHING MADE SENSE AS LONG AS I WAS DOING THAT.
BUT, I'VE NEVER BEEN GOOD AT BEING ALONE, KATE. I GUESS I'VE BEEN SELFISH. I KEPT YOU CLOSE BECAUSE I WAS SCARED WHAT WOULD HAPPEN IF I WAS FLYING SOLO AGAIN.
BUT YOU'RE BETTER THAN THAT. YOU DESERVE TO FIND OUT WHAT BEING HAWKEYE MEANS TO YOU.
SO, YOU'RE NOT MAD? I MEAN, IF I WANT TO GO SOLO FOR A WHILE?
HOW COULD I BE MAD AT YOU, KATIE? YOU'RE MY BEST FRIEND.
AND YOU'RE STILL MY HERO.

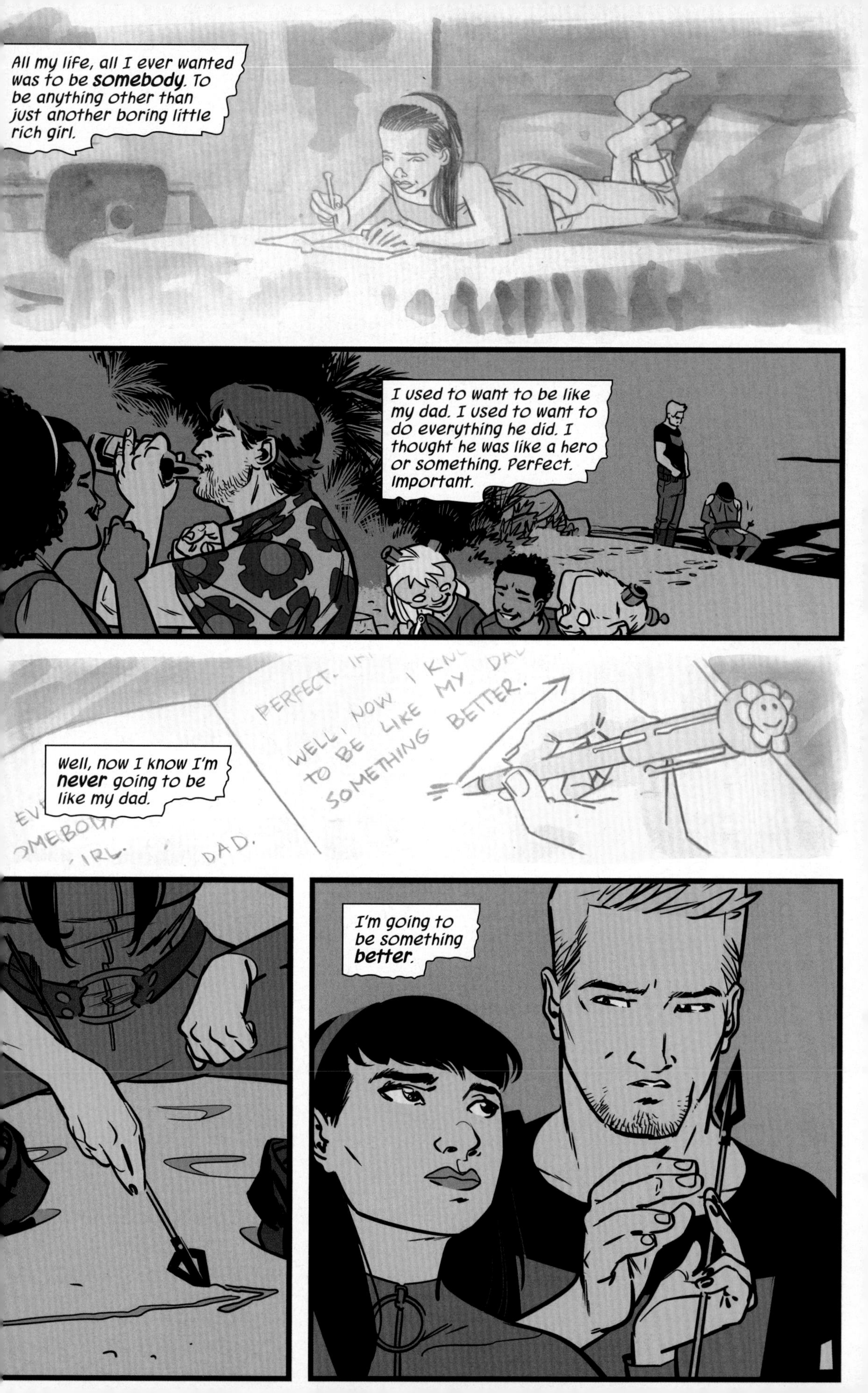
All my life, all I ever wanted was to be **somebody**. To be anything other than just another boring little rich girl.
I used to want to be like my dad. I used to want to do everything he did. I thought he was like a hero or something. Perfect. Important.
PERFECT.
TO BE LIKE MY DAD
SOMETHING BETTER.
Well, now I know I'm **never** going to be like my dad.
DAD.
I'm going to be something **better**.

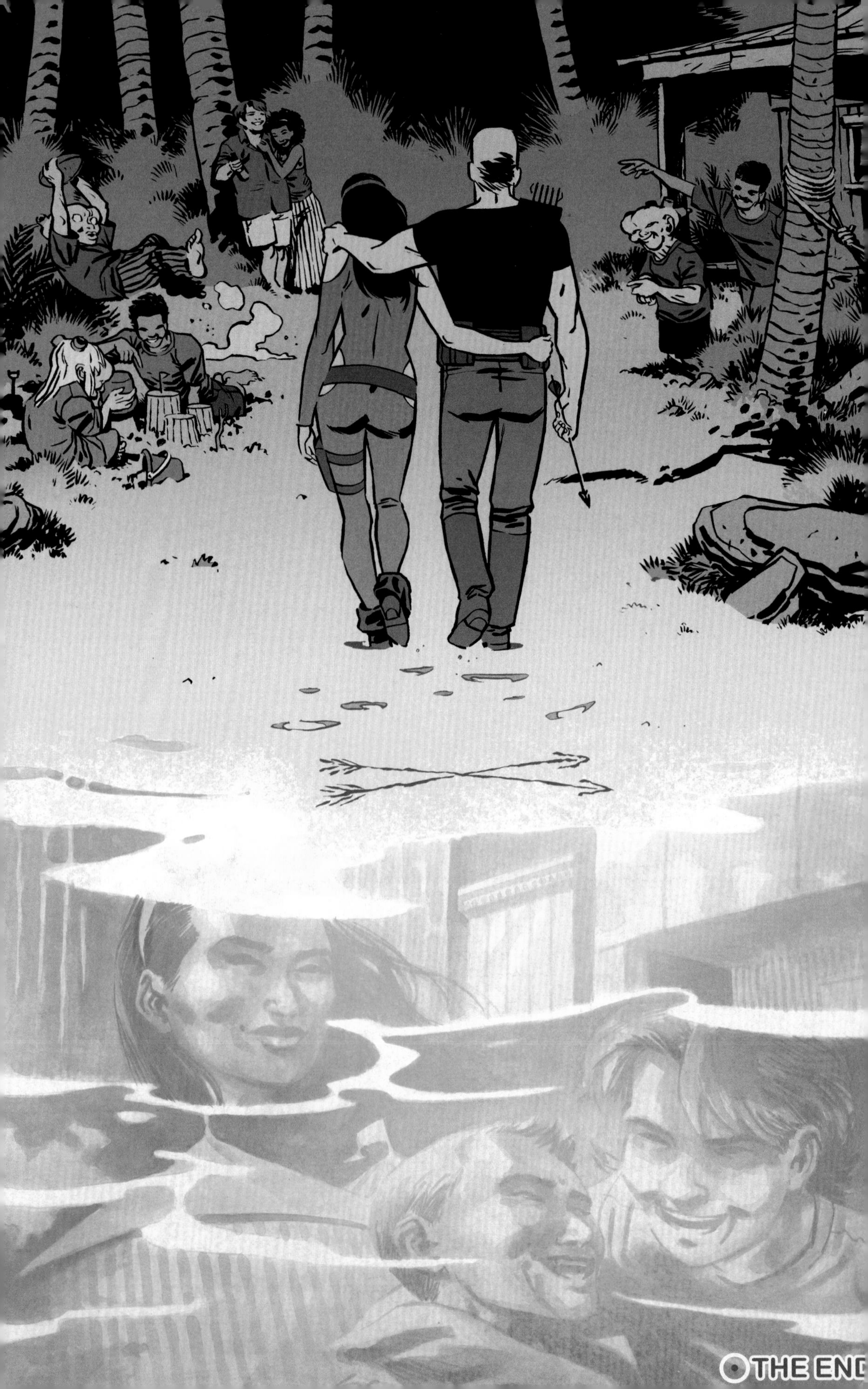
THE END